CRITICAL ACCLAIM FOR *ROSE WATER & ORANGE BLOSSOMS*

IACP Award Finalist ✤ Michigan Notable Book

"A terrific and important book!"
—Anthony Bourdain

"Compelling . . . an ebullient mix of the authentic classics . . . with fresh, modern twists on many of them. The recipes . . . are carefully created and sprinkled with helpful details that will ensure success. . . . You'll be sure to come back often."
—New York Times

"If you're a cookbook fanatic who reads them like novels, you'll find this book to be a good read. Maureen Abood provides detailed instructions and shares family stories all in a breezy conversational tone."
—Detroit Free Press

"The recipes are straightforward, painstakingly tested, and presented more often than not with a story about how she came up with the recipe or where she first experienced the flavors. . . . Every word . . . is a love letter to her family, her culture, and her kitchen. The writing is . . . always exquisite."
—Lansing City Pulse

"A contemporary, sophisticated Lebanese cookbook."
—Lansing State Journal

"Maureen Abood takes readers on a Lebanese journey, meal by meal . . . a full-on exploration of her Lebanese heritage through food. . . . Every recipe comes with a memory and tips to help the home cook."
—Milwaukee Journal Sentinel

"A gorgeous primer for those who want to learn more. The ingredients alone are intoxicating."
—San Diego Union-Tribune

"Not just a book of recipes but the story of Arabian life which revolves around great tasting foods . . . Maureen Abood does it so well . . . a must-read and essential reference. . . . You will enjoy reading it."
—Arab Daily News

"Maureen Abood infuses Lebanese food with a sense of gravitas. . . . This book is not simply an ode to the cuisine of Lebanon, but a discussion of the lifestyle around the food. . . . Abood invites the reader to a family meal."

LEBANESE BAKING

Also by Maureen Abood

Rose Water & Orange Blossoms:
Fresh & Classic Recipes from My Lebanese Kitchen

LEBANESE BAKING

More Than 100 Recipes for Sweet and Savory Baked Goods

MAUREEN ABOOD

PHOTOGRAPHY BY Kristin Teig

Countryman Press

An Imprint of W. W. Norton & Company
Independent Publishers Since 1923

This is a general information resource. The commercial products that the author recommends in this book are ones that the author personally likes. You need to do your own research to find the ones that are best for you.

Copyright © 2025 by Maureen Abood
Photography © by Kristin Teig

All rights reserved
Printed in Malaysia
First Edition

For information about permission to reproduce selections from this book, write to Permissions, Countryman Press, 500 Fifth Avenue, New York, NY 10110

For information about special discounts for bulk purchases, please contact W. W. Norton Special Sales at specialsales@wwnorton.com or 800-233-4830

Manufacturing through Imago
Book design by Allison Chi
Production manager: Devon Zahn

Countryman Press
www.countrymanpress.com

An imprint of W. W. Norton & Company, Inc.
500 Fifth Avenue, New York, NY 10110
www.wwnorton.com

978-1-68268-898-4

1 2 3 4 5 6 7 8 9 0

For my mother, Maryalice Abood, the ultimate habibti. I find you again in my heart every time I bake.

Contents

- ix Introduction
- xiii How to Use This Book
- xv Equipment
- xvii Ingredients

1 BAKLAWA

- 6 Baklawa Diamonds with Homemade Phyllo
- 10 Baklawa Spirals with Homemade Phyllo
- 15 Baklawa Diamonds
- 19 *Arabic Cardamom Coffee*
- 20 Baklawa Rolls
- 22 Burma Baklawa
- 24 Baklawa Nests
- 26 Baklawa Crinkle
- 29 Cream Baklawa
- 31 Nut-Free Baklawa
- 33 Triple Chocolate Baklawa

37 KNAFEH

- 40 Shortcut Knafeh Crust
- 40 Combo Knafeh Crust
- 42 Kataifi Knafeh Crust
- 43 Smooth Knafeh Crust
- 45 Cheese Knafeh
- 46 Knafeh bil Ka'ak
- 49 Nut-Filled Knafeh
- 50 Shredded Wheat Knafeh Biscuits
- 53 Knafeh Nests
- 54 Chocolate Pistachio Knafeh Bars
- 57 Cream Knafeh
- 59 *Café Blanc*

61 SWEET YEAST BREADS

- 64 Zalabia Donuts
- 67 Honey Buns
- 70 Cardamom Date Rings
- 73 Qurban Holy Bread
- 76 Glazed Ka'ak Bread
- 79 Orange Blossom Caramel Pecan Rolls
- 83 Orange Date Tea Ring
- 85 *Green Tea with Warm Spices*

87 COOKIES

- 89 Glazed Mak'rouns
- 91 Walnut Orange Blossom Mak'roun Fingers
- 95 Toasted Coconut Mak'rouns
- 96 Raspberry Rose Water Macarons
- 101 Glazed Zalabia
- 102 Apricot Gems
- 105 Ma'amoul
- 110 Ma'amoul Mad Cream Bars
- 113 Ma'amoul Mad Date Bars
- 115 *Mint Lemonade*
- 117 Millionaire Ma'amoul Mad
- 119 Fig Crescents
- 123 Barazek Sesame Cookies
- 124 *Date Ice Cream Shake*
- 126 Awamet
- 129 Sesame Ka'ak Rings
- 131 Mocha Brownies with Olive Oil and Tahini Swirl
- 134 White Chocolate Pistachio Cookies
- 137 Apricot Walnut Cookies
- 138 Ghraybeh
- 141 *Raspberry Basil Iced Tea*
- 142 Glazed Ka'ak Shortbread

145 CAKES

146 Orange Blossom Cake
150 Atayef
153 Pistachio Cream Atayef
154 Walnut Atayef
155 Orange Blossom Madeleines with Apricot Glaze
158 *Michigan Tart Cherry Limeade*
159 Mini Sticky Date Cakes with Orange Blossom Caramel Sauce
162 Pistachio Cupcakes with Strawberry Rose Water Buttercream
165 Mocha Cardamom Snack Cake
169 Apricot Upside-Down Cake
171 Lemon Yogurt Cake with Strawberry Rose Water Sauce and Labneh
175 Turmeric Tea Cake
176 *Matcha Orange Blossom Latte*
177 Michigan Tart Cherry Bundt Cake
181 Lebanese Nights Cream Cake with Berry Compote
185 Coconut Semolina Cake
186 Baklawa Cheesecake
191 Pomegranate Mousse Cake with Lime Icing

195 FATAYER

199 Fatayer Dough
200 Cheese Fatayer
202 Cheese Fatayer XL
204 Sfeha
206 Spinach Fatayer
208 Kale and Feta Fatayer
210 Kousa Fatayer
213 Sambousek
215 *Mulberry Manhattan*

217 SAVORY YEAST BREADS

221 Manakeesh Dough
222 Za'atar Manakeesh
225 Labneh Mint Manakeesh
226 Cheese Manakeesh
227 Muhammara Manakeesh
230 Lamb and Tomato Manakeesh
233 Talami Bread
235 Za'atar Cheese Dome
238 Sesame Purse Bread
240 Pita
243 Pita Chips
245 *Orange Blossom Gin Fizz*
247 Arayes
248 Za'atar Garlic Knots
252 Saj Bread
259 Za'atar Croissants

265 BAKING STAPLES

266 Toasted Nuts
267 Blanched Pistachios
269 Toasted Sesame Seeds
270 Dried Mint
271 Clarified Butter
272 Date Paste
273 Flower Water Syrup

275 *Glossary and Pronunciation Guide*
277 *Acknowledgments*
279 *Index*

Introduction

أَلْهَسَوَ أَلْهَأَ
Ahlan wa sahlan.
Welcome!

AS A SECOND-GENERATION Lebanese American, I don't use that Arabic welcome often, but the phrase exists deep in the recesses of my memories. Sitto (Grandma) said it when she answered her green telephone in the galley kitchen of her apartment. I heard it, learned it, embraced it, and then obsessed over it when studying Arabic in college. My friend-cousin Patti Haddad and I walked across campus, emphasizing the accent of our grandparents using words that now we could read and write, too. We laughed so hard at ourselves for sounding like Jiddo (Grandpa) and Sitto, and we reveled in it, as we did with all things Lebanese. This simple expression helped illuminate and crystalize my Lebanese-ness, a world that I wanted to know and hold.

Growing up, we employed a mash-up of Arabic and English that anyone could understand for its intonations but that struck us as comedic. This Arabanglish still thrives among me, my husband, kids, siblings, nieces, nephews, and our billions of cousins: the blood cousins and the love-you-like-a-cousin friends. Our parents used it, too. As kids, we started easy, using "honey" with one another, replicating how our elders affectionately spoke to us. Just imagine someone in the grocery store hearing 14-year-old me say to my 12-year-old sister, Peg: "Honey, we need two gallons, not one." Over the years, we added *deenie* (my heart) and *habibi* (my dear) or *habibti 'albi* (darling of my heart). Then, perhaps just from my own parents: kousa (summer squash), a perfect parallel to the American English use of "pumpkin" as a term of endearment.

My baking language evolved in much the same way. It also started easy, sitting on the counter in the early morning dark while Sitto made the dough for a day of baking. She mixed by hand, gold bangles clinking on her wrists. "Feel that dough, how good it feels," she whispered. She made a cross in the top of the dough, with an Arabic blessing that I remember only in English: *I worked with you and grew tired. Now God bless you.* In the basement, the furnace room had an oven, which was set with a hot baking steel because Sitto

Saj bread baking day with Sitto in her amazing little kitchen, circa 1991

INTRODUCTION

didn't have a saj dome, a folding table for the dough, and a kara—a flat, round pillow that holds thin rounds of saj bread dough—for stretching the edges of the dough before flipping it into the oven. Later, as I studied words and stories in school, a parallel education took place in Sitto's kitchen and my mother's, allowing me to absorb their ways with a keen awareness of what I was doing and why.

That awareness has become one of the greatest gifts of my life. It's not a talent, not an accomplishment for my pride. It's a gift from God, who sprinkled me with a passion to share Lebanese culture and cuisine. For years, I pined to attend culinary school, to visit Lebanon, and to write a book of recipes that included the stories that gave them meaning. Those aims all came to fruition on my website, MaureenAbood.com, and in my first cookbook, *Rose Water & Orange Blossoms*.

Among the more business-minded, the idea for this book first met with consternation: *how small, how niche. How about Mediterranean baking?*—or no baking at all. But Lebanese baking kept calling me, shaping my mission with experiences that broadened my understanding of the canon. In Beirut, the pastry chef at the Four Seasons Hotel topped golden puffed pitas with black sesame seeds and filled glossy croissants with za'atar. Street vendors turned out the ultimate

Lebanese breakfasts: za'atar-topped manakeesh rolled in paper cones to eat on the go, or hot cheese knafehs drizzled with flower water syrup and tucked into ka'ak sesame purse bread, also to eat on the move.

Lebanon itself deepened my quest to understand and share its stunning repertoire of classic and innovative baking. Michigan, where I grew up and live, has an enormous Lebanese American population. Lebanese bakeries in Dearborn offer a dizzying array of pastries and breads. Baking groups have arisen among my circle, too, perhaps born of loss, a collective absence of sittos, mothers, and aunts. The passing of my sister-in-law at age 40 catalyzed me to attend culinary school and focus on food full time. Likewise, this book blossomed in the wake of my mother's death. As someone said to me in empathy, "Plates shift when a mother dies." Thankfully, that generation raised me, my husband, and all our siblings with the strength to weather tectonic loss, instilling in us the ability to hold the hard with the good at once.

With that mother-dearth came a series of realizations. Recipes give us access to memories, wisdom, connection. Baking offers beauty in solitude and in community. We continue the conversations with those who baked for us in the past by continuing to bake and by sharing those conversations and traditions with future generations. Baking enacts a rich, braided conversation that never ends. No compendium of Lebanese baking, both savory and sweet, existed before this book. It may fill a niche, but it's far from small because nothing tastes better than a piece of crisp, syrup-laden baklawa; a slice of coconutty namoura (semolina cake); or a tender fatayer filled with spinach and nuts—all homemade.

The aromatic hallmarks of Lebanese cuisine fill this book: flower waters and spearmint, pomegranate and pistachios, sumac and za'atar. We'll venture through the magical world of baklawa and knafeh, simplifying and streamlining where possible, while still embracing homemade phyllo for the connection it makes with our forebears and for the pure, immense satisfaction and fun of it. We'll fry crisp tidbits and treats worth the indulgence. We'll bake khubz, breads of all kinds: soft, thick talami; thin saj bread that we call Syrian bread; puffed pita; fatayer pies; and manakeesh, which are flatbreads with toppings. We'll make cookies and cakes galore, with numerous variations of ka'ak and mak'rouns, including macarons and other French-inspired treats because, after the Ottoman Empire collapsed, the League of Nations handed control of what became Lebanon to France. The French mandate, which lasted almost 20 years, influenced Lebanese language, baking, and so much more.

All these recipes—whether passed down, handwritten, or researched—include as much of the Lebanese baking repertoire as possible. If, by not growing up in Lebanon, I've missed something important—come, tell me, and let's talk. I'll serve us a plate of ghraybeh and barazek and hot cardamom qahwa. Tell me about your beloved recipe so I can know it, too, and work on it to share. You'll find my own ideas in these pages, as well. We'll fill ma'amoul with apricots, stud a rose water Bundt cake with Michigan tart cherries, make chewy brownies with olive oil and tahini, dust chocolate baklawa with sea salt, and drizzle ghraybeh with chocolate, too.

Can you smell the aroma from the oven yet? Habibi, let's bake!

> "Everything we crave points to something greater beyond it."
> —C. S. Lewis

How to Use This Book

Like reading a good story or watching a meaningful movie, the pleasure of baking doesn't lie just in the result. Getting there is half the fun! If you're a seasoned baker, dive in and make every recipe. If you're new or bake with trepidation, don't be afraid. You have me by your side with all the instructions, suggestions, and other wisdom that you need. Keep these four key tips in mind.

BEFORE YOU BEGIN, READ THE ENTIRE RECIPE

This step eliminates unfortunate surprises, such as not having the right equipment on hand. Recipe headnotes indicate approximate times for prep and cooking, but reading ahead might save you time in the kitchen if you decide to prep certain ingredients in advance or use an alternative method.

By the same token, read the secrets first! In six different places—baklawa (page 2), knafeh (page 38), yeasted doughs (page 62), fatayer (page 196), manakeesh (page 218), and saj bread (page 250)—I reveal my baking secrets. Knowing what to do before you start doing it makes baking an even greater pleasure.

TAKE NOTES

No matter how beautiful you think this or any cookbook is, we all need permission to write in our books. Marginalia are your friends and continue the conversation. Record your thoughts and reactions about what is meaningful to you, such as:

Teta made this for us when kids.
Made for Christmas 2025.
Actually served only two of us.
So good, we ate it all in one day!

With the decline of handwritten recipes, handwritten notes in cookbooks have become more powerful. Someday, your copy of this book will become someone else's, hopefully in your family, and that person will treasure your notes, which will connect future generations back to you.

USE ALL THE TOOLS YOU WANT

Tools are liberating. The checklist of possibilities seemingly never ends, but it starts with some essentials. Look to the next section for a list of necessary equipment and some nice-to-have items, too.

BE KIND TO YOURSELF

Sometimes it takes a try or two to get the hang of particular methods, especially shaping. A light heart, patience, and practice will get you where you want to go.

Equipment

Here's what you'll need . . .

KITCHEN SCALE: Weighing ingredients ensures accuracy that makes for better baking. Ingredients in quantities of less than 1 teaspoon do not have an equivalent gram measurement provided, as many kitchen scales don't measure fractions of grams and can be less accurate when weighing those small amounts.

STAND MIXER: Sticky doughs, such as those for Fatayer (page 199), Pita (page 240), and Saj Bread (page 252), make kneading by hand something of a challenge. A stand mixer does the job swiftly, and its ease of use opens a vast world of baking.

ROLLING PIN: Old pins have an internal axle and handles separated from the body that allow the pin to roll with ease, making them a pleasure to use. They can become heirlooms worth handing down. The older the better for their smooth, worn patina that glides over doughs with ease and channels the bakers before us. Of the new pins available, look for one with adjustable guides that help you roll dough evenly to a specific thickness.

KITCHEN TOWELS: A stash of clean towels covers phyllo and bowls of yeast dough, wipes up spills and surfaces, and keeps hands clean during shaping with fillings.

KNIVES AND SCRAPERS: Make sure your knives are sharp and, depending on how much work they do, sharpen them at least once a year. Use a sharp chef's knife. A metal bench knife makes quick work of moving chopped ingredients from place to place, and the sharp edge makes easy work of dividing dough. (Aunt Louise—technically my mother-in-law but called "aunt" since my childhood in affinity, as I know you understand!—used an electric knife to cut baklawa. She must have given one to my husband, Dan. I've never used it, but he keeps reminding me how much she liked hers.) A flexible bench scraper helps remove sticky doughs from bowls with ease, and it clears dried dough off surfaces nicely.

PASTRY BRUSHES: Avoid silicone brushes, which don't hold liquids well and drip too heavily. Natural bristles provide more control for brushing butter on phyllo, for example. You can find them in the craft aisle or at a hardware store.

MISTING BOTTLE: Delicate doughs—phyllo, kataifi, fatayer, saj—require hydration for shaping. A spray bottle emits too much water at once, which can ruin the dough. A misting bottle emits just the right amount of moisture.

BREAD PEEL OR PIZZA PEEL: This giant offset spatula allows you to transfer flatbread doughs from counter to oven and back again with ease.

BAKING STEEL OR STONE: A baking steel delivers the best results for making flatbread and pita, but even a simple pizza stone transforms the experience.

PIPING BAGS AND TIPS: Piping isn't just for fancy cake decorating; it often offers the most efficient, lovely way to dollop frosting on cupcakes (page 162), insert cream in baklawa (page 29), or squeeze dough into hot oil for frying (page 126). Buy disposable piping bags and a few basic tips, especially a plain ½-inch (1.25-cm) tip.

THERMOMETER: A candy, deep fry, or instant-read thermometer tells you the exact temperature, so you don't have to guess.

Nice-to-have tools include the following . . .

NUT GRINDER: Many recipes call for coarsely chopped nuts, a consistency that can prove difficult to achieve in a food processor and is excessively time-consuming to do by hand. An old-fashioned, hand-cranked nut grinder does just the job, and its usefulness for baking never goes out of style.

MA'AMOUL AND KA'AK MOLDS: These little forms turn out cookies in traditional shapes. They feature a variety of pretty designs that will imprint on top of cookies. Look for deep designs expertly carved in wood. Mass-produced molds are often rough-hewn and shallow. A small metal tong huller makes an excellent alternative to molds. The sawtooth tong tips make beautiful ma'amoul designs with ease.

DOWEL: To shape baklawa for burma (page 22) and nests (page 24), use a metal, plastic, or wooden dowel that is ½ by 13 inches (1.25 cm by 33 cm).

KARA PILLOW: For making saj bread (page 252), this tool holds the delicate dough for shaping and transporting to the oven in a way that hands or even a peel can't. Buy one or make your own with a pillowcase over a round pillow or piece of crafting foam at least 16 inches (41 cm) wide.

SAJ DOME OVEN: This wonderful, specialized piece of equipment may not be easy to procure, but it's worth it. Like a convex frying pan, it makes baking saj bread (page 252) easier because you can flip the dough from the kara pillow onto the heated dome with simplicity.

Find more information about the tools, ingredients, and other items that you need to bake with from this book on my website at MaureenAbood.com.

Ingredients

Before gathering your ingredients, keep these notes in mind.

FLOUR

For recipes that call for all-purpose flour, always use unbleached. Bleach makes flour whiter, but it also makes it behave differently. Don't substitute! Many bread recipes call for bread flour, which has a higher protein content than all-purpose, making it stronger and easier to withstand shaping, as with fatayer (page 199).

Quantity is crucial, which is why you should use a scale to weigh your flour. Measuring by volume can be remarkably arbitrary, even with the same flour and tools. If you do measure by volume, stir the flour first and spoon it into the measuring cup lightly, over the top. Level it across the top with the flat edge of a knife or bench scraper. Don't try to spoon in the exact amount. To catch the excess, place the cup on a plate or paper towel, or hold it over the flour bag itself or another container.

I developed these recipes with King Arthur Unbleached All-Purpose Flour and King Arthur Bread Flour. Use those flours for the same results.

YEAST

Most of my recipes call for instant yeast, which activates without needing to dissolve in liquid. Often the labels will say "fast acting," "rapid rise," or "bread machine." Add instant yeast with the other dry ingredients. Dough containing instant yeast rises faster than dough containing dry yeast. Buy yeast in jars rather than packets so you can measure it easily. My recipes don't call for yeast by packet amount but by weight and the occasional imperial measure. Store yeast in an airtight container in the refrigerator.

> **SHAGGY DOUGH**
> In recipes that call for mixing together a dough, you will often see the term "shaggy." A shaggy dough means lumpy yet well mixed, with no dry spots of flour.

BUTTER

Most of my recipes that include butter call for Clarified Butter (page 271).

Across the board, I use unsalted butter. This allows me to control the amount of salt in the finished dish. It's also why a recipe might call for unsalted butter plus salt: Different salted butters have different sodium contents, so as with measuring by weight, this combination provides a way to be more precise and consistent. Does it hurt to use salted butter? No. If you use salted butter, though, reduce or eliminate other instances of salt in the recipe.

European or cultured butter has a higher butterfat content than standard American butter, enriching both aroma and flavor. You can use cultured butter in any of the recipes here.

OIL

My recipes use two basic types of oil: neutral and extra virgin olive. Neutral oils come from nuts, grains, seeds, and fruits. They have little to no flavor, don't weigh down a dough, and have a high smoke point, meaning they won't burn at high temperatures. My favorite neutral oils include expeller-pressed grapeseed, sunflower, safflower, canola, coconut, peanut, and avocado.

NUTS

Lebanese baking generously uses nuts—pistachios, walnuts, almonds, cashews—in practically everything: baklawa, knafeh, cookies, and more. Use your favorite(s) in any of the recipes. Nuts are so close in weight that substituting almonds for pistachios, for example, will work just fine. Walnuts and almonds taste excellent toasted (page 266). Pistachios, when blanched raw, add a bright, natural pop of green. For ground nuts, use a nut grinder (page xvi). For longevity and freshness, store nuts in an airtight container in the freezer.

YOGURT

Lebanese cuisine employs yogurt, called laban, in baking as much as in cooking. An acidic fermented food, yogurt imparts tenderness and moisture. Labneh, a thickened yogurt, resembles Greek yogurt, which you can substitute for labneh 1:1. But you can't swap labneh or Greek yogurt for plain yogurt. Plain yogurt has a higher water content, which will affect the recipe. If you need to use labneh or Greek yogurt in place of plain yogurt, add 14 grams (1 tablespoon) of water for every 57 grams (¼ cup) of labneh.

DATES

This royal fruit, tamar, appears throughout Lebanese cuisine, often as filling for breads and cookies. Big, soft, chewy medjool dates taste divine. Date Paste (page 272), also available in many Middle Eastern and Mediterranean markets, makes a quick and easy filling for cookies, such as ma'amoul. It's quite thick and often needs softening on the stovetop, in the microwave, or in a food processor with water, particularly for recipes that use it as a spread filling.

FLAVORINGS

Lebanese spices—especially Dried Mint (page 270), sumac, and za'atar—add zest to savory baking. Za'atar blends wild thyme, sumac, and sesame seeds. Mix it with oil to top breads or to use as a dip. Rose water and orange blossom water serve as essential flavorings in Lebanese baking, added directly or in syrups. These pure essences distill the aromas and flavors of flower petals. Rose and orange blossom extracts are *not* the same as flower water. Don't substitute!

PHYLLO AND KATAIFI DOUGH

Unleavened and paper-thin, commercial phyllo dough contains flour, water, and oil. Various preparations typically layer it with butter or oil. It dries quickly, though, so have everything else for the recipe ready before making it or opening the package. The same goes for kataifi dough. Its long, thin strands come bundled in a box. Both come frozen.

POMEGRANATE MOLASSES

A key pantry item in Lebanese cuisine, pomegranate molasses imparts a sweet-tart flavor to many dishes. Find this thick syrup in a local grocery store or online.

Baklawa

Like higher math, making baklawa can feel overwhelming at first. But breaking it into its fundamental parts and taking each step at a time transform the impressive whole into a solvable triumph. Its nuances, when fully understood, can combine to make a seemingly impossible pastry a centerpiece of your baking repertoire. Baklawa is one of the most beloved pastries of the Middle East and beyond. In my mother's and grandmothers' generations, everyone who baked made baklawa (even Aunt Hilda, who said, "I'm more cook than baker, honey"). The pastry forms part of the finery of any celebration, as essential as the savory foods, the flowers, the clothing. It's celebration itself made edible!

Secrets to Making Baklawa

This pastry includes many styles, but all share the basic components of phyllo, clarified butter, nuts, and flower water syrup. The word phyllo comes from the ancient Greek φύλλον (fúllon) meaning "leaf" or "sheet," like feuille in French. In Turkey, it goes by yufka. Lebanese baklawa differs in flavor from Greek and some Turkish baklavas. In commercial bakeries, baklawa comes in a variety of shapes and sizes, but home bakers typically roll or layer it, cutting it into diamonds. Prepare the components in advance so baking day calls only for assembling, buttering, cutting, baking, syruping, and devouring it.

PHYLLO

The baklawa chapter begins with two recipes using homemade phyllo dough. One of my old Lebanese cookbooks states: "I wouldn't even suggest that you attempt to make the paper-thin, transparent pastry used for this dessert. Instead, buy it." I don't disagree! But ease isn't the only metric. Learning how to make phyllo unlocks the past, connecting us with the many women who had no choice but to make it from scratch by hand if they wanted baklawa. At times, this reality has struck me as a burden, a bitter comment on the state of things for women then. My thinking changed as my interest in pastry deepened, though. These women who stretched the dough paper thin over the dining table, each doing her delicate job—they were pastry superheroines! They mastered and kept the tradition, and it brought them together. Making homemade phyllo feels like a reunion with them.

Homemade

You can make phyllo dough in two ways: dry and wet. The dry method takes more time, and each yields different results. I find dry works best for diamonds, and wet for spirals. For the dry method, it takes a *lot* of cornstarch to keep the sheets from sticking together. A fine mesh sieve makes even distribution of cornstarch a breeze, and it's much more effective than dusting freehand. Roll pieces of dough in a stack, creating all the delicate layers. While rolling, keep a light touch on the pin and roll just to the size indicated. Pressing too firmly can meld the sheets together, making it difficult or impossible to separate them. The sheets will run close in size, but they won't match exactly, and that's OK.

Another way with the dry method rolls giant sheets of phyllo with an oklava or long dowel rolling pin (24 to 30 inches by ¾ inch, 61 to 75 cm by 2 cm). Halve the dough, coat each half well in the dusting mixture, and roll it into a 10-inch (25-cm) circle. Wind the dusted dough around the pin, leaving about 2 inches (5 cm) loose at the long edge. (Rolling that edge of dough onto the rest will make it difficult to unroll the sheet.) With both hands, press and draw the dough from the middle to the end three times and no more. Unroll the dough, rotate it 90 degrees, dust with more cornstarch, and roll again. Repeat until the dough sheet stretches thin and large. Cut it to fit your pan and layer from there.

To store phyllo for later use, layer the dusted sheets between sheets of parchment paper, roll the layered stack, and then wrap the roll in plastic wrap and place it in an airtight container or food storage bag. Refrigerate for up to 2 days or freeze for up to 4 weeks. Thaw frozen phyllo in the refrigerator overnight before using.

For the wet method, follow the recipe for Baklawa Spirals with Homemade Phyllo (page 10).

Store-Bought

Commercial phyllo runs thinner and crunches crispier all the way through in a way that thicker, crispy-chewy homemade phyllo can't. At the grocery store, you can find phyllo in the frozen dessert section. The sheets typically come in two sizes: 9 by 14 inches (23 by 35 cm) and 14 by 18 inches (35 by 45 cm). More grocery stores carry the smaller size, so if that's the case where you shop, buy that one. All the recipes here work with that smaller size, which fits neatly into a 9-by-13-by-2-inch (23-by-33-by-5-cm) baking pan. This smaller size yields 35 to 45 pieces, which seems like plenty, but they disappear quickly!

The larger sheets come in varying, numbered thicknesses. Of those, #4—the ideal thickness—bakes to a perfect crisp. You often can find it at specialty food stores. Larger size sheets work well for making big-event baklawa. That said, it feels easier to me to make a double batch of the smaller size rather than a single batch of the larger size in a larger pan. If you do use the larger size sheets in a half sheet pan, double the quantity of nuts, butter, and syrup as you would for a double batch of the smaller size.

Thaw the phyllo overnight in the refrigerator and, a couple of hours before baking, bring it to room temperature. Cold phyllo doesn't obey as well as phyllo at room temperature; it breaks and tears more easily. Removing the sleeves of phyllo from the box speeds thawing, but don't open the sleeves until right before you begin assembly. Even then, keep the phyllo under a kitchen towel. The sheets dry out faster than lightning, so work with purposeful energy once the phyllo meets the air.

SYRUP

Flower Water Syrup (page 273), or attar, flavored with pure orange blossom water and/or rose water—not to be confused with flower extracts—drenches baklawa. In baking, it often goes by the name simple syrup, even though simple syrup technically consists of sugar dissolved 1:1 in water. The syrup in Lebanese pastry has more sugar than water, but it's still pretty simple. Don't cook the syrup too long. Always use a timer to get it right. Double or even triple the recipe so you always have syrup in the refrigerator.

BUTTER

My cousin John Abowd once said that the best baklawa he ever made used cultured butter from France. I tried it, and the flavor it produced tasted so much richer than what came from standard American butter that I never looked back! When people ask why my baklawa tastes so much better than any they've eaten, this is one major reason. In baklawa, the solids in regular butter can burn and look spotty. Clarifying butter (page 271) removes those solids and water, leaving pure, golden, translucent butterfat.

FILLING

Use your favorite nuts. For me, walnuts taste the best, and their scent and flavor (and even the bag!) conjure a lifetime of wonderful memories. Pistachios, almonds, cashews—all traditional and delightful—are excellent solo or in combinations. Feel free to set tradition aside and try pecans, hazelnuts, or even peanuts. Toasting your nuts (page 266) deepens the flavor and texture, and doing this in advance makes baking day easier. You can grind, sugar, and freeze them in advance, too.

Grinding nuts coarsely requires a careful hand. You don't want big chunks, but you also don't want nut powder or nut butter. Aim for little nuggets, easiest to achieve with a hand grinder (page xvi). Another cousin, Jimmy Abood, sent me the grinder that our mothers and grandmothers preferred, which I do, too. You *can* use a food processor, but pace your pulses with care so as not to go too far. Finely ground nuts tend to fall from the pastry when cutting and eating.

ASSEMBLY

Baklawa consists fundamentally of buttery layers of phyllo. How the butter reaches its destination becomes part of the art of making them. Aunt Rita baked so much baklawa—clarifying 50 pounds of butter every Christmas!—that she came up with brilliant efficiencies. For example, she stacked phyllo in the pan, then nuts, then more phyllo. She cut it, poured butter over everything, and let it soak in. Habibi, it works! But for baklawa rolls, the layers need buttering individually before rolling, or else they'll dry and crack.

For diamonds, pour the butter over the whole assembly. For all the other recipes, butter each layer.

CUTTING

To achieve diamond shapes, cut straight and diagonal rows (or just diagonal if making rolls). It helps enormously to mark the cuts lightly before making them, so always mark your cuts first. Align the knife blade with where you're about to cut to visualize the shape first. If it veers more toward rhomboid than rhombus (more math!), realign and correct course before and as you cut.

Always cut the baklawa *before* baking, and—very important—cut to the bottom of the pan to allow the butter and syrup to soak and absorb all the way through. After baking and syruping, follow the existing lines to cut the pieces again before carefully removing them from the pan.

BAKING

Use a metal cake pan or baking pan. Metal holds heat well and bakes evenly from all contact points. When the baklawa comes out of the oven, immediately pour the cold syrup on it slowly and evenly. The temperature differential of cold syrup on hot pastry encourages absorption. (Hot syrup on cooled baklawa also works.) Don't forget to listen for the sizzle of cold syrup sinking into hot pastry, another sensation of baking baklawa. The pastry lightens in color over time; it's not an illusion! But it is another reason, besides great flavor and texture, to bake it to a deep golden brown.

EATING

Baklawa needs time to rest, set, and absorb the syrup before the final cutting. But that doesn't stop Dan, my husband, from eating the end pieces hot and bragging about it to anyone who will listen. Keep the baklawa in the baking pan until serving. After you remove the pieces, they'll begin to dry. Aunt Louise kept a squeeze bottle of syrup on the dining table. As she cut and served, she squeezed a little more syrup on each piece to refresh it.

Baklawa cut from the pan tastes best within 2 or 3 days. In a covered baking pan, baklawa will keep for 2 weeks by my calendar and a month by Aunt Hilda's—assuming you have the discipline not to eat it all before then. (I don't!) Cover it lightly with wax paper or parchment, leaving it loose on all sides and barely touching the top of the pastry. Transport or gift it by placing pieces in foil mini-muffin cups.

BAKLAWA DIAMONDS
with Homemade Phyllo

This recipe uses the dry method to make phyllo sheets that roll out just right for a 10-inch pan. It's not difficult, but it's more hands-on and takes longer than the wet method used for Baklawa Spirals (page 10). Homemade phyllo is fun, satisfying, and yields its own kind of pastry. The crunchy, beautiful layers have a delightful cookie-like flavor. Before you begin, give yourself space and time to read my secrets (page 2) and the entire recipe. This will help you understand the whole process before you dive in.

PREP: **45 MINUTES**
REST: **1 HOUR 15 MINUTES**
COOK: **2 HOURS 10 MINUTES**
COOL: **2 HOURS**
TOTAL: **6 HOURS 10 MINUTES**

MAKES: **32 PIECES**

DOUGH
151 grams (⅔ cup) water, warm (105–110°F, 40–43°C)
8 grams (2 teaspoons) white vinegar
½ teaspoon fine sea salt
25 grams (2 tablespoons) extra virgin olive oil
254 grams (2 cups plus 2 tablespoons) unbleached all-purpose flour

DUSTING MIXTURE
84 grams (¾ cup) cornstarch
8 grams (1 tablespoon) unbleached all-purpose flour, plus more for surfaces

FILLING
225 grams (1¼ cups) toasted nuts of choice (page 266)
100 grams (½ cup) granulated white sugar
8 grams (2 teaspoons) orange blossom water or 4 grams (1 teaspoon) rose water, or a 2:1 combination
112 grams (½ cup plus 1 tablespoon) Clarified Butter (page 271), melted
160 grams (½ cup) Flower Water Syrup (page 273), cold

1. In a small mixing bowl, combine the water, vinegar, salt, and olive oil. Stir to dissolve the salt.

2. In the bowl of a stand mixer fitted with the dough hook, add the flour and set the mixer speed to low. Slowly add the liquid mixture until the dough becomes shaggy, about 30 seconds.

3. Bring the dough together in a rough, sticky ball and knead it on medium just until the dough becomes cohesive, about 1 minute.

4. Cover the dough ball with a damp towel tucked directly on it. Let the dough rest for 1 hour. Any lumps will dissolve as the dough rests.

5. Meanwhile, make the dusting mixture and filling. In a small mixing bowl, whisk together the cornstarch and flour. Set aside with a small fine-mesh sieve.

6. In a nut grinder or food processor, coarsely chop the nuts. Transfer them to a small mixing bowl and combine them with the sugar and flower water. Set aside.

7. Arrange an oven rack in the middle position and preheat the oven to 325°F (165°C). Brush the bottom of a 10-inch (25-cm) cake pan with 12 grams (1 tablespoon) of the clarified butter. Lightly dust a baking sheet with flour.

8. Form the rested dough into a smooth ball and divide it into 16 pieces, 27 grams each. Shape each piece into a smooth ball. Place the balls on the floured baking sheet as you go. Cover them with a kitchen towel and let them rest for no more than 15 minutes.

9. Generously sift the dusting mixture on the counter. Dip 1 dough ball in the bowl of cornstarch and flour. On the dusted counter, roll it out into to a 5-inch (13-cm) disc. Repeat with 3 more dough balls, setting each aside after rolling.

10. Generously sift the dusting mixture over the counter and the 4 discs. Stack the discs in the middle of the counter, gently press the rolling pin across the top of the stack to start rolling, and roll the stack into an 8-inch (20-cm) circle. Don't roll it larger than that.

11. Gently separate the sheets.

12. Thoroughly dust each sheet with the cornstarch mixture and stack them again. Roll the stack to a 10-inch (25-cm) circle. Don't roll it larger than that.

13. Gently separate the sheets again. Dust off as much of the cornstarch mixture as possible.

14. Lay 1 sheet flat in the buttered cake pan, stretching it to fit if needed and folding over any excess around the perimeter. Sprinkle it lightly with clarified butter. Repeat with the 3 remaining sheets.

15. Roll the next 4 sheets, repeating steps 9 through 14.

16. Bake for 10 minutes.

17. Meanwhile, roll the next 4 sheets, repeating steps 9 through 13.

18. After 10 minutes, remove the cake pan from the oven, keeping the oven on. Place the cake pan on a cooling rack and top the par-baked sheets with the filling.

continues

19. Repeat step 14 with the 4 rolled sheets, then repeat steps 9 through 14 for the final 4 sheets.

20. Of the final 4 sheets, set the smoothest aside for the top of the baklawa. One at a time, carefully lay the other 3 sheets in the pan, drizzling butter over each. Top with the reserved sheet but don't butter it yet.

21. Using the tip of a long, sharp chef's knife, mark 6 diagonal cuts for 7 rows in one direction and 6 diagonal cuts for 7 rows in the opposite direction. Hold the knife perpendicular to the pastry, cutting straight down into it.

22. Brush the remaining clarified butter evenly over the top.

23. Bake until the baklawa turns a deep golden brown, about 2 hours.

24. Remove the pan from the oven and immediately pour the cold syrup slowly and evenly over the hot baklawa. Let it cool at room temperature for at least 2 hours.

25. Following the diamond lines, cut the pieces of baklawa from the pan with a sharp knife. Serve them in foil mini-muffin cups or on a plate, arranged in a circle with the tips pointing to center.

Note

In the cake pan, keep the baklawa lightly covered with plastic wrap or wax paper at room temperature for up to 2 weeks.

VARIATION: Cut the baklawa in narrow slices for a **TURKISH** appearance. Use a 2-inch (5-cm) round cutter to mark a circle in the center and cut the circle through to the bottom. Mark 16 even wedges into the top of the baklawa and cut them through to the bottom.

BAKLAWA SPIRALS
with Homemade Phyllo

PREP: **40 MINUTES**
REST: **30 MINUTES**
COOK: **1 HOUR**
COOL: **2 HOURS**
TOTAL: **4 HOURS 10 MINUTES**

MAKES: **2 SPIRALS (16 SERVINGS)**

This recipe employs the wet method to stretch two giant phyllo sheets by hand. This dough shapes best in rolls, which, as in Turkish and other cultures' pastry, coil easily into pretty spirals. The wedges cut from the spirals have beautiful cross sections through the slice.

BASTING MIXTURE
57 grams (¼ cup) Clarified Butter (page 271)
50 grams (¼ cup) extra virgin olive oil

DOUGH
151 grams (⅔ cup) water, warm (105–110°F, 40–43°C)
25 grams (2 tablespoons) extra virgin olive oil
8 grams (2 teaspoons) white vinegar
½ teaspoon fine sea salt
300 grams (2½ cups) unbleached all-purpose flour

FILLING
170 grams (1⅓ cups) toasted nuts of choice (page 266)
100 grams (½ cup) granulated white sugar
4 grams (1 teaspoon) orange blossom water, rose water, or a 1:1 combination
160 grams (½ cup) Flower Water Syrup (page 273), cold

1. In a small mixing bowl, whisk together the basting mixture. Set aside.
2. In another small mixing bowl, add the water, oil, vinegar, and salt. Stir to dissolve the salt.
3. In the bowl of a stand mixer fitted with the dough hook, add the flour and set the speed to low. Slowly add the liquid mixture until the dough becomes shaggy, about 30 seconds.
4. Bring the dough together in a rough, sticky ball and knead it on medium speed until the dough becomes soft and smooth, about 3 minutes.
5. Generously coat a 10-inch plate with some of the basting mixture.
6. Halve the dough and shape the halves (approximately 220 grams or ½ pound each) into smooth balls. Roll out one ball into an 8-inch (20-cm) disc. Place the dough disc on the oiled plate.
7. Roll out the second ball and lay the second disc on the first. Generously brush the top with the basting mixture. Let the dough rest, uncovered, for 30 minutes.
8. Meanwhile, make the filling. In a nut grinder or food processor, coarsely chop the toasted nuts. Transfer them to a small mixing bowl and combine them with the sugar and flower water. Set aside.
9. Arrange an oven rack in the middle position and preheat the oven to 375°F (190°C).
10. On the counter or a table, clear a space at least 30 inches (75 cm) square. Lightly brush the surface with some of the basting mixture. Lay a dough disc in the center of the work area, with room in all directions to stretch it.
11. Lift the edge farthest from you and gently stretch it away from the center. Set it back down, pressing the edge to anchor it back to the surface. Repeat with the edge closest to you.
12. Moving 2 inches (5 cm) at a time clockwise, pick up the edge of the dough, gently stretch it outward, and set it back down. As you move all the way around to the starting point, occasionally lift the sheet, placing your hand underneath it, and

continues

BAKLAWA

gently stretch the dough from the center, drawing it upward and outward. When done, the sheet should measure roughly 28 inches by 30 inches (71 cm by 75 cm). Leave any tears that may occur while stretching.

13. Lightly sprinkle the sheet with some of the basting mixture and fold it in half toward you. Sprinkle with more of the basting mixture.

14. Along the long edge of the sheet closer to you, spoon the nut mixture in a straight line.

15. Pick up that long edge and carefully roll it into a log, lifting the long edges of the dough up over the nuts and then rolling. Pinch the seam closed and finish with the seam underneath the log.

16. Coil the log into a spiral. Finish by tucking the narrow outer end slightly underneath the spiral. Carefully transfer the spiral to an unlined baking sheet. Brush the top liberally with more of the basting mixture.

17. Repeat steps 9 through 15 with the second dough ball. On the baking sheet, place the second spiral about 2 inches from the first.

18. Bake until the spirals turn golden brown, 1 hour.

19. Remove the baklawa from the oven and immediately pour the cold syrup slowly and evenly over the pastry. Direct the syrup into the seams of the spirals and over the edges. Some of the syrup will run off.

20. Let the spirals cool at room temperature for at least 2 hours.

21. To serve, cut the baklawa into wedges.

Note
Keep the baklawa lightly covered with plastic wrap or wax paper at room temperature for up to 1 week.

BAKLAWA DIAMONDS

My fast and easy method for this ultimate classic doesn't require buttering every layer, and it still comes out just as light and crisp. Brushing the top layers does help hold down the phyllo for cutting, though. Because phyllo often runs a little longer or shorter than the size on the box, you'll use your pan as a guide to trim it for a perfect fit.

PREP: 20 MINUTES
COOK: 50 MINUTES
COOL: 2 HOURS
TOTAL: 3 HOURS 10 MINUTES

MAKES: 38 PIECES

226 grams (1 cup) Clarified Butter (page 271), melted
One 9-by-14-inch (23-by-35.5-cm) package phyllo dough (32 sheets, 454 grams, 1 pound), room temperature

FILLING
384 grams (3 cups) toasted nuts of choice (page 266)
100 grams (½ cup) granulated white sugar
8 grams (2 teaspoons) orange blossom water or 4 grams (1 teaspoon) rose water, or a 2:1 combination
320 grams (1 cup) Flower Water Syrup (page 273), cold

1. Arrange an oven rack in the middle position and preheat the oven to 350°F (177°C).

2. Brush the bottom of a 9-by-13-by-2-inch (23-by-33-by-5-cm) metal baking pan with 12 grams (1 tablespoon) of the butter.

3. In a nut grinder or food processor, coarsely chop the nuts. Transfer them to a small mixing bowl and combine them with the sugar and flower water. Set aside.

4. Open one sleeve of the phyllo and unroll it on the plastic packaging, leaving the other sleeve unopened. Lay the baking pan over the stack of phyllo, aligning a short side of the pan with a short side of the phyllo. Use the pan as a guide to trim the stack with kitchen scissors so the dough will fit inside the pan. You likely will trim about 1 inch (2.5 cm) from the short side.

5. Lay the trimmed dough in the pan and top it evenly with the nut mixture. With the back of a spoon, firmly press the nuts down.

6. Open the second sleeve of dough and unroll it on the plastic packaging. Trim it as in step 4. If the top layer of phyllo shows any damage, such as tears or folding, pull a sheet from the middle and place it on top. Remove 2 sheets from the top of the stack and set them aside. Lay the rest of the stack in the pan over the filling.

7. Lightly brush the top layer in the pan with butter. Lay 1 of the 2 reserved sheets, not the clean top sheet, in the pan and brush it with butter. Repeat with the second and top sheets.

8. Using the tip of a long, sharp chef's knife, mark 5 lengthwise cuts for 6 columns and 9 crosswise diagonal cuts for 10 rows. (For smaller pieces, make 6 lengthwise cuts for 7 rows and 10 crosswise diagonal cuts for 11 rows.) Hold the knife perpendicular to the pastry, cutting straight down into the phyllo and nuts. Use your nondominant hand to hold the top layers of phyllo down while cutting with your dominant hand all the way through to the bottom of the pan. (The small end pieces will go automatically to the baker!)

9. Pour the butter evenly over the baklawa. Allow the butter to soak in for 3 minutes, tilting the pan to distribute it evenly if needed.

10. Bake until the baklawa turns a deep golden brown, 45 to 55 minutes.

continues

11. Remove the pan from the oven and immediately pour the cold syrup slowly and evenly over the hot baklawa. Let it cool at room temperature for at least 2 hours.

12. Following the diamond lines, cut the pieces of baklawa from the pan with a sharp knife. Serve them in foil mini-muffin cups or on a plate, arranged in a circle with the tips pointing to center.

> *Note*
>
> In the pan, keep the baklawa lightly covered with plastic wrap or wax paper at room temperature for up to 2 weeks.
>
> **VARIATION:** For **VEGAN BAKLAWA DIAMONDS**, replace the butter with 125 grams (½ cup plus 2 tablespoons) extra virgin olive oil or melted coconut oil. Both have subtle flavor; the taste of the nuts and syrup shine through.

Something to Drink

ARABIC CARDAMOM COFFEE

This coffee, *Qahwa Arabi*, is a way of life. Coffee bean grinders often have an Arabic or Turkish setting, which creates grounds so fine that the coffee mostly dissolves as it boils in an ibrik, a special stovetop pot. Often this intense brew is sipped from Arabic coffee cups that don't have handles.

PREP: **1 MINUTE**
COOK: **5 MINUTES**
TOTAL: **6 MINUTES**
MAKES: **4 SERVINGS**

454 grams (2 cups) water, cold
21 grams (2 tablespoons) finely ground dark-roast coffee
⅛ teaspoon ground cardamom
4 grams (1 teaspoon) granulated white sugar (optional)

VARIATION: Albi, an eatery in Washington, DC, makes an amazing **ARABIC COFFEE AFFOGATO**. You can make it, too. In a small dessert bowl, add a brownie (page 131) and 1 scoop of vanilla frozen yogurt. Pour 1 serving of Arabic Cardamom Coffee over it and, if desired, finish it with a splash of Kahlúa or amber rum.

1. In an ibrik or small saucepan over high heat, add the water, coffee, cardamom, and, if using, the sugar. Bring it to a boil, stirring occasionally.

2. When it just comes to a boil, remove the vessel from the heat and gently stir to prevent the coffee from boiling over.

3. Return the vessel to the heat and, stirring constantly, bring the coffee to a boil again.

4. Remove the coffee from the heat and divide it, along with any foam, among four Arabic coffee cups or demitasse cups and serve.

BAKLAWA ROLLS

For much of my family, baklawa is all about these rolls that form a tidy bundle that's easy to pick up and eat. This shape doesn't take to pour-over buttering, though, which makes it a slower process to create. As my cousin Celine says, "It's like a meditation." My mother-in-law, Louise, always made this style, and my husband, Dan, and his brothers, Ralph and Jim, call these the best for the texture, flavor, and nostalgia for their sweet mother's baking.

PREP: **45 MINUTES**
COOK: **40 MINUTES**
COOL: **2 HOURS**
TOTAL: **3 HOURS 25 MINUTES**

MAKES: **40 PIECES**

FILLING
384 grams (3 cups) toasted nuts of choice (page 266)
50 grams (¼ cup) granulated white sugar
8 grams (2 teaspoons) orange blossom water or 4 grams (1 teaspoon) rose water, or a 2:1 combination
226 grams (1 cup) Clarified Butter (page 271), melted
One 9-by-14-inch (23-by-35.5-cm) package phyllo dough (32 sheets, 454 grams, 1 pound), room temperature
320 grams (1 cup) Flower Water Syrup (page 273), cold

1. Arrange an oven rack in the middle position and preheat the oven to 350°F (177°C).

2. In a nut grinder or food processor, coarsely chop the nuts. Transfer them to a small mixing bowl and combine them with the sugar and flower water. Set aside.

3. Brush a 9-by-13-by-2-inch (23-by-33-by-5-cm) metal baking pan with 12 grams (1 tablespoon) of the clarified butter.

4. Open one sleeve of the phyllo and unroll it on the plastic packaging, leaving the other sleeve unopened. Lay a kitchen towel over the phyllo.

5. Place 1 sheet of phyllo on the surface in front of you, long side toward you. Brush the sheet with butter but don't worry about coating every inch. Place a second sheet of phyllo on the buttered sheet and brush it with butter. Repeat three times more for a total of 5 sheets.

6. In a line along the long edge of the stack closer to you, spoon 63 grams (about 7 tablespoons) of the filling. Leave ½ inch (1.25 cm) of space along the edge and sides.

7. Fold the left and right edges of the phyllo over the filling by ½ inch (1.5 cm) and press to crease the folds from edge to edge. Holding the phyllo at either folded edge, lift the long edge of the phyllo closer to you over the nuts, tuck the long edge tightly under the filling, and roll into a tight log.

8. Carefully transfer the log to the buttered pan, seam side down. Fit it snugly against the long edge of the pan. Brush the top and sides of the log with more butter.

9. Repeat steps 5 through 8 with the rest of the phyllo and nuts, opening the second sleeve halfway through making the fourth roll. Lay each roll snugly against the last one in the pan and brush the top and sides with butter. If an extra sheet or two of phyllo remain, don't add them to the roll, which will make the roll too thick.

10. Using the tip of a long, sharp chef's knife, mark 9 crosswise diagonal cuts for 10 rows. (Again, the small, folded end pieces will go to the baker!)

11. Pour the rest of the butter evenly over the cut rolls.

12. Bake until the baklawa turns a deep golden brown, 35 to 40 minutes.

13. Remove the pan from the oven and immediately pour the cold syrup slowly and evenly over the hot

baklawa. Let it cool at room temperature for at least 2 hours.

14. Following the lines, cut the pieces of baklawa from the pan with a sharp knife. Serve them in foil mini-muffin cups or on a serving platter.

Note
In the pan, keep the baklawa lightly covered with plastic wrap or wax paper at room temperature for up to 2 weeks.

TIP: To prevent the baklawa from drying out, remove only the pieces you're about to eat and keep the rest in the pan.

VARIATIONS
- Use the rolls to make **BAKLAWA FINGERS**, another traditional shape with a nice, crispy ratio of nuts to phyllo. Create 12 narrow rolls by using 3 sheets of phyllo and 30 grams (4 tablespoons) of filling per roll. Make 5 crosswise (rather than diagonal) cuts for 6 straight-sided rows of 60 fingers total. Bake for 30 to 35 minutes.
- For **VEGAN BAKLAWA ROLLS**, replace the butter with 125 grams (½ cup plus 2 tablespoons) extra virgin olive oil or melted coconut oil.

BURMA BAKLAWA

In Turkish, *burma* means a twist. Like Baklawa Nests (page 24), this form calls for shaping on a dowel and accordian pleating, and the style eats light as air! Because the delicate phyllo can tear when shaped, a quick misting of water makes the dough more pliable. Finely chopped nuts scatter lightly over the phyllo, allowing for more air in the shape and a lighter bite.

PREP: 25 MINUTES
COOK: 45 MINUTES
COOL: 2 HOURS
TOTAL: 3 HOURS 10 MINUTES

MAKES: 32 ROLLS (BURMA)
SPECIAL EQUIPMENT: MISTING BOTTLE; DOWEL, ½-BY-13 INCHES (1.25-BY-33-CM) WOOD, METAL, OR PLASTIC

FILLING
256 grams (2 cups) toasted nuts of choice (page 266)
50 grams (¼ cup) granulated white sugar
8 grams (2 teaspoons) orange blossom water or 4 grams (1 teaspoon) rose water, or a 2:1 combination
1 sleeve phyllo dough (18 sheets, 227 grams, ½ pound) from one 9-by-14-inch (23-by-35.5-cm) box, room temperature
113 grams (½ cup) Clarified Butter (page 271), melted
160 grams (½ cup) Flower Water Syrup (page 273), cold

1. Arrange an oven rack in the middle position and preheat the oven to 350°F (177°C).
2. Coat a 9-inch (23-cm) square pan with 12 grams (1 tablespoon) of butter.
3. In a nut grinder or food processor, finely chop the nuts. Transfer them to a small mixing bowl and combine them with the sugar and flower water. Set aside.
4. Set up a workstation with the misting bottle, dowel, pastry brush, baking sheet, and a bowl of the melted butter.
5. Open the sleeve of the phyllo and unroll it on the plastic packaging. Lay a kitchen towel over the phyllo.
6. Place 1 sheet of phyllo on the surface in front of you, short side toward you. Mist the top of the phyllo very lightly with water. Fold in the short edge closer to you by ½ inch (1.25 cm) and each long side by the same amount.
7. Brush the phyllo with butter but don't worry about coating every inch. Don't butter the folded edges.
8. Evenly scatter 38 grams (2 tablespoons) of the filling over the buttered phyllo, again avoiding the folded edges.
9. Lay the dowel along the folded short side of the pastry. Lift the edge over the dowel and roll it tightly around the dowel. When you reach the opposite edge, position that seam downward and press gently on the dowel to seal it.
10. Lift the phyllo-wrapped dowel, wrap your hands around each end of the phyllo, and gently push the ends to the center to scrunch the roll.
11. Gently slide the burma off the dowel into the prepared pan and nudge it to one side of the pan, seam side still facing down. Generously brush the top and sides of the burma with butter.
12. Repeat steps 4 through 11 with the rest of the phyllo. In the pan, place the burma directly against one another to make two columns. Adjust to fit as needed.
13. With the tip of a sharp chef's knife, cut down the middle of each column, creating four pieces per row.

14. Bake until golden brown, about 45 minutes.

15. Remove the pan from the oven and immediately pour the cold syrup slowly and evenly over the burma. Let them cool at room temperature for at least 2 hours.

16. When ready to serve, cut the pieces from the pan row by row.

Note

In the pan, keep the burma lightly covered with plastic wrap or wax paper at room temperature for up to 2 weeks.

VARIATION: To make **NUT-FREE BAKLAWA**, change the filling to 120 grams (1 cup) pepitas, 70 grams (½ cup) sunflower seeds, 72 grams (½ cup) Toasted Sesame Seeds (page 269), 100 grams (½ cup) granulated white sugar, and 8 grams (2 teaspoons) flower water.

BAKLAWA NESTS

This pretty, delicate style of baklawa enjoys popularity throughout the Middle East. In various countries, it goes by the names Nightingale's Nest and Lady's Navel. Like Burma Baklawa (page 22), making it also requires the use of a dowel and the technique of accordion pleating, made easier with a light misting of water. Nests require far less butter than the other baklawas, because too much will make shaping it difficult. When it comes to the fillings, run with your imagination! These crispy, light-as-air nests work wonderfully with all kinds of nuts, melted chocolate, nut butters, and even seeds (see variation on page 23).

PREP: **20 MINUTES**
COOK: **40 MINUTES**
TOTAL: **1 HOUR**

MAKES: **18 NESTS**
SPECIAL EQUIPMENT: **MISTING BOTTLE; DOWEL, ½-BY-13 INCHES (1.25-BY-33-CM), WOOD, METAL, OR PLASTIC**

FILLING

- 90 grams (¾ cup) raw or Blanched Pistachios (page 267), toasted nuts of choice (page 266), or desiccated coconut
- 12 grams (1 tablespoon) granulated white sugar
- ½ teaspoon orange blossom water or rose water, or a 1:1 combination of the two
- 113 grams (½ cup) Clarified Butter (page 271), melted
- 18 sheets phyllo dough (1 sleeve, 227 grams, ½ pound) from a 9-by-14-inch (23-by-35.5-cm) package, room temperature
- 320 grams (1 cup) Flower Water Syrup (page 273), cold

1. Arrange an oven rack in the middle position and preheat the oven to 350°F (177°C).
2. In a nut grinder or food processor, coarsely chop the nuts. Transfer them to a small mixing bowl and combine them with the sugar and flower water. Set aside.
3. Brush a baking sheet with 12 grams (1 tablespoon) of the butter.
4. Open the sleeve of the phyllo and unroll it on the plastic packaging. Lay a kitchen towel over the phyllo.
5. Set up a workstation with the dowel, pastry brush, the prepared baking sheet, and a bowl of the melted butter.
6. Place 1 sheet of phyllo on the surface in front of you, short side toward you. Mist the top of the phyllo very lightly with water. Fold in the short edge closer to you by 1 inch (2.5 cm).
7. Brush the phyllo with butter but don't worry about coating every inch. Don't butter the folded edge.
8. Lay the dowel along the folded short side of the pastry. Lift the edge over the dowel and roll it tightly around the dowel. Leave a 2-inch (5-cm) flap loose at the opposite end.
9. Lift the phyllo-wrapped dowel, wrap your hands around each end of the phyllo, and gently push the ends to the center to scrunch the roll.
10. Gently slide the roll off the dowel into the prepared baking sheet and bring the ends together so the flap forms the bottom of the nest. Gently brush the nest generously with butter.
11. Repeat steps 6 through 10 with the rest of the phyllo. Place the nests touching one another, side by side, to fill the sheet.
12. Bake until the nests turn a deep golden brown, 17 to 20 minutes.
13. Remove the sheet from the oven and immediately pour the syrup slowly and evenly over the nests. Use approximately 40 grams (2 tablespoons) of syrup per nest.

14. Spoon 5 grams (2 teaspoons) of filling into the center of each nest and drizzle more syrup over the filling.

15. Serve immediately or let cool for 1 hour.

Note
On the baking sheet, store the nests lightly covered with wax paper at room temperature for up to 1 week.

TIP: Easily double the recipe by using 2 sleeves (1 package) of phyllo and doubling the other ingredients.

BAKLAWA CRINKLE

Who doesn't love an innovation that makes baking easier and retains such delicious results? For this quick and easy crinkle, you'll scrunch sheets of phyllo into the pan; bake it three times, adding butter, syrup, and a custardy filling; then shower it all with bright pistachios and rose petals.

PREP: **15 MINUTES**
COOK: **55 MINUTES**
COOL: **1 HOUR**
TOTAL: **2 HOURS 10 MINUTES**

MAKES: **12 (3-INCH, 7.5-CM) SQUARES**

One 9-by-14-inch (23-by-35.5-cm) package phyllo dough (32 sheets, 454 grams, 1 pound), room temperature
226 grams (1 cup) Clarified Butter (page 271), melted

CUSTARD
2 large eggs
150 grams (¾ cup) granulated white sugar
227 grams (1 cup) whole milk
4 grams (1 teaspoon) orange blossom water
4 grams (1 teaspoon) rose water

TOPPING
160 grams (½ cup) raw or Blanched Pistachios (page 267)
160 grams (½ cup) orange blossom syrup (page 273), cold
1 tablespoon edible dried rose petals

1. Arrange an oven rack in the middle position and preheat the oven to 350°F (177°C).

2. Butter the bottom of a 9-by-13-by-2-inch (23-by-33-by-5-cm) metal baking pan.

3. Open one sleeve of the phyllo and unroll it on the plastic packaging, leaving the other sleeve unopened. Place the entire stack in front of you, long side toward you.

4. Working with 2 sheets at a time, lift the short ends from the stack and push them toward the middle, making a loose accordion fold. Transfer the crinkled sheets to the baking pan and nestle the bundle against a short side of the pan.

5. Repeat step 4 with the rest of the phyllo, placing each crinkled sheet against the last one. When you finish the first sleeve, open and crinkle the second.

6. Bake just until the phyllo turns pale gold, 10 minutes.

7. Remove the pan from the oven and pour the butter evenly over the phyllo. Return it to the oven and bake until golden, 10 more minutes.

8. Meanwhile, make the custard. In a large liquid measuring cup or medium mixing bowl with a spout, whisk together the eggs and sugar. Add the milk, orange blossom water, and rose water and whisk to combine.

9. When the second bake has finished, remove the phyllo from the oven and pour the custard evenly over the top.

10. Bake until it turns a deep golden brown, 30 to 35 more minutes.

11. Meanwhile, finely grind the nuts in a food processor or nut grinder.

12. When the third bake has finished, remove the pan from the oven and immediately pour the cold syrup slowly and evenly over the top, followed by the ground pistachios and rose petals.

13. Let the baklawa cool to room temperature, at least 1 hour.

14. To serve, cut it into twelve 3-inch squares.

> **Note**
> In the pan, store the baklawa, covered with plastic wrap, in the refrigerator for up to 2 days.
>
> **VARIATIONS**
> * **STRAWBERRIES** taste divine in this recipe. Use 167 grams (1 cup) chopped strawberries, tucking them evenly into the folds between steps 5 and 6.
> * Another delight: add ½ teaspoon **COCONUT EXTRACT** to the custard and replace the rose petals with toasted coconut.

CREAM BAKLAWA

Cream-filled baklawa triangles combine layers of crispy, buttery phyllo with ashta filling, a rich, aromatic Lebanese cream popular in all kinds of desserts, including Ma'amoul Mad Cream Bars (page 110), Pistachio Cream Atayef (page 153), Lebanese Nights Cream Cake with Berry Compote (page 181), and more. Known as *warbat bil ashta* or *shaabiyat*, this dish often accompanies special feasts. As with most ashta pastries, the filling needs to chill in advance. The pastry tastes best when served right after being filled.

PREP: **1 HOUR 15 MINUTES**
COOK: **25 MINUTES**
COOL: **1 HOUR 30 MINUTES**
TOTAL: **3 HOURS 10 MINUTES**

MAKES: **12 (4-INCH, 10-CM) TRIANGLES**

FILLING
341 grams (1½ cups) whole milk
341 grams (1½ cups) heavy whipping cream
100 grams (½ cup) granulated white sugar
56 grams (½ cup) cornstarch
20 grams (2 tablespoons) fine semolina flour
4 grams (1 teaspoon) orange blossom water
4 grams (1 teaspoon) rose water

TRIANGLES
One 9-by-14-inch (23-by-35.5-cm) package phyllo dough (32 sheets, 454 grams, 1 pound), room temperature
113 grams (½ cup) Clarified Butter (page 271), melted

TOPPING
20 grams (2 tablespoons) orange blossom syrup (page 273), cold
60 grams (½ cup) raw or Blanched Pistachios (page 267)

1. In a small saucepan over medium-low heat, whisk together all the filling ingredients.

2. Increase the heat to medium-high and, whisking constantly, bring the mixture to a boil.

3. As soon as the mixture begins to boil, reduce the heat to medium-low and continue whisking until the ashta (filling) thickens and the whisk leaves a trail, about 5 minutes.

4. Transfer the ashta to a bowl and cover the surface with plastic wrap to prevent it from forming a skin. Let it cool to room temperature for 30 minutes and refrigerate until cold, at least 30 minutes and up to 3 days.

5. Arrange an oven rack in the middle position and preheat the oven to 400°F (200°C).

6. Open one sleeve of the phyllo and lay it flat. Using kitchen scissors, trim the stack to 12 inches (30 cm) wide by cutting 1 inch (2.5 cm) off a short side. Discard the trimmed phyllo and cover the stack with a kitchen towel.

7. Brush 1 sheet of phyllo with the butter. Lay another sheet evenly over it, butter, and repeat with 13 more sheets for a total of 15 buttered layers. (Reserve the 3 remaining sheets of phyllo for another use.)

8. Halve the stack lengthwise and cut it crosswise twice to create six equal squares. Use your hands to flip the squares upside down and diagonally fold each square in half to form a triangle with the unbuttered bottom layer on the inside.

9. Place the triangles on an unlined baking sheet. Arrange them in a group of four that forms a square with the obtuse points touching one another. Start a second group of four with the two remaining triangles.

10. Repeat steps 6 through 9 with the second sleeve of phyllo.

11. Bake the triangles until they puff and turn golden brown, 20 minutes.

continues

12. Remove the pan from the oven and immediately drizzle each triangle slowly and evenly with cold syrup. Let them cool for 30 minutes.

13. Meanwhile, finely grind the nuts in a food processor or nut grinder. Set aside.

14. Fill the triangles using a piping bag or spoon. Stir the cold ashta until smooth. If piping, transfer the ashta to a piping bag fitted with a ½-inch (1.25-cm) round tip. Gently open the center of a triangle, pipe or spoon 60 grams (2 tablespoons) of cream into it, and spread the cream all the way to the edges. Don't overfill.

15. Dip the open sides of each triangle in the pistachios, plate them on a serving platter, and serve immediately.

Notes
- It may be tempting to use the 6 extra phyllo sheets, but they'll make the triangles too thick. For these, 15 layers are exactly right.
- Store any uneaten triangles, uncovered, in the refrigerator for up to 2 days.

NUT-FREE BAKLAWA

A hearty blend of seeds makes an excellent baklawa for nut-free eaters, as I learned from my cousin Holly. This recipe creates a baklawa that tastes just as delicious as those with nuts. The seed mixture runs finer than its nutty counterparts, so for the pieces to hold together, not one but three layers of filling separate the phyllo. The easy pour-over butter method works nicely here.

PREP: 20 MINUTES
COOK: 50 MINUTES
COOL: 2 HOURS
TOTAL: 3 HOURS 10 MINUTES

MAKES: 38 PIECES

226 grams (1 cup) Clarified Butter (page 271), melted
One 9-by-14-inch (23-by-35.5-cm) package phyllo dough (32 sheets, 454 grams, 1 pound), room temperature

FILLING
120 grams (1⅓ cups) pepitas, roasted or raw
45 grams (½ cup) roasted or raw unsalted sunflower seeds
72 grams (½ cup) Toasted Sesame Seeds (page 269)
67 grams (⅓ cup) granulated white sugar
12 grams (3 teaspoons) orange blossom water, or 8 grams (2 teaspoons) rose water, or 8 grams (2 teaspoons) orange blossom water plus 4 grams (1 teaspoon) rose water

320 grams (1 cup) Flower Water Syrup (page 273), cold

1. Arrange an oven rack in the middle position and preheat the oven to 350°F (177°C).

2. Butter the bottom of a 9-by-13-by-2-inch (23-by-33-by-5-cm) metal baking pan with 12 grams (1 tablespoon) of the butter.

3. In a food processor, pulverize the pepitas and sunflower seeds until the mixture resembles coarse bread crumbs. In a small mixing bowl, combine the pepita-sunflower mixture with the sesame seeds, sugar, and orange blossom water. Set aside.

4. Open one sleeve of the phyllo and unroll it on the plastic packaging, leaving the other sleeve unopened. Lay the baking pan over the stack of phyllo, aligning a short side of the pan with a short side of the phyllo. Use the pan as a guide to trim the stack with kitchen scissors so the dough will fit inside the pan. You likely will trim about 1 inch (2.5 cm) off the short side.

5. Lay a stack of 10 phyllo sheets in the pan and spread a third (161 grams, 1 cup) of the filling mixture evenly over it.

6. Lay a stack of 8 phyllo sheets over the filling and spread another third of the seed mixture evenly over it.

7. Open the second sleeve of dough and unroll it on the plastic packaging. Trim it as in step 4. If the top layer of phyllo shows any damage, such as tears or folding, pull a sheet from the middle and set it on top. Remove the top 3 layers of the stack and set them aside.

8. Lay a stack of 8 phyllo sheets over the filling and spread the final third of the seed mixture evenly over it. Lay a stack of 7 phyllo sheets over the top.

9. Lightly brush the top layer in the pan with butter. Lay one of the 3 reserved sheets, not the clean top sheet, in the pan and brush it with butter. Repeat with the second and top sheets.

10. Using the tip of a long, sharp chef's knife, mark 5 lengthwise cuts for 6 columns and 9 crosswise diagonal cuts for 10 rows. Hold the knife perpendicular to the pastry, cutting straight down into

continues

the phyllo and filling. Use your nondominant hand to hold the top layers of phyllo down while cutting with your dominant hand all the way through to the bottom of the pan. (Once more, the small end pieces will go automatically to the baker!)

11. Pour the butter evenly over the baklawa. Allow the butter to soak in for 3 minutes, tilting the pan to distribute it evenly if needed.

12. Bake until the baklawa turns a deep golden brown, 45 to 55 minutes.

13. Remove the pan from the oven and immediately pour the cold syrup slowly and evenly over the hot baklawa. Let it cool at room temperature for at least 2 hours.

14. Following the diamond lines, cut the pieces of baklawa from the pan with a sharp knife. Serve them in foil mini-muffin cups or on a plate, arranged in a circle with the tips pointing to center.

> **Note**
> In the pan, keep the baklawa lightly covered with plastic wrap or wax paper at room temperature for up to 2 weeks.

TRIPLE CHOCOLATE BAKLAWA

At one time, none of the children in the family wanted anything to do with baklawa. *If only it were chocolate*, I thought, sparking the genesis of this recipe. If you need baklawa in your life as much as chocolate, you've come to the right place. Both chocolate and cocoa powder impart deep flavor to all the elements: butter, syrup, and filling. A dusting of flaky sea salt elevates this pastry's hallmark crisp texture and nutty notes like nothing else.

PREP: **20 MINUTES**
CHILL: **20 MINUTES**
COOK: **50 MINUTES**
COOL: **2 HOURS**
TOTAL: **3 HOURS 30 MINUTES**

MAKES: **38 PIECES**

CHOCOLATE SYRUP
170 grams (¾ cup) water
300 grams (1½ cups) granulated white sugar
22 grams (¼ cup) cocoa powder of choice
8 grams (2 teaspoons) orange blossom water or 4 grams (1 teaspoon) rose water, or a 2:1 combination

CHOCOLATE FILLING
256 grams (2 cups) toasted almonds (page 266)
85 grams (½ cup) dark chocolate, 60% cacao, chopped or chips
100 grams (½ cup) granulated white sugar
8 grams (2 teaspoons) orange blossom water, or 4 grams (1 teaspoon) rose water, or a 2:1 combination

CHOCOLATE BUTTER
226 grams (1 cup) Clarified Butter (page 271)
22 grams (¼ cup) cocoa powder of choice

One 9-by-14-inch (23-by-35.5-cm) package phyllo dough (32 sheets, 454 grams, 1 pound), room temperature
1 tablespoon flaky sea salt, such as Maldon

1. In a small saucepan over medium-high heat, combine the water and sugar and bring the syrup to a boil. Reduce the heat to low and simmer for 5 minutes.
2. Remove the pan from the heat and whisk in the cocoa powder and orange blossom water.
3. Pour the chocolate syrup into a heatproof liquid measuring cup or small mixing bowl with a spout. To chill the syrup quickly, fill a large bowl with ice water and gently place the vessel holding the syrup into it. Don't let the ice water splash into the syrup. Occasionally stir the syrup until it chills through, about 20 minutes, or refrigerate until cold, at least 2 hours.
4. Meanwhile, make the filling. In a food processor or nut grinder, finely grind the nuts and chocolate.
5. In a small bowl, combine the chocolate-nut mixture with the sugar and orange blossom water. Set aside.
6. Next, make the chocolate butter. In a small saucepan over medium heat, melt the butter. Whisk in the cocoa powder until it combines completely. Reduce the heat to low to keep it warm.
7. Arrange an oven rack in the middle position and preheat the oven to 350°F (177°C).
8. Brush the bottom of a 9-by-13-by-2-inch (23-by-33-by-5-cm) metal baking pan with 12 grams (1 tablespoon) of the melted chocolate butter.
9. Open one sleeve of the phyllo and unroll it on the plastic packaging, leaving the other sleeve unopened. Lay the baking pan over the stack of phyllo, aligning a short side of the pan with a short side of the phyllo. Use the pan as a guide to trim the stack with kitchen scissors so the dough will fit inside the pan. You likely will trim about 1 inch (2.5 cm) off the short side.

continues

10. Lay the trimmed dough in the pan and top it evenly with the nut mixture. With the back of a spoon, firmly press the nuts into the dough.

11. Open the second sleeve of dough and unroll it on the plastic packaging. Trim it as in step 9. If the top layer of phyllo shows any damage, such as tears or folding, pull a sheet from the middle and set it on top. Remove the top 3 layers of the stack and set them aside. Lay the rest of the stack in the pan over the filling.

12. Lightly brush the top layer in the pan with chocolate butter. Lay one of the 3 reserved sheets, not the clean top sheet, in the pan and brush it with butter. Repeat with the second and top sheets.

13. Using the tip of a long, sharp chef's knife, mark 5 lengthwise cuts for 6 columns and 9 crosswise diagonal cuts for 10 rows. (For smaller pieces, make 6 cuts for 7 rows lengthwise and 10 crosswise diagonal cuts for 11 rows.) Hold the knife perpendicular to the pastry, cutting straight down into the phyllo and nuts. Use your nondominant hand to hold the top layers of phyllo down while cutting with your dominant hand all the way through to the bottom of the pan. (You guessed it, the small end pieces will go automatically to the baker!)

14. Pour the rest of the chocolate butter evenly over the baklawa. Allow the butter to soak in for 3 minutes, tilting the pan to distribute it evenly if needed.

15. Bake for 45 to 55 minutes.

16. Stir the cold chocolate syrup to loosen it. Add 1 teaspoon of cold water if needed.

17. Remove the pan from the oven and immediately pour the cold chocolate syrup slowly and evenly over the hot baklawa. Sprinkle the sea salt evenly over the top. Let it cool at room temperature for at least 2 hours.

18. Following the diamond lines, cut the pieces of baklawa from the pan with a sharp knife. Serve them in foil mini-muffin cups or on a plate, arranged in a circle with the tips pointing to center.

Note

In the pan, keep the baklawa lightly covered with plastic wrap or wax paper at room temperature for up to 2 weeks.

VARIATIONS
- Use any type of **NUTS**. Pistachios, walnuts, or cashews all work well.
- For **"ALMOND JOY" BAKLAWA**, replace 64 grams (½ cup) of the nuts with 63 grams (¾ cup) desiccated coconut.

Knafeh

As with baklawa, knafeh encompasses not a single pastry but a broader category, and it dates at least to the 10th century. Spellings vary a great deal: kanafe, kanafeh, kenafeh, knafeh, knéfé, konafa, kunafa, kunafah, kunafeh, kunafeh, and so on. The standard English spelling comes from the Arabic كُنافة, *kunāfa*, likely from the Coptic *kenephiten*, meaning pastry or cake. The name for kataifi—the bulky, thin-stranded, store-bought dough in the recipes—comes, by way of the Greek καταΐφι, from the Arabic قطايف, *qatayef*. Some people call the long strands shredded phyllo—though they're not phyllo per se—or, less frequently, vermicelli or rishta for their resemblance to the pasta. In multiple thin streams, the batter drops onto a spinning hot griddle to form bundles of pastry. Also as with baklawa, the dough can make several kinds of knafeh. The spun pastry soaks in syrup and supports layers of cheese, cream, nuts, and other toppings.

Secrets to Making Knafeh

The several ways to make knafeh all use the same basic ingredients: kataifi dough or semolina, clarified butter, nuts, white cheese or ashta cream, and a generous drizzle of syrup. It tastes rich and crisp when toasted to a deep golden brown. You can use any crust with any filling, so this chapter provides separate recipes for each. Hot cheese knafeh tucked into sesame purse bread is a crazy-good Lebanese breakfast or treat on the go. In Lebanon, our driver took us to his favorite spot: Hallab in Tripoli. While sipping a little cup of Arabic coffee, he inhaled the pastry faster than seemed humanly possible. I think of that every time I eat knafeh!

CRUSTS

Variations include a rough-chopped or "shredded" crust (kishneh); a medium-fine crust made with ground kataifi and bread crumbs (muhayarah); a fine, smooth crust (na'ameh or sometimes Nabulseyeh after its origins in Nablus, Palestine) made with ground semolina dough (called farkeh); shredded wheat cereal biscuits as a substitute for kataifi; and nests made with rough-chopped kataifi dough. Some knafeh glows with a bright orange hue, achieved with standard food coloring or powdered knafeh coloring sold in Middle Eastern markets.

FILLINGS

Akkawi, a traditional brined white cheese, tastes so salty that you need to rinse and soak it for use in knafeh. It's not readily available everywhere, so you can substitute a combination of block and fresh mozzarella. As with baklawa, ground nuts also fill knafeh. Ashta cream balances the crisp kataifi dough like a dream. You can substitute it with sweetened ricotta, but pastry cream tastes even better.

BAKING

Cheese knafeh tastes best warm. Professional bakers often place trays of knafeh directly on a large heating element. The direct heat browns the crust perfectly. Moved to a warming counter, the trays retain heat as the baker cuts away the pastry, piece by piece. Use dark cake pans for even browning of the crust in the oven.

For knafeh filled with Akkawi or mozzarella, don't overbake. To achieve a soft, stretchy texture, the cheese should hit its melting point and stop right there. Browning forms a crust on the cheese, making it difficult to bite through.

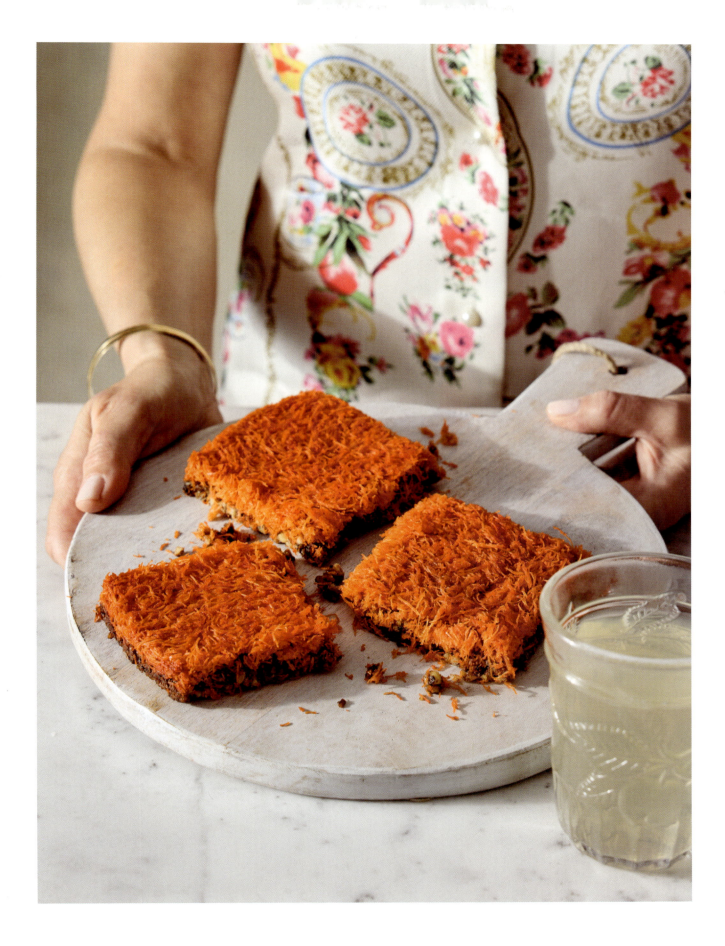

SHORTCUT KNAFEH CRUST

This lovely recipe approximates a Smooth Knafeh Crust (page 43) with ease. The trick consists of using only panko bread crumbs, which hold the butter and syrup beautifully and toast in the pan like a dream.

PREP: **3 MINUTES**
TOTAL: **3 MINUTES**
MAKES: **DOUGH FOR 1 (9-INCH, 23-CM) KNAFEH**

150 grams (2½ cups) panko bread crumbs
113 grams (½ cup) unsalted butter, melted
160 grams (½ cup) Flower Water Syrup (page 273)

1. In a medium mixing bowl, combine all the ingredients and stir to coat the bread crumbs well.
2. Proceed with the Cheese Knafeh (page 45), Nut-Filled Knafeh (page 49), or Cream Knafeh (page 57).

COMBO KNAFEH CRUST

This combo offers the best of both worlds: the crispness of a kataifi crust with smooth bread crumbs that bind everything together. In the food processor, the kataifi will break down only so far, creating tiny shreds. The result is a wonderfully delicate crust with a gentle crunch.

PREP: **7 MINUTES**
TOTAL: **7 MINUTES**
MAKES: **DOUGH FOR 1 (9-INCH, 23-CM) KNAFEH**

114 grams (¼ pound) kataifi dough, room temperature
50 grams (1 cup) panko or plain dry bread crumbs
113 grams (½ cup) unsalted butter, melted
80 grams (¼ cup) Flower Water Syrup (page 273)

1. In a food processor, pulse the kataifi dough until finely shredded, about 1 minute. It will reduce to small shreds, not fine crumbs.
2. Transfer the kataifi shreds to a medium mixing bowl. Add the panko, butter, and syrup and stir to coat well.
3. Proceed with the Cheese Knafeh (page 45), Nut-Filled Knafeh (page 49), or Cream Knafeh (page 57).

KATAIFI KNAFEH CRUST

This coarse crust (khishneh) uses chopped kataifi dough. Use room temperature kataifi, which you can slice more easily; thoroughly rubbing the pieces separates strands that otherwise will stick together. Marshal a little elbow grease to press the buttered pieces into the baking pan to make a compact, crisp crust for any of the fillings. You can color the butter with orange food coloring dissolved in water to make orange-colored (not flavored) knafeh.

PREP: 15 MINUTES
TOTAL: 15 MINUTES
MAKES: DOUGH FOR 1 (9-INCH, 23-CM) KNAFEH

151 grams (⅓ pound) kataifi dough, room temperature
113 grams (½ cup) unsalted butter, melted
½ teaspoon fine sea salt
40 grams (2 tablespoons) Flower Water Syrup (page 273)
1 drop orange food coloring (optional)

1. Remove the kataifi from the packaging and lay it on a large cutting board. Use a sharp chef's knife to cut one-third of the bundle. Return the remaining dough to an airtight container and freeze for another use.

2. Cut the kataifi bundle into ½-inch (1.25-cm) slices. Chop any long strands. Use your hands to separate the pieces thoroughly, rubbing apart any that have stuck together.

3. In a large mixing bowl, add the butter, salt, and syrup. If using food coloring, dissolve it in 10 grams (2 teaspoons) water and add to the butter mixture. Stir to combine.

4. Add the kataifi pieces to the bowl. With your hands or tongs, mix until the butter mixture evenly coats the kataifi. Use food-grade gloves if using food coloring.

5. Proceed with the Cheese Knafeh (page 45), Nut-Filled Knafeh (page 49), or Cream Knafeh (page 57).

SMOOTH KNAFEH CRUST

The fine, buttery, crisp texture of *na'ameh* (smooth) knafeh hints at a graham cracker crust. This process makes bread crumbs from a baked flour and semolina dough, pressed into a crust.

PREP: 10 MINUTES
COOK: 10 MINUTES
COOL: 15 MINUTES
TOTAL: 35 MINUTES

MAKES: DOUGH FOR 1 (9-INCH, 23-CM) KNAFEH

---

120 grams (1 cup) unbleached all-purpose flour
41 grams (¼ cup) fine semolina flour
¼ teaspoon baking powder
¼ teaspoon fine sea salt
86 grams (6 tablespoons) unsalted butter, melted
57 grams (¼ cup) whole milk
40 grams (2 tablespoons) Flower Water Syrup (page 273)

1. Arrange an oven rack in the middle position and preheat the oven to 400°F (177°C). Line a baking sheet with parchment paper.

2. In a large mixing bowl, combine the flour, semolina, baking powder, salt, 43 grams (3 tablespoons) of the melted butter, and milk. Stir well until the mixture becomes shaggy, then lightly knead it to form a dough.

3. On the prepared baking sheet, press the dough into a rough rectangle, about 9 by 6 inches by ¼ inch (23 by 15 cm by 6 mm).

4. Bake until it just cooks through but still looks pale, 10 minutes.

5. Remove from the oven and let it cool enough to handle, about 5 minutes.

6. Break the cooked dough into 2-inch (5-cm) pieces. Transfer them to a cooling rack and let them cool for 15 minutes.

7. In a food processor, pulverize the pieces to fine crumbs.

8. Transfer the crumbs to a medium mixing bowl. Add the remaining melted butter and syrup and stir well to coat the crumbs evenly.

9. Proceed with the Cheese Knafeh (page 45), Nut-Filled Knafeh (page 49), or Cream Knafeh (page 57).

CHEESE KNAFEH

The flavors of this supreme knafeh (knafeh jibneh) offer the finest in sweet-and-savory eating. It tastes like a board of soft cheese and excellent crackers drizzled in honey. Par-bake the crust up to one day ahead of time and keep it covered with plastic at room temperature until ready to use. Add the cheese and complete the bake just before serving this pastry that eats like a melty warm hug.

PREP: 10 MINUTES
COOK: 24 MINUTES
COOL: 5 MINUTES
TOTAL: 39 MINUTES

MAKES: 1 (9-INCH, 23-CM) KNAFEH (9 SERVINGS)
SPECIAL EQUIPMENT: DARK 9-INCH (23-CM) CAKE PAN

1 recipe Shortcut Knafeh Crust (page 40), Combo Knafeh Crust (page 40), Kataifi Knafeh Crust (page 42), or Smooth Knafeh Crust (page 43)

FILLING
- 113 grams (1 cup) fresh mozzarella
- 113 grams (1 cup) block mozzarella or soaked Akkawi cheese (see Notes)
- 454 grams (2 cups) whole milk
- 62 grams (⅓ cup) coarse semolina (Cream of Wheat)

TOPPING
- 15 grams (2 tablespoons) raw or Blanched Pistachios (page 267)
- 240 grams (¾ cup) Flower Water Syrup (page 273), cold

1. Arrange an oven rack in the middle position and preheat the oven to 400°F (200°C).
2. Firmly press the crust recipe of your choice into the cake pan first with your hands, then with the flat bottom of a cup or similar implement.
3. Par-bake the crust for 10 minutes.
4. Meanwhile, make the filling. Slice the fresh mozzarella and pat it dry with a paper towel. Cut the block mozzarella into pieces. Add all the cheese to the food processor and process it into a coarse meal.
5. In a small saucepan over medium-high heat, heat the milk until hot but not boiling. Add the semolina and cook, stirring constantly, until the mixture starts thickening, 2 minutes.
6. Reduce the heat to medium, add the cheese, and stir constantly until it melts, 1 to 2 minutes.
7. When the crust has par-baked, remove it from the oven. Pour the cheese mixture into it and smooth the top with an offset spatula.
8. Bake until the cheese bubbles and the edges turn a deep golden brown, 10 more minutes. Remove from the oven and let cool for 5 minutes.
9. Meanwhile, finely chop the pistachios.
10. Place a serving platter slightly larger than the cake pan upside down over the pan. Use hot pads, kitchen gloves, or pot holders to grasp the hot pan and platter and quickly invert the knafeh. Lift the pan. The crust has become the top of the knafeh.
11. Drizzle the knafeh evenly with 160 grams (½ cup) of the syrup and garnish with the chopped pistachios.
12. Cut the knafeh into squares or slices, pour the remaining syrup over the pieces, and serve.

Notes
- A soft cow's milk cheese, Akkawi traditionally fills cheese knafeh. Named for the Aker region of Palestine, this very salty cheese requires soaking before using. Slice it and submerge it in a large bowl of cold water for at least 3 hours and up to 1 day. Change the water every hour. Drain, pat dry, taste for saltiness, and use.
- In the refrigerator, keep any leftover knafeh lightly covered with plastic wrap or wax paper for up to 2 days. To reheat it, warm it in a 250°F (120°C) oven for 10 minutes and serve with more syrup.

KNAFEH BIL KA'AK

Take knafeh to the next level as we Lebanese do. Tuck a slice of Cheese Knafeh (page 45) into the pocket of Sesame Purse Bread (page 238). Heat one right before you eat it for breakfast on the run, or enjoy it as a treat any time of the day.

PREP: 5 MINUTES
COOK: 10 MINUTES
TOTAL: 15 MINUTES
MAKES: 1 SERVING

1 Sesame Purse Bread (page 238)
1 slice Cheese Knafeh (page 45)
20 grams (1 tablespoon) Flower Water Syrup (page 273)

1. Preheat the oven to 250°F (120°C).
2. On an unlined baking sheet, place the bread and knafeh (crust side facing down) and cover both with foil.
3. Bake until both warm through, 10 minutes.
4. Separate the bread at the base of the "purse," like pita.
5. Tuck the knafeh into the opening of the bread and drizzle the knafeh with the syrup. Eat immediately.

NUT-FILLED KNAFEH

This dish, knafeh Arabiyeh, with its filling of nuts and cinnamon, evokes baklawa but in a different form. The flavor and texture of the nuts plus the crispness of the knafeh crust create a cookie-like experience, and the syrup adds another dimension of deliciousness. Choose your favorite nut, including almonds or cashews, or go for a combination. My favorite is a mix of walnuts and pistachios.

PREP: **10 MINUTES**
COOK: **20 MINUTES**
COOL: **20 MINUTES**
TOTAL: **50 MINUTES**

MAKES: **1 (9-INCH, 23-CM) KNAFEH (9 SERVINGS)**
SPECIAL EQUIPMENT: **DARK 9-INCH (23-CM) CAKE PAN**

1 recipe Shortcut Knafeh Crust (page 40), Combo Knafeh Crust (page 40), Kataifi Knafeh Crust (page 42), or Smooth Knafeh Crust (page 43)

FILLING
256 grams (2 cups) toasted walnuts (page 266) or 240 grams (2 cups) roasted whole pistachios
½ teaspoon ground cinnamon
160 grams (½ cup) Flower Water Syrup (page 273)

TOPPING
15 grams (2 tablespoons) raw or Blanched Pistachios (page 267)
160 grams (½ cup) Flower Water Syrup (page 273)

1. Arrange an oven rack in the middle position and preheat the oven to 400°F (200°C).
2. Firmly press the crust recipe of your choice into a dark 9-inch (23-cm) cake pan first with your hands, then with the flat bottom of a cup or similar implement.
3. Par-bake the crust for 10 minutes.
4. Meanwhile, make the filling. Coarsely grind the whole nuts and transfer them to a small mixing bowl along with the cinnamon and syrup. Stir to combine.
5. When the crust has par-baked, remove it from the oven. Spoon the nut mixture into it and spread it evenly by pressing it gently with an offset spatula. Take care not to lift the nuts. Nestle back any that stick to the spatula.
6. Bake for 10 more minutes, then let it cool for 20 minutes.
7. Meanwhile, finely grind the pistachios.
8. Run a knife around the perimeter of the knafeh in the pan to loosen the edges. Place a serving platter slightly larger than the cake pan upside down over the pan. Use hot pads, kitchen gloves, or pot holders to grasp the hot pan and platter and quickly invert the knafeh. Lift the pan. The crust has become the top of the knafeh.
9. Drizzle the knafeh evenly with 80 grams (¼ cup) of syrup and garnish with the ground pistachios.
10. Cut the knafeh into squares or slices, pour the remaining syrup over the pieces, and serve immediately.

Note
In the refrigerator, keep the knafeh lightly covered with plastic wrap or wax paper for up to 2 days.

VARIATION: Use ½ teaspoon of **CARDAMOM** in place of the cinnamon or in addition to it for even more lovely warm flavor.

SHREDDED WHEAT KNAFEH BISCUITS

This knafeh, which I remember Sitto making long ago, populates the old Lebanese cookbooks in my kitchen. Bakeries in Lebanon and Michigan offer an array of crusty, cheesy knafehs, but this recipe still holds my heart not only for its lovely simplicity but also because it highlights the ingenuity of my sitto's generation. Few specialty markets sold boxed kataifi dough then, and the strenuous path to a homemade version no doubt inspired this clever substitution. When you can't find ingredients commonplace in the old country, forge a new path. Shredded wheat biscuits look like perfect kataifi rolls, and they take butter and syrup like a dream.

PREP: **10 MINUTES**
COOK: **50 MINUTES**
TOTAL: **1 HOUR**

MAKES: **6 KNAFEH BISCUITS**

FILLING
128 grams (1 cup) toasted walnuts (page 266)
50 grams (¼ cup) granulated white sugar
4 grams (1 teaspoon) orange blossom water

CRUST
127 grams (½ cup plus 1 tablespoon) Clarified Butter (page 271), melted
227 grams (1 cup) whole milk
6 big shredded wheat cereal biscuits (approximately 142 grams)

TOPPING
30 grams (2 tablespoons) raw or Blanched Pistachios (page 267)
160 grams (½ cup) Flower Water Syrup (page 273), cold

1. Arrange an oven rack in the middle position and preheat the oven to 300°F (150°C). Place a colander in the sink.
2. Finely chop the walnuts and transfer them to a small mixing bowl.
3. Add the sugar and orange blossom water, stir to combine, and set aside.
4. Brush the bottom of an 8-inch (20-cm) square pan with 14 grams (1 tablespoon) of the butter.
5. Pour the milk in another small bowl.
6. Dunk a biscuit in the milk and soak it for 5 seconds on each side. With your hands or tongs, lift the biscuit, letting the milk drain into the bowl. Place the biscuit in the colander to continue draining.
7. Repeat with 2 more biscuits.
8. Use a sharp knife to slice the drained biscuits along the seam of one long side and place them in the prepared pan, forming 2 rows.
9. Repeat steps 6, 7, and 8 with the remaining 3 biscuits.
10. Carefully open and fill each biscuit with 29 grams (2 tablespoons) of the filling. Liberally brush the tops of the biscuits with the remaining butter. Use all of it.
11. Bake until golden brown, 40 minutes.
12. Meanwhile, finely chop the pistachios.
13. Remove the knafeh biscuits from the oven and immediately pour the cold syrup evenly over them.
14. Garnish the biscuits with the pistachios and let them cool for 10 minutes.
15. Serve warm or let them cool to room temperature.

Note
You can store the knafeh in an airtight container at room temperature for up to 2 days.

VARIATIONS
- For the filling, use finely **GROUND RAW OR ROASTED PISTACHIOS** instead of toasted walnuts.
- Replace the orange blossom water with 4 grams (1 teaspoon) **ROSE WATER**.

KNAFEH NESTS

Individual servings make a great presentation for gatherings of all kinds, whether in a buffet or for a formal dessert course at the table. Fill these nests with nuts or cream or a combination of the two. Toasted coconut also tastes wonderful atop the cream filling.

PREP: 10 MINUTES
COOK: 12 MINUTES
COOL: 10 MINUTES
TOTAL: 32 MINUTES

MAKES: 12 NESTS
SPECIAL EQUIPMENT: DARK 12-WELL MUFFIN PAN

1½ recipes Kataifi Knafeh Crust (page 42)
30 grams (2 tablespoons) raw or Blanched Pistachios (page 267)
1 recipe filling from Nut-Filled Knafeh (page 49) or ½ recipe filling from Cream Knafeh (page 57)
80 grams (¼ cup) Flower Water Syrup (page 273)

1. Arrange an oven rack in the middle position and preheat the oven to 350°F (177°C).
2. Divide the crust mixture evenly among the 12 muffin wells, approximately 38 grams (2 heaping tablespoons) each. Firmly press the mixture into the bottom and up the sides of each well.
3. Bake the nests until golden brown, 10 to 12 minutes.
4. Meanwhile, finely chop the pistachios.
5. Remove the nests from the oven and let them cool to room temperature, 10 minutes.
6. With a knife, carefully loosen the perimeter of each nest. Transfer the nests to a serving platter.
7. Divide the filling mixture evenly among the 12 wells, approximately 30 grams (2 tablespoons) each.
8. Drizzle each nest evenly with flower water syrup and a pinch of pistachios. Serve immediately.

> *Note*
> You can make the nests up to 2 days in advance, but eat them on the same day that you fill them. You can keep leftover nests in an airtight container for up to 2 days at room temperature if they are filled with nuts and in the refrigerator for up to 2 days if they are filled with cream.

CHOCOLATE PISTACHIO KNAFEH BARS

This recipe riffs on the kataifi chocolate bars from Dubai that went viral in 2024. Toasted kataifi creates a buttery, crunchy knafeh consistency and an irresistible flavor. The knafeh serves as a base layer and adds incredible texture to the pistachio cream. The twist? The chocolate layer goes on the inside.

PREP: **25 MINUTES**
COOK: **15 MINUTES**
COOL: **1 HOUR 10 MINUTES**
TOTAL: **1 HOUR 50 MINUTES**

MAKES: **32 PIECES**

- 227 grams (1 cup) unsalted butter
- 340 grams (¾ pound) kataifi dough, room temperature
- 3 grams (1 teaspoon) fine sea salt
- 80 grams (¼ cup) Flower Water Syrup (page 273)
- 283 grams (10 ounces) dark chocolate, 60% or more, chips or coarsely chopped
- 180 grams (1½ cups) raw or Blanched Pistachios (page 267)
- 113 grams (1 cup) confectioners' sugar
- 28 grams (¼ cup) powdered milk
- 113 grams (½ cup) whole milk

1. Arrange an oven rack in the middle position and preheat the oven to 400°F (200°C).
2. Line a 9-inch (23-cm) square pan with parchment paper, leaving a few inches of overhang on opposing sides to help lift the pastry from the pan.
3. Remove the bundle of kataifi from the packaging and lay it on a large cutting board. Use a sharp chef's knife to cut three-fourths from the bundle (340 grams, ¾ pound). Return the remaining dough to an airtight container and freeze it for another use.
4. Cut the dough into 1-inch (2.5-cm) pieces. Use your hands to separate the pieces, rubbing apart any that have stuck together.
5. In a large sauté pan over medium-high heat, melt the remaining 226 grams (1 cup) of butter. Add the chopped kataifi and salt and cook until it toasts and turns golden brown, about 8 minutes. Use tongs to turn and stir the kataifi frequently.
6. In a large mixing bowl, add half of the toasted kataifi (283 grams) and the syrup and stir well to coat it evenly.
7. Into the bottom of the prepared pan, firmly and evenly press the kataifi mixture first with your hands, then with the flat bottom of a cup or similar implement.
8. Bake the crust until it turns a deep golden brown, 5 minutes. Let it cool in the pan for 10 minutes.
9. In a microwave-safe bowl, melt the chocolate in three increments of 30 seconds each. Stir after each increment until it melts completely.
10. Use an offset spatula to spread the melted chocolate evenly over the kataifi. Refrigerate.
11. In a food processor, pulverize the pistachios until they resemble bread crumbs. Scrape down the bowl, add the sugar and powdered milk, and process again to combine.
12. With the food processor running, slowly add the milk until a smooth paste forms.
13. Transfer the pistachio mixture to large mixing bowl. Add the remaining toasted kataifi and stir to coat it completely.

continues

14. Remove the chocolate kataifi pan from the refrigerator and use an offset spatula to spread the pistachio cream evenly over the chocolate.

15. Refrigerate until firm, 1 hour.

16. Use the overhanging parchment flaps to lift the knafeh block from the pan. Place the block on a cutting board and use a serrated knife to cut 16 squares. Halve each square diagonally to form 32 triangles.

> **Note**
> You can store the bars in an airtight container at room temperature for up to 5 days.

CREAM KNAFEH

This dish provides a blissful textural contrast: a crisp crust topped with luscious cream. Many traditional cream knafehs call for sweetened ricotta, but this recipe uses pastry cream for richer flavor. The knafeh stays in the pan, the crust and cream crowned with a generous layer of bright pistachios. No need to invert the crust for this one; slice it directly from the pan.

PREP: 40 MINUTES
CHILL: 1 HOUR
COOK: 28 MINUTES
COOL: 20 MINUTES
TOTAL: 2 HOURS 28 MINUTES

MAKES: 1 (9-INCH, 23-CM) KNAFEH (9 SERVINGS)
SPECIAL EQUIPMENT: DARK 9-INCH (23-CM) CAKE PAN, ROUND OR SQUARE

PASTRY CREAM
227 grams (1 cup) whole milk
227 grams (1 cup) heavy cream
5 large egg yolks
100 grams (½ cup) granulated white sugar
14 grams (2 tablespoons) cornstarch
28 grams (2 tablespoons) unsalted butter
4 grams (1 teaspoon) pure vanilla extract
4 grams (1 teaspoon) orange blossom water
½ teaspoon rose water

1 recipe Shortcut Knafeh Crust (page 40), Combo Knafeh Crust (page 40), Kataifi Knafeh Crust (page 42), or Smooth Knafeh Crust (page 43)
135 grams (1 cup plus 2 tablespoons) raw or Blanched Pistachios (page 267)
80 grams (¼ cup) Flower Water Syrup (page 273), cold

1. In a medium saucepan over medium heat, heat the milk and cream until steaming but not boiling. In a medium heatproof mixing bowl, whisk the egg yolks and sugar until pale and thick. Add the cornstarch and whisk to combine.
2. Ladle ¼ cup of the milk mixture into the yolk mixture and whisk it quickly to incorporate.
3. Repeat with another ¼ cup of the milk mixture.
4. Pour the yolk mixture into the milk mixture in the saucepan. Increase the heat to medium-high and whisk constantly until the mixture thickens, about 3 minutes.
5. Remove from the heat and add the butter, vanilla, orange blossom water, and rose water. Whisk to combine.
6. Transfer the pastry cream to a heatproof container. Lay a piece of plastic wrap or wax paper on the surface of the cream to prevent a skin from forming. Refrigerate for at least 30 minutes and up to 3 days.
7. Arrange an oven rack in the middle position and preheat the oven to 400°F (200°C).
8. Firmly press the crust recipe of your choice into a dark 9-inch (23-cm) cake pan first with your hands, then with the flat bottom of a cup or similar implement.
9. Bake the crust until golden brown, 20 to 30 minutes.
10. Remove the crust from the oven and let it cool completely in the pan, at least 20 minutes.
11. Meanwhile, finely chop the pistachios.

continues

12. Whisk the cold pastry cream until smooth. Spoon it over the cooled crust and spread it evenly with an offset spatula.
13. Scatter the pistachios evenly onto the pastry cream.
14. Chill the knafeh for at least 30 minutes and up to 2 hours.
15. To serve, use a sharp chef's knife to cut the knafeh into 9 pieces, carefully removing them from the pan with an offset spatula. Drizzle each piece with syrup before serving.

> **Notes**
> Cream knafeh has the best texture the day you make it, when the crust tastes crispest. In the refrigerator, keep the knafeh pan covered with plastic wrap for up to 3 days.

Something to Drink

CAFÉ BLANC

The aromatic goodness of Lebanese "white coffee" will help you savor the start of the day, soothe a sore throat or heart, fortify against winter's chill, or cool the soul on a summer day. It contains no coffee or dairy and traditionally is served in a demitasse.

PREP: **1 MINUTE**
COOK TIME: **5 MINUTES**
TOTAL: **6 MINUTES**

MAKES: **1 SERVING**

284 grams (1¼ cups) water
4 grams (1 teaspoon) orange blossom water
7 grams (1 teaspoon) honey

1. In a kettle or saucepan over high heat, bring the water to a boil.
2. In a heatproof demitasse or mug, add the orange blossom water and honey. Pour the boiling water into the mug, stir, and serve immediately.

> **VARIATION:** For **ICED CAFÉ BLANC**, dissolve the honey in 28 grams (2 tablespoons) hot water, stirring constantly for 1 minute. Fill a glass with ice, add the honey syrup, orange blossom water, and cold water. Stir to combine and serve immediately.

Sweet Yeast Breads

My passion for Lebanese baking began with breads. As a girl, the greatest fun I had was helping make dough and bake bread with my mother, grandmothers, and aunts. In Lebanon, communal ovens and baking still remain a way of life. For much of my life, I thought that khubz, Lebanese bread, consisted of just three items: thin, chewy "Syrian" bread that Sitto masterfully threw with ease; talami baked into different shapes and sizes; and the large, thin, pillowy pita from Detroit that we used to scoop juicy goodness from our plates. An entire lifetime couldn't uncover all the distinctions among Lebanese breads, it turns out, because they vary from village to village, family to family, baker to baker, oven to oven. Here are some of my favorites.

Secrets to Making Yeasted Doughs

Dough feels personal . . . because it is. It has nuances as distinct as the kitchen where it rises. Dough contains the same atmosphere that we breathe. The bread that it makes becomes a part of us, close like a cousin. Every ingredient matters, but the most essential of all is you, the baker, the habibi! Baking requires all kinds of investments, including money, tools, ingredients, and time for reading, shopping, cooking, and cleaning. It also requires another investment—in yourself. Your role for joyful, successful baking with yeasted dough includes three steps.

1. Follow my notes on using this book (page xiii).

2. Use all your senses to understand the dough. My recipes cover many details, as they should, but in your home, you're doing the baking. As you add ingredients, watch the dough, feel it with your hands and your heart, too, and correct course as needed. Never shy from rechecking the recipe to make sure that you followed it correctly.

3. Consider the atmosphere of your kitchen. Temperature and humidity affect rise times. What takes an hour in my brother Dick's Florida kitchen in summer takes many hours in my niece Maria's Minneapolis kitchen in winter. She once called me, *five* hours into testing a recipe, to ask whether it should have risen yet! Poor habibti in that cold clime! With practice you will come to know how the seasons and your kitchen environment affect what you're doing.

The more you bake, the more these facets of baking will become intuitive. You may find, like me, that the journey tastes so deeply rewarding that you crave going back for more.

HANDLING

Many doughs made from the recipes in this book have a high hydration, which means they feel quite soft and sticky. When you touch them, the dough adheres to your fingers. To handle sticky dough, use a lightly oiled soft spatula, oiled scraper, or oiled hands. Use a light touch, too, and handle the dough as little as possible to move or divide it.

SHAPING

After dough rises the first time in a bulk ferment (one big mass), the next step often consists of dividing it into pieces and shaping them into balls that will rise again (preshaping). The second rise allows the gluten strands, activated during dividing, to relax for the final shaping. When shaping dough into smaller balls, you want to create a smooth surface and remove any folds at the base of the ball. Don't knead or overwork the dough, though. Shaping also requires a light touch. Here's how to shape dough balls.

Divide the dough into the number of pieces indicated. Work with one piece at a time and stretch the edges down under the ball to smooth and tighten the top and side surfaces. Bring those edges together underneath, cupping the ball in your palms as you use the edges of the pinkie sides of your hands to pull the dough together, and pinch them closed.

If the ball has deep seams where pinched closed, place the ball, seam side down, on the counter and, with a slightly cupped hand, palm the dough. Pressing with your palm, roll the ball around, using the cupped sides of your hand to keep the ball centered under your palm. This action creates surface tension and rubs the bottom seams into the dough. It may take more effort than seems reasonable!

As you work, check the bottom of the ball to ensure that the folds incorporate and become nearly invisible. Now you have a homogenous ball of dough ready to rise again.

STORING

The key to storing homemade bread lies in keeping it in an airtight container and, if eating it soon, at room temperature. In my kitchen, that often means a sealable plastic bag, but larger containers with tight lids work well, too. Homemade breads hold beautifully at room temperature for at least a couple of days.

The freezer is a good friend to bread. Frozen bread won't degrade as refrigerated bread will. Wrap bread tightly with plastic wrap and store it in the same kind of sealable plastic bag or tight-lidded container in the freezer for up to 3 months. In spring, I've pulled bread from the freezer that went into it the summer before, and it was just fine, so check older frozen bread before tossing it. Let frozen bread thaw to room temperature or, per recipe instructions, do a quick warm up in the oven before serving, and you're ready to feast.

ZALABIA DONUTS

Years ago, when I first wrote about this dish on my website, plenty of Lebanese readers gently informed me that the zalabia of my childhood—a soft stretch of dough with a hole in the middle, fried and dusted with sugar—didn't qualify as proper zalabia. They described it as something else entirely: batter shaped by a squeeze bottle, fried into a lattice, and glazed with syrup—a Glazed Zalabia (page 101). Thankfully *Sweet Delights from a Thousand and One Nights* by Habeeb Salloum, Muna Salloum, and Leila Salloum Elias affirmed both styles as traditional! Among my extended family, still more versions exist, including anise-spiced fritters. These donuts celebrate the Epiphany, just after Christmas. In my childhood home, Mom and Sitto always set aside some dough to fry for us at the end of a baking day, just before dinner. Whenever I want to rekindle those happy memories, I do the same and make this zalabia for the kids in our family, with mugs of thick hot chocolate for dipping.

PREP: **15 MINUTES**
REST: **2 HOURS**
COOK: **8 MINUTES**
TOTAL: **2 HOURS 23 MINUTES**
MAKES: **12 DONUTS**

360 grams (3 cups) unbleached all-purpose flour
6 grams (2 teaspoons) instant yeast
100 grams (½ cup) plus 50 grams (¼ cup) granulated white sugar
6 grams (1 teaspoon) fine sea salt
227 grams (1 cup) water, warm (105–110°F, 40–43°C)
70 grams (⅓ cup plus 1 teaspoon) neutral oil
Neutral oil for frying

1. In the bowl of a stand mixer, add the flour, yeast, 100 grams (½ cup) of the sugar, and salt and stir to combine with a wooden spoon or a dough hook (not attached). Slowly add the water and 66 grams (⅓ cup) of the oil and mix until a shaggy dough forms, 1 minute.

2. Attach the dough hook, set the mixer speed to medium-high, and knead the dough until smooth, 3 minutes.

3. Coat a medium mixing bowl with the remaining 4 grams (1 teaspoon) of the oil. Ball the dough, transfer it to the prepared bowl, and flip the dough to coat it completely with oil. Cover the bowl with plastic wrap and lay a kitchen towel over that. Let the dough rise until it doubles in size, 1 hour 30 minutes.

4. Onto a lightly floured surface, turn out the dough and divide it into 12 pieces, approximately 60 grams each. Shape them into balls (page 62), dust them lightly with flour, cover them with the plastic wrap and towel again, and let them rise for 30 more minutes.

5. Next, set up the frying station. Over medium heat, fill a medium sauté pan 2 inches (5 cm) deep with oil and heat it to 350°F (177°C). Line a baking sheet or platter with paper towels and place it nearby.

6. When ready to fry, stretch a dough ball into an oval 6 inches (15 cm) wide. Poke a hole in the middle and stretch it to 2 inches (5 cm) wide. Repeat with 3 more dough balls.

7. Carefully lower each of the dough pieces into the hot oil by hand. Fry until the bottoms turn golden brown, about 1 minute.

continues

8. Use tongs to turn the zalabia over. Fry for 1 more minute.

9. Transfer the donuts to the paper towel–lined baking sheet and immediately sprinkle both sides of each donut with some of the remaining sugar.

10. Bring the oil temperature back to 350°F (177°C) before repeating steps 6 through 9 with the rest of the balls.

> **Notes**
> - For even frying, the oil must stay at 350°F (177°C). Throughout the frying process, measure the temperature and reduce or increase the heat level as necessary.
> - In step 7, lower the donuts by hand because the heat of the oil will cause the dough to stick to any utensil that dips into it.
>
> **TIP:** Fried dough tastes best when eaten fresh, but you can make the dough ahead of time, through step 3. In an oiled bowl covered with plastic wrap, refrigerate the dough for up to 1 day. When ready to fry, let it come to room temperature and rise to double in size, at least 2 hours, then proceed, starting with step 4.

HONEY BUNS

A serious contender for my favorite bite from the recipes in this book, these heavenly buns resemble a honeycomb, which gives them their name in Arabic: khaliat al nhal (honeycomb bread). Nestled tightly in a round pan and glazed with glossy honey syrup, the cloudlike rolls draw rave reviews and make a beautiful gift.

PREP: **18 MINUTES**
REST: **1 HOUR 40 MINUTES**
COOK: **30 MINUTES**
TOTAL: **2 HOURS 28 MINUTES**

MAKES: **21 ROLLS**

DOUGH

300 grams (2½ cups) unbleached all-purpose flour, plus more as needed
6 grams (2 teaspoons) instant yeast
8 grams (2 teaspoons) baking powder
½ teaspoon fine sea salt
227 grams (1 cup) whole milk, lukewarm
32 grams (2 tablespoons plus 2 teaspoons) neutral oil
42 grams (2 tablespoons) honey
113 grams (4 ounces) cream cheese, cold

EGG WASH

1 large egg
5 grams (1 teaspoon) water

GLAZE

75 grams (⅓ cup) water
150 grams (¾ cup) granulated white sugar
42 grams (2 tablespoons) honey
6 grams (2 teaspoons) sesame seeds
6 grams (2 teaspoons) nigella seeds

1. In the bowl of a stand mixer, add the flour, yeast, baking powder, and salt and stir to combine with a wooden spoon or the dough hook (not attached). Slowly add the milk, 24 grams (2 tablespoons) of the oil, and honey and mix until a shaggy dough forms, 1 minute.
2. Attach the dough hook, set the mixer speed to medium-high, and knead the dough until smooth, 3 minutes.
3. Coat a medium mixing bowl with 4 grams (1 teaspoon) of the oil. Ball the dough, transfer it to the prepared bowl, and flip the dough to coat it completely with oil. Cover the bowl with plastic wrap and lay a kitchen towel over that. Let the dough rise until it doubles in size, 1 hour.
4. With the remaining oil, lightly brush the bottom and sides of a 9-inch (23-cm) round cake pan with oil, line it with a circle of parchment paper, and brush the paper with more oil.
5. Turn the dough out onto the counter and divide it into 21 pieces, approximately 31 grams each.
6. Cut the cream cheese into 21 pieces, about 5 grams each.
7. Use your fingers to flatten a piece of dough to ¼ inch (6 mm) thick and place a piece of cream cheese in the middle. Wrap the dough around the cream cheese, tightly pinching it closed and creating a smooth ball. Repeat with the other 20 pieces of dough and cream cheese.
8. In the prepared cake pan, arrange the dough balls, seam side down with spaces between them, in concentric circles to create a honeycomb pattern. Cover the pan with a kitchen towel and let the balls rise until puffy and no spaces remain among them, 40 minutes.
9. Arrange an oven a rack in the middle position and preheat the oven to 350°F (177°C).
10. In a small mixing bowl, make the egg wash by whisking together the egg and water. Lightly brush the tops of the risen dough balls with egg wash. You'll have some egg wash left over.

continues

11. Bake until the buns turn golden brown, 25 minutes.

12. Meanwhile, make the glaze. In a small saucepan over medium-high heat, combine the water, sugar, and honey. Bring the mixture to a boil, reduce the heat to medium-low, and simmer for 5 minutes. Set aside until the buns finish baking.

13. Immediately after removing the buns from the oven, pour the glaze over them. Let the glaze absorb for 1 minute.

14. Sprinkle each bun with a pinch of sesame seeds and a pinch of nigella seeds.

15. Allow the glaze to continue absorbing for 10 more minutes.

16. Serve warm or let cool to room temperature.

> *Note*
> You can keep the buns in an airtight container in the refrigerator for up to 2 days.
>
> **TIP:** You can make the glaze ahead of time, from several days to several weeks. In a jar, it will keep in the refrigerator or at room temperature. Reheat the glaze before pouring it on the buns in step 13.

CARDAMOM DATE RINGS

To test store-bought bread for freshness and worthiness, I squeeze the bag to gauge its softness. For that test, these rings set the gold standard. At one of my favorite bakeries, I discovered them when doing my squeeze test near the checkout line. The bread's bright yellow color and puffiness looked so inviting that—from that first squeeze, then taste—the rings had me hooked. I had to figure out how to bake them at home so I could enjoy the soft, warm cardamom flavor fresh from the oven. This bread is worth it!

PREP: **30 MINUTES**
REST: **2 HOURS**
COOK: **18 MINUTES**
TOTAL: **2 HOURS 48 MINUTES**

MAKES: **3 (8-INCH, 20-CM) RINGS**
SPECIAL EQUIPMENT: **MISTING BOTTLE**

DOUGH
57 grams (¼ cup) unsalted butter, melted
57 grams (¼ cup) whole-milk yogurt
57 grams (¼ cup) whole milk, warm (105–110°F, 40–43°C)
57 grams (¼ cup) water, warm (105–110°F, 40–43°C)
2 large eggs, room temperature
4 grams (1 teaspoon) pure vanilla extract
420 grams (3½ cups) unbleached all-purpose flour
6 grams (2 teaspoons) instant yeast
50 grams (¼ cup) granulated white sugar
½ teaspoon ground cardamom
½ teaspoon turmeric powder
½ teaspoon fine sea salt
4 grams (1 teaspoon) neutral oil

EGG WASH
1 large egg
5 grams (1 teaspoon) water
9 grams (1 tablespoon) sesame seeds

FILLING
1 recipe Date Paste (page 272)

1. In a large liquid measuring cup, whisk together the butter, yogurt, milk, water, eggs, and vanilla.
2. In the bowl of a stand mixer, add the flour, yeast, sugar, cardamom, turmeric, and salt and stir to combine with a wooden spoon or the dough hook (not attached). Slowly add the butter-milk mixture and mix until a shaggy dough forms, 1 minute.
3. Attach the dough hook, set the mixer speed to medium, and knead the dough until cohesive but still soft and sticky, 5 minutes.
4. Coat a medium mixing bowl with the oil. Ball the dough, transfer it to the prepared bowl, and flip the dough to coat it completely with oil. Cover the bowl with plastic wrap and lay a kitchen towel over that. Let the dough rise until it doubles in size, 1 to 2 hours.
5. Arrange an oven rack in the top third of the oven and preheat it to 350°F (177°C). Line a baking sheet with parchment paper and place it on a second unlined baking sheet.
6. In a small mixing bowl, make the egg wash by whisking together the egg and water. Set aside.
7. Divide the dough into three equal pieces, approximately 260 grams (2 cups) each.
8. Pat one piece into a rough rectangle. With the long side toward you, roll the dough into a 5-by-10-inch (13-by-25-cm) rectangle, lifting the dough off the counter a couple of times as you roll to allow it to contract.
9. Gently use an offset spatula to spread a third of the date paste, about 60 grams (¼ cup), evenly onto the dough, all the way to the edges.
10. Starting at the long side toward you, roll the dough tightly into a log. Pinch the seam to seal it. Stretch the log to 14 inches (36 cm) in length.
11. Transfer the log to the prepared baking sheet, seam side down. To form the ring, join the two

continues

ends of the dough. Lightly mist or dab the join with water and pinch the seam again.

12. Grasp the side of the ring opposite the join and gently draw the dough around to even the thickness at the narrower seam area. Move the first ring to make room for the remaining two.

13. With the tip of a sharp knife or kitchen scissors, cut four equally spaced vertical slits in the outside of the ring, avoiding the seam area. Make partial cuts to expose the filling but don't cut all the way through the ring.

14. Brush the egg wash lightly over the top and sides of the ring. Sprinkle it with a third of the sesame seeds.

15. Repeat steps 8 through 14 to make two more rings and place them on the baking sheet, a few inches apart.

16. Bake until the bottoms of the rings turn golden brown, 16 to 18 minutes.

17. Transfer the rings to a cooling rack and let them cool for 10 minutes.

18. Slice and serve warm.

> *Notes*
> - The second baking sheet under the rings protects the bottoms from getting too dark before the rings fully bake.
> - You can store the rings in an airtight container at room temperature for up to 3 days. You also can freeze them, wrap them in plastic wrap or foil, and store them for up to 3 months. To serve, let them thaw to room temperature, then wrap them in foil and warm them in a 250°F (120°C) oven for 10 minutes.

QURBAN HOLY BREAD

In Arabic, *qurban* means sacrifice, but these sacred loaves don't feel like one! Tradition names the five ingredients as flour, yeast, water, salt, and prayer. Many in our wider family circle, including some of my grandparents, come from the Eastern Orthodox tradition. When they came to Lansing, Michigan, they became a welcome part of the Greek Orthodox Church, which, for the sacrament of the Eucharist, calls this holy bread προσφορά (*prosforá*). When any of my siblings and I went to church with Sitto, we waited patiently for it—so different than our Catholic communion wafers! When my friend and neighbor Alexis Branoff heard that I was including holy bread in this book, she couldn't wait to bring over her mother's heirloom mold for me to use. This recipe adds more fragrance and flavor to the traditional version, but it still works for religious services. It also tastes especially good when sliced, toasted, and slathered with butter and jam.

PREP: 15 MINUTES
REST: 3 HOURS
COOK: 12 MINUTES
TOTAL: 3 HOURS 27 MINUTES

MAKES: 4 LOAVES
SPECIAL EQUIPMENT: ORTHODOX HOLY BREAD MOLD (OPTIONAL)

DOUGH
360 grams (3 cups) bread flour, plus more for dusting
150 grams (¾ cup) granulated white sugar
6 grams (2 teaspoons) instant yeast
4 grams (1 teaspoon) baking powder
½ teaspoon fine sea salt
1 pebble mastic, ground (see Notes)
2 grams (1 teaspoon) ground mahleb
¼ teaspoon ground nutmeg
200 grams (¾ cup plus 2 tablespoons) whole milk, warm (105–110°F, 40–43°C)
14 grams (1 tablespoon) orange blossom water
14 grams (1 tablespoon) rose water
28 grams (2 tablespoons) unsalted butter, room temperature

GLAZE
57 grams (2 tablespoons) whole milk, warm (105–110°F, 40–43°C)
28 grams (2 tablespoons) unsalted butter, melted
4 grams (1 teaspoon) orange blossom water
4 grams (1 teaspoon) rose water

1. In the bowl of a stand mixer, add the flour, sugar, yeast, baking powder, salt, mastic, mahleb, and nutmeg. Stir to combine with a wooden spoon or a dough hook (not attached). Slowly add the milk, orange blossom water, rose water, and butter and mix until a shaggy dough forms, 1 minute.

2. Attach the dough hook, set the mixer speed to medium-high, and knead the dough until smooth, 3 minutes.

3. Cover the bowl with plastic wrap and lay a kitchen towel over that. Let the dough rise until it doubles in size, at least 1 hour.

4. Turn out the dough onto a lightly floured counter. Quarter it. Each piece should weigh approximately 114 grams. Shape each piece into a smooth ball (page 62). Cover them on the counter with plastic wrap and lay a kitchen towel over that. Let the dough rise until it doubles in size, 1 hour.

5. Roll each ball into a 6-inch (15-cm) disc. Dust the discs lightly with flour, cover them with plastic wrap, and lay a kitchen towel over that. Let the dough rise for 1 more hour.

6. Arrange an oven rack in the middle position and preheat the oven to 400°F (200°C). Line a baking sheet with parchment paper.

continues

7. Onto each disc, sift a thin layer of flour. If using the mold, press the seal firmly into the top of each disc. If not using a mold, use a toothpick, skewer, or fork to poke a 1-inch (2.5-cm) square in the center of each disc, piercing all the way through the dough. For either method, make five evenly spaced pricks in the perimeter of each disc to prevent puffing while baking. Place the discs on the prepared baking sheet, about 1 inch (2.5 cm) apart.

8. Bake until the loaves turn golden brown, 10 to 12 minutes.

9. Meanwhile, make the glaze. In a small bowl, stir together all the glaze ingredients.

10. Immediately after baking, brush each loaf with glaze and serve warm.

Notes
- You can keep the bread in an airtight container at room temperature for up to 3 days or frozen for up to 3 months. To serve, let it thaw to room temperature, wrap it in foil, and warm it in a 250°F (120°C) oven for 10 minutes.
- Mastic is the dried resin of the mastic tree, sold in small jars of pebbles or "tears." This aromatic ingredient originates in Greece (called μαστίχα there), and it imparts an aromatic pine or cedar flavor to many Greek and Lebanese dishes. A spice grinder won't work for one tiny pebble. Grind it, as needed, in a mortar and pestle or on a cutting board with a mallet.

GLAZED KA'AK BREAD

My mother-in-law, Louise, was a beloved matriarch in all ways, including of this recipe. She made the finest soft, sweet anise bread. The moment that Ash Wednesday ended, she began her Easter "test-baking" of ka'ak. She lived just a few houses down, so we wandered down the street to watch and taste, enveloped in the heady aroma and warmth of her kitchen. You can mold the dough or simply pinch the perimeter and prick it with a fork, as she did. My sister-in-law Trisha enjoys recalling her VIP childhood assignment of decorating ka'ak with the tip of a feather. Molds are traditional, too, and fun to use. My recipe uses Louise's as a foundation but increases the anise flavor and swaps dry yeast for instant.

PREP: **15 MINUTES**
REST: **3 HOURS**
COOK: **30 MINUTES**
TOTAL: **3 HOURS 45 MINUTES**

MAKES: **12 SMALL LOAVES**
SPECIAL EQUIPMENT: **KA'AK MOLD(S)**

DOUGH
227 grams (1 cup) whole milk
75 grams (⅓ cup) Clarified Butter (page 271)
57 grams (¼ cup) water, warm (105–110°F, 40–43°C)
18 grams (1 tablespoon) pure anise extract
480 grams (4 cups) unbleached all-purpose flour, plus more for dusting
133 grams (⅔ cup) granulated white sugar
20 grams (2 tablespoons) ground anise seed
12 grams (1½ tablespoons) instant yeast
7 grams (1 tablespoon) ground mahleb
¼ teaspoon ground nutmeg
6 grams (2 teaspoons) sesame seeds
¼ teaspoon fine sea salt
4 grams (1 teaspoon) extra virgin olive oil

GLAZE
100 grams (½ cup) granulated white sugar
57 grams (2 tablespoons) whole milk, warm (105–110°F, 40–43°C)
28 grams (2 tablespoons) unsalted butter
4 grams (1 teaspoon) rose water

1. In the microwave, heat the milk, clarified butter, and water just until the butter melts and the mixture reaches 105°F (40°C). Add the anise extract and stir to combine.

2. In the bowl of a stand mixer, add the flour, sugar, anise seed, yeast, mahleb, nutmeg, sesame seeds, and salt. Stir to combine with a wooden spoon or a dough hook (not attached). Slowly add the milk mixture and mix until a shaggy dough forms, 1 minute.

3. Attach the dough hook, set the mixer speed to medium-high, and knead the dough until smooth, 3 minutes.

4. Coat a medium mixing bowl with the olive oil. Ball the sticky dough, transfer it to the prepared bowl, and flip the dough to coat it completely with oil. Cover the bowl with plastic wrap and lay a kitchen towel over that. Let the dough rise until it doubles in size, 2 to 3 hours.

5. For the second rise, place kitchen or bread towels on the counter or on two baking sheets. Cover them with plastic wrap.

6. Divide the dough into 12 pieces, approximately 80 grams each. Shape them into smooth balls (page 62).

7. On the prepared counter or baking sheets, place the balls 2 inches (5 cm) apart. Cover them with more plastic wrap and towels. Let them rise for 15 minutes, uncover the dough, and let them rise for 15 more minutes.

continues

8. Arrange an oven rack in the middle position and preheat the oven to 325°F (165°C). Line two baking sheets with parchment paper. Dust the counter and mold(s) lightly with flour.

9. To shape the dough, lightly coat a dough ball with flour and flatten it with your hands. With force, repeatedly press the flattened dough into the mold. Don't let the dough lift from the mold. Push in any dough that runs over the edges. To unmold, turn the mold over and wait for gravity to do its work. Gently peel the dough away from the edges. Place the molded loaves on the prepared baking sheets. To shape by hand, flatten a dough ball with your palm. Pinch the edges five or six times around the disc and use the tines of a fork to poke the top liberally.

10. Repeat with the remaining dough, placing 6 loaves on each baking sheet.

11. Bake one sheet at a time until the bread turns golden brown, 25 to 30 minutes.

12. Transfer the ka'ak to cooling racks and let the loaves cool for 15 minutes.

13. Meanwhile, make the glaze. In a small saucepan over medium heat, add all the glaze ingredients, bring them to a simmer, and cook for 1 minute. Transfer the glaze to a wide bowl.

14. Place parchment paper under the cooling racks. Dip each loaf entirely in the glaze and hold the bread over the bowl to allow excess glaze to drip back into it.

15. Return the ka'ak to the cooling racks and let the glaze dry for at least 15 minutes before serving.

Notes

In airtight containers, store the loaves at room temperature for up to 5 days. The bread will harden slowly over time, which makes it perfect to dip in coffee or tea. To soften it, heat it in the microwave for 15 to 20 seconds before serving.

TIPS
- Make the loaves larger or smaller, as you like them. Simply divide the dough into smaller or larger balls.
- If you have additional baking sheets, double them when baking to prevent overbaking the bottoms of the ka'ak.

ORANGE BLOSSOM CARAMEL PECAN ROLLS

A restaurant in northern Michigan serves pecan rolls in their breadbasket for brunch *and* dinner. My friend Hollye has a sweet tooth like me, and she always sets one aside for dessert, which I take as permission to enjoy these decadent rolls for any occasion, morning or evening, that calls for a bite of soft, sweet, nutty goodness.

PREP: **30 MINUTES**
REST: **3 HOURS**
COOK: **40 MINUTES**
TOTAL: **4 HOURS 10 MINUTES**

MAKES: **20 ROLLS**

DOUGH

2 large eggs, room temperature
57 grams (¼ cup) water, warm (105–110°F, 40–43°C)
114 grams (½ cup) whole-milk yogurt, room temperature
510 grams (3¾ cups) unbleached all-purpose flour
6 grams (2 teaspoons) instant yeast
50 grams (¼ cup) granulated white sugar
6 grams (1 teaspoon) fine sea salt
57 grams (¼ cup) unsalted butter, room temperature
4 grams (1 teaspoon) neutral oil for coating

FILLING

113 grams (½ cup) unsalted butter, room temperature
159 grams (¾ cup packed) light brown sugar
5 grams (2 teaspoons) ground cinnamon
3 grams (1 teaspoon) ground cardamom

CARAMEL

170 grams (¾ cup) unsalted butter
265 grams (1¼ cups packed) light brown sugar
104 grams (⅓ cup) light corn syrup
¼ teaspoon fine sea salt
57 grams (¼ cup) heavy cream
6 grams (1 teaspoon) pure vanilla extract
12 grams (2 teaspoons) orange blossom water
168 grams (1½ cups) whole pecans

1. In a small bowl, whisk together the eggs, water, and yogurt until lightly beaten.
2. In the bowl of a stand mixer, add the flour, yeast, sugar, and salt and stir to combine with a wooden spoon or a dough hook (not attached). Slowly add the egg mixture and butter and mix until a shaggy dough forms, 1 minute.
3. Attach the dough hook, set the mixer speed to medium-high, and knead the dough until smooth, 3 minutes. Once or twice during kneading, stop to scrape down the sides of the bowl to incorporate everything.
4. Turn out the dough onto a lightly floured counter and knead by hand until smooth, 1 minute.
5. Lightly coat a large mixing bowl with the oil. Ball the dough, transfer it to the prepared bowl, and flip the dough to coat it completely with oil. Cover the bowl with plastic wrap and lay a kitchen towel over that. Let the dough rise until it doubles in size, 2 hours.
6. Meanwhile, make the filling. In a small saucepan over medium-low heat, melt the butter.
7. Add the brown sugar, cinnamon, and cardamom and whisk to combine. Cook, whisking constantly, until the sugar dissolves and the mixture becomes cohesive and sandy, 3 minutes. Transfer to a bowl and set aside.
8. In the same saucepan, make the caramel. Over medium heat, melt the butter.
9. Add the brown sugar, corn syrup, and salt. Cook, stirring constantly, until the sugar dissolves and the mixture becomes cohesive, 3 minutes.
10. Remove the sugar mixture from the heat. Add the cream, vanilla, and orange blossom water. Whisk to combine.

continues

11. Pour the caramel into a 9-by-13-by-2-inch (23-by-33-by-5-cm) baking dish. Sprinkle the pecans evenly on the caramel. Set aside.

12. Turn out the dough onto a lightly floured counter. Pat the dough into a rough rectangle and roll it out to 10 by 20 inches (25 by 50 cm), a long side toward you.

13. Use an offset spatula to spread the filling evenly on the dough, leaving a 1-inch (2.5-cm) border around the perimeter.

14. Starting at the long side toward you, roll the dough tightly into a log, seam side down.

15. With a sharp chef's knife, halve the log crosswise, then cut each half into 6 equal pieces, about 1½ inches (4 cm) thick, for a total of 12 pieces.

16. In the baking dish, place the slices, a cut side up, on the caramel. Cover the dish with plastic wrap and let the dough rise until the rolls become puffy and double in size, at least 1 hour.

17. When the dough has risen, arrange a rack in the middle of the oven and preheat the oven to 350°F (177°C).

18. Remove the plastic wrap and bake until the rolls turn golden brown and reach an internal temperature of 200°F (95°C), 35 to 40 minutes.

19. Remove the rolls from the oven and let them cool in the pan for 10 minutes.

20. Turn the block of rolls out onto a large serving platter, cutting board, or baking sheet. Cut it into pieces and serve.

Note

You can store leftover buns in an airtight container in the refrigerator for up to 2 days. To reheat, heat them in the foil in a 250°F (120°C) oven for 15 minutes.

TIP: To prep rolls ahead of time, follow the recipe through adding the raw rolls to the baking dish in step 17, then refrigerate the pan overnight. When ready to bake, let the rolls come to room temperature, let them rise for at least 1 hour after that until puffy, and proceed with the rest of the recipe. You also can freeze the raw rolls. Thaw the pan at room temperature overnight and let them rise until puffy.

ORANGE DATE TEA RING

The glory of this ring lies in its beautiful shape, the fun of fanning the pieces, and of course the captivating flavor combination of orange and dates. A longtime favorite among Lebanese bakers, this ring appears in most older Lebanese cookbooks. For me, it makes such a lovely hospitality helper, ready to slice for friends who visit. Make a cup of Arabic Cardamom Coffee (page 19) or Green Tea with Warm Spices (page 85), and do as earlier bakers did: welcome, sit, eat, and share.

PREP: **35 MINUTES**
REST: **2 HOURS**
COOK: **25 MINUTES**
TOTAL: **3 HOURS**

MAKES: **12 SERVINGS**
SPECIAL EQUIPMENT: **MISTING BOTTLE**

DOUGH
114 grams (½ cup) whole milk
57 grams (¼ cup) unsalted butter
28 grams (2 tablespoons) water
1 large egg
300 grams (2½ cups) bread flour, plus more for dusting
3 grams (1 teaspoon) instant yeast
50 grams (¼ cup) granulated white sugar
½ teaspoon fine sea salt
4 grams (1 teaspoon) neutral oil

FILLING
1 recipe Date Paste with orange juice (page 272)

EGG WASH
1 large egg
5 grams (1 teaspoon) water
9 grams (1 tablespoon) sesame seeds

1. In a small heatproof bowl, warm the milk and butter in the microwave to 105–110°F / 40–43°C in 30-second increments, stirring after each increment. Add the water and stir to combine.
2. In another small bowl, lightly beat the egg with a whisk.
3. In the bowl of a stand mixer, add the flour, yeast, sugar, and salt and stir to combine with a wooden spoon or the dough hook (not attached). Slowly add the milk mixture and the beaten egg and mix until a shaggy dough forms, 1 minute.
4. Attach the dough hook, set the mixer speed to medium-high, and knead the dough until smooth, 5 minutes. Once or twice during kneading, stop to scrape down the sides of the bowl to incorporate everything.
5. Coat a medium mixing bowl with the oil. Ball the dough, transfer it to the prepared bowl, and flip the dough to coat it completely with oil. Cover the bowl with plastic wrap and lay a kitchen towel over that. Let the dough rise until it doubles in size, 1 to 2 hours.
6. Line a baking sheet with parchment paper.
7. On a lightly floured surface, roll the dough into a 12-by-15-inch (30-by-38-cm) rectangle, a long side toward you.
8. Use an offset spatula to spread the date paste evenly onto the dough.
9. Starting at the long side toward you, roll the dough tightly into a log. Pinch the seam to seal it.
10. Transfer the log to the prepared baking sheet, seam side down. To form the ring, join the two ends of the dough. Lightly mist or dab the join with water and pinch the seam again.
11. Grasp the side of the ring opposite the join and gently draw the dough around to even the thickness at the narrower seam area.

continues

12. With the tip of a sharp knife or kitchen scissors, cut 12 to 14 equally spaced vertical slits in the outside of the ring, each 1 inch (2.5 cm) apart, avoiding the seam area. Make partial cuts to expose the filling without cutting through the ring.

13. Holding the outer edges of a slice, gently turn it on its side to fan it out. Repeat with all the pieces.

14. Cover the ring with plastic wrap and lay a kitchen towel over that. Let the ring rise until puffy, 1 hour.

15. Arrange an oven rack in the middle position and preheat the oven to 350°F (177°C).

16. In a small mixing bowl, make the egg wash by whisking together the egg and water. Lightly brush the top of the risen tea ring with egg wash and sprinkle sesame seeds evenly on it.

17. Bake until the ring turns golden brown, 20 to 25 minutes.

18. Transfer the ring to a cooling rack and let it cool for at least 15 minutes before serving.

19. Cut slices and serve warm.

> **Notes**
> - In an airtight container, you can store the ring at room temperature for up to 3 days. You also can freeze it; wrap it in plastic wrap or foil, and store it for up to 3 months.
> - To serve, let it thaw to room temperature, wrap it in foil, and warm it in a 250°F (120°C) oven for 10 minutes.
>
> **VARIATION: GLAZE** adds even more sweetness and beauty to the ring. Whisk together 113 grams (1 cup) confectioners' sugar, 10 grams (2 teaspoons) water, ½ teaspoon rose water, and 7 grams (1 teaspoon) corn syrup. After the ring has cooled to room temperature, drizzle it with glaze and finish it with sesame seeds.

Something to Drink

GREEN TEA WITH WARM SPICES

The anise and cinnamon flavors in this tea beautifully complement the Orange Date Tea Ring (page 83). This tea also amplifies the flavors of Sesame Ka'ak Rings (page 129), Walnut Orange Blossom Mak'roun Fingers (page 91), and pretty much every sweet bread and cookie in the book!

PREP: **1 MINUTE**
REST TIME: **5 MINUTES**
TOTAL: **6 MINUTES**

MAKES: **4 SERVINGS**

17 grams (4 teaspoons) loose green tea or 2 green tea bags
8 grams (2 teaspoons) anise seeds
2 cinnamon sticks
908 grams (4 cups) hot water (185°F, 85°C)
28 grams (4 teaspoons) honey (optional)

1. Chafe a teapot with hot water. Discard the water and add the loose tea or bags. Set aside.

2. In a large heatproof measuring cup, add the anise seeds and cinnamon sticks. Pour the hot water over the spices and let them infuse for 3 minutes.

3. Through a fine mesh strainer, strain the spiced water into the prepared teapot. Steep the tea for 2 minutes.

4. Strain the brewed tea into four teacups. Stir 1 teaspoon of honey, if desired, into each cup and serve.

Cookies

The cookie holds a place of honor as the ideal ambassador of warmth, hospitality, and love from the kitchen. Everyone enjoys a cookie tradition for every season and for a fulfilling way to spend an afternoon, especially with your habibis. This chapter surveys a baker's dozen of different styles that invite you to bake, taste, and share their goodness. Discover here the many types of mak'rouns. Try your hand at ma'amoul, that most iconic of Middle Eastern cookies, with an array of fillings and shaping methods. Overheard while baking with my sister, Peg: "You want a controversy, you open your mouth and say 'ma'amoul!'" because two camps have formed concerning ma'amoul dough: all-purpose flour or semolina as the foundation. Find out where I land on page 105!

The Mak'roun Menu

Mak'rouns constitute a special tradition, with several styles, in Lebanese baking. First, a quick overview of the word. Almost as many types exist as spellings: makdrouns, makaroons, mak'rouns, mak'roons, macaroons, and macarons. The English *macaroon* comes from the French *macaron*, itself from the Italian *maccaroni*. From there, it gets a little murky. The Italian word could derive from Byzantine Greek μακαρία (*makaría*, barley food), from Latin *maccare* (to bruise or crush), or ancient Greek μακάριος (*makários*, blessed by the gods). Each makes its own kind of sense. Here are the four main varieties of mak'rouns:

1. **TOASTED COCONUT COOKIES**, typical in Lebanese bakeries, never dipped in chocolate but instead feature a cherry on top.

2. **NUT-FILLED FINGERS**, with a pie-like crust, originate in the southern Lebanese village of Deir Mimas (if you know otherwise, let's hear it!), from which my father's family hails.

3. **GLAZED FINGERS** feature a waffle design from being pressed onto a rack or mold, fried or baked, and take a glaze of flower water syrup.

4. **FRENCH MACARONS** appear here because they share the name; and with their historical French influence on Lebanon, plus my own love of macarons, we have the perfect opportunity to marry both traditions in one beautiful confection.

GLAZED MAK'ROUNS

Shaping these cookies always recalls memories of my brief stint in high school making waffle cones for the Melting Moments ice cream shop (my poor burned fingertips). This recipe skips a hot waffle iron in favor of using a cooling rack to imprint the design. Frying yields the best crisp texture and flavor, but you can bake them instead, as in the variation that follows.

PREP: **20 MINUTES**
COOK: **10 MINUTES**
TOTAL: **30 MINUTES**

MAKES: **17 (3-INCH, 7.5-CM) COOKIES**
SPECIAL EQUIPMENT: **METAL COOLING RACK**

Neutral oil for frying

DOUGH
210 grams (1 cup plus 3 tablespoons) unbleached all-purpose flour
163 grams (1 cup) fine semolina flour
½ teaspoon instant yeast
8 grams (2 teaspoons) granulated white sugar
¼ teaspoon fine sea salt
9 grams (1 tablespoon) ground anise seed
113 grams (½ cup) whole milk, warm (105–110°F, 40–43°C)
66 grams (⅓ cup) neutral oil

GLAZE
480 grams (1½ cups) Flower Water Syrup (page 273), cold

1. Set a medium sauté pan over medium heat, fill it 2 inches (5 cm) deep with oil, and heat it to 375°F (190°C). Line two baking sheets with parchment paper.

2. In a medium mixing bowl, combine the flour, semolina, yeast, sugar, salt, and anise. With a large spoon, stir in the milk and 66 grams (⅓ cup) of oil until the dough becomes crumbly and resembles piecrust dough.

3. Turn out the dough onto a lightly floured counter and knead until smooth and pliable, 3 minutes.

4. Divide the dough into 17 pieces, approximately 28 grams each, and roll each piece into a log 2½ inches by 1 inch (6.25 by 2.5 cm), with tapered ends.

continues

5. Press the dough into the rack grid on the diagonal, flattening it to create a waffle imprint in the dough. (If the rack has wires in just one direction, press the dough twice to create the pattern.) Make hollow fingers by rolling or folding one long edge carefully over to the other side, creating a central cavity but still retaining pointed ends. Transfer them to the prepared baking sheets.

6. Pour the flower water syrup into a medium bowl.

7. When the oil has heated, use a slotted spoon or spider skimmer to lower 5 cookies carefully into the hot oil. To ensure even frying, don't fry more than 5 at once. Fry until the bottoms turn golden brown, about 2 minutes.

8. Flip them over and continue frying until they turn golden all over, 1 more minute.

9. Remove the cookies with the slotted spoon and immediately immerse them in the syrup. Stir to coat them evenly and let them rest in the glaze for 5 minutes.

10. Meanwhile, fry the next batch of cookies. With tongs or the slotted spoon, transfer the glazed cookies to a sheet of parchment to dry. Repeat until you've fried and glazed all the cookies.

11. Serve immediately or let them dry completely.

Note

Store the glazed mak'rouns, lightly covered with wax paper, at room temperature for up to 3 days.

VARIATION: To bake the **MAK'ROUNS**, arrange an oven rack in the middle position and preheat the oven to 375°F (190°C). On the baking sheets, space them 1 inch (2.5 cm) apart. Bake until they turn a deep golden brown, 20 to 25 minutes. Soak them, fresh from the oven, in the syrup in batches of 5 cookies at a time.

WALNUT ORANGE BLOSSOM MAK'ROUN FINGERS

So many in my tribe remember Sitto's famous holiday mak'rouns, yet no one has her recipe, which means that none of us had baked them since she passed away in 1994. Over the years, Aunt Gloria Nakfoor often made her own version, so she worked with me to re-create the recipe. As we baked and tasted, memories flooded back and filled the day, giving us both a beautiful new baking memory to savor. This cookie has a pastry-like crust filled with orange blossom–coated nuts, delivering an unforgettable texture and aroma. I was tempted to include toasted nuts in these cookies, but Aunt Gloria instructed otherwise!

PREP: 25 MINUTES
COOK: 24 MINUTES
TOTAL: 49 MINUTES

MAKES: 24 (4½-INCH, 11.5-CM) **COOKIES**

360 grams (3 cups) unbleached all-purpose flour
18 grams (2 tablespoons) ground anise seed
½ teaspoon fine sea salt
226 grams (1 cup) unsalted butter, room temperature
1 large egg
124 grams (½ cup plus 2 tablespoons) granulated white sugar
14 to 42 grams (1 to 3 tablespoons) whole milk as needed

FILLING
160 grams (1¼ cups) walnut halves or pieces
50 grams (¼ cup) granulated white sugar
9 grams (2 teaspoons) orange blossom water

1. Arrange an oven rack in the middle position and preheat the oven to 400°F (200°C). Line a baking sheet with parchment paper.
2. In a medium mixing bowl, whisk together the flour, anise, and salt. Set aside.
3. In the bowl of a stand mixer fitted with the paddle attachment or with a hand mixer, beat the butter until light and fluffy, 1 minute.
4. Add 100 grams (½ cup) of the sugar to the butter and cream it until it combines, 1 minute.
5. Meanwhile, in a small bowl, lightly beat the egg.
6. Stop the mixer, add the egg, and beat until it combines as well, 1 more minute.
7. With a wooden spoon or using your hands, add the flour mixture and mix to combine. Add the milk 1 tablespoon at a time, mixing well after each addition, until the dough becomes soft and pliable. Squeeze the dough to test it. If it cracks, add 1 more tablespoon of milk, mix well, and test again.
8. Next, make the filling. In a nut grinder or food processor, coarsely chop the nuts.
9. In a small mixing bowl, stir together the walnuts, sugar, and orange blossom water.
10. Divide the dough into 24 pieces, approximately 30 grams each.
11. On a dry counter, pat a piece of dough into an oval 4 to 5 inches long, 2½ inches wide, and ⅛ inch thick (10 to 12.5 cm long, 6.25 cm wide, and 3 mm thick). With your fingers or a thin metal spatula, gently loosen the flattened dough from the counter and turn it over so the smooth side faces down.
12. Spoon 7 grams (1 tablespoon) of the nut mixture lengthwise down the dough, leaving the edges clear.
13. Starting at one end, lift the sides of the dough over the filling. Pinch the edges together with one hand,

continues

keeping the nuts in place with the other, to close the seam. Crimp the seam between your thumb and index knuckle four times. The crimp should stand ⅛ inch (3 mm) tall.

14. Repeat steps 11 through 13 with the remaining dough and filling. As you go, place the raw fingers 1 inch (2.5 cm) apart on the prepared baking sheet.

15. Bake until the fingers turn golden brown, 10 to 12 minutes.

16. Remove the baking sheet from the oven and immediately sprinkle the cookies evenly with the remaining 2 tablespoons sugar. Let them cool to room temperature before serving.

> *Notes*
> - You can store the mak'roun fingers in an airtight container at room temperature for up to 1 week or frozen for up to 3 months.
> - To prep the recipe in advance, you can make the dough, wrap it in plastic wrap, and store it in the refrigerator for up to 3 days or the freezer for up to 2 months. Let it come to room temperature before shaping.
>
> **TIP:** Shaping these mak'roun fingers can be a sticky process! Keep a damp cloth or paper towel handy to wipe your fingers as you go.
>
> **VARIATION:** Aunt Gloria tops the fingers with a smattering of **SUGARED NUTS** before baking. Sitto sprinkled them with **GREEN AND RED DECORATING SUGAR**, also before baking.

TOASTED COCONUT MAK'ROUNS

This bakery staple has become my favorite impulse buy at the checkout line in Middle Eastern markets after the hard work of grocery shopping. But these cookies taste even better when homemade. The cherry on top of this sundae-like treat grabs my attention, and I love the contrast between the toasted exterior and chewy interior. Work at least one day ahead with this recipe because the batter needs at least 12 hours to chill.

PREP: 15 MINUTES
CHILL: 12 HOURS
COOK: 26 MINUTES
TOTAL: 12 HOURS 41 MINUTES
MAKES: 12 (2-INCH, 5-CM) COOKIES

3 large egg whites (105 grams)
160 grams (1½ cups) confectioners' sugar
128 grams (1¾ cups) desiccated coconut or shredded unsweetened coconut
4 grams (1 teaspoon) pure vanilla extract
6 maraschino cherries (35 grams)

1. In the bowl of a double boiler or a medium heat-proof bowl that fits over a small saucepan, whisk together the egg whites and the sugar until the sugar completely dissolves, 3 minutes.
2. Add the coconut and vanilla extract and use a spoon to combine.
3. Fill the bottom of a double boiler or saucepan with 1 inch (2.5 cm) of water, taking care that the water doesn't touch the bottom of the upper bowl when assembled. Over high heat, bring the water to a boil, then reduce the heat to low to simmer.
4. Place the upper bowl containing the batter on the lower vessel. Cook, stirring constantly, until the mixture thickens, 3 to 5 minutes.
5. Remove the upper bowl and dry the bottom of it. Let the batter cool to room temperature and cover the bowl with plastic wrap or transfer the batter to an airtight container. Refrigerate it for at least 12 hours and up to 3 days.
6. Arrange an oven rack in the middle position, preheat the oven to 350°F (177°C), and line a baking sheet with parchment paper or use a silicone baking mat.
7. Halve the cherries.
8. Using a cookie scoop, spoon, or your hands coated lightly with oil, form the cold dough into 12 balls, approximately 28 grams (1 ounce) each.
9. On the prepared baking sheet, place the dough balls at least 1 inch (2.5 cm) apart.
10. Lightly press half a maraschino cherry, cut side down, in the center of each raw cookie.
11. Bake until the cookies turn golden brown, 24 to 26 minutes.
12. Remove the cookies from the oven and let them cool to room temperature before serving.

Note
Immediately store any leftover cookies in an airtight container, where they will keep at room temperature for up to 4 days.

RASPBERRY ROSE WATER MACARONS

In 1516, the Ottoman Empire wrested control of the lands of Lebanon from the sultans of Egypt. Four centuries later, when the Empire collapsed, the League of Nations handed control of the region to France. The French mandate lasted for 20 years, until Charles de Gaulle recognized Lebanese independence. But those two decades left their mark on Lebanon, including its language and cuisine in a way that has transcended time and borders. Like so many Lebanese everywhere, I studied French and developed an affinity for all things French, especially pastry. When I lived and worked in downtown Chicago, I went out of my way to walk past Pierrot Gourmet, the kind of French café that helps you forget your troubles and transports you straight to Paris. I almost hated to bite into the perfection of their raspberry rose macarons—*almost*.

PREP: **38 MINUTES**
REST: **1 HOUR 15 MINUTES**
CHILL: **1 DAY**
COOK: **36 MINUTES**
TOTAL: **1 DAY 2 HOURS 29 MINUTES**

MAKES: **6 EXTRA-LARGE (3-INCH, 8-CM) MACARONS**
SPECIAL EQUIPMENT: **PIPING BAG WITH ½-INCH (1.5-CM) ROUND PIPING TIP**

SHELLS
- 4 grams (1 teaspoon) neutral oil
- 150 grams (1½ cups plus 1 tablespoon) finely ground blanched almond flour
- 150 grams (1¼ cups plus 1 tablespoon) confectioners' sugar
- ⅛ teaspoon fine sea salt
- 4 egg whites (105 grams), room temperature
- ⅛ teaspoon cream of tartar

SYRUP
- 150 grams (¾ cup) granulated white sugar
- 60 grams (¼ cup plus 1 teaspoon) water
- 4 grams (1 teaspoon) rose water
- 4 drops pink gel food coloring

FILLING
- 170 grams (¾ cup) unsalted butter, room temperature
- 143 grams (1¼ cups) confectioners' sugar
- 4 grams (1 teaspoon) rose water
- 4 grams (1 teaspoon) pure vanilla extract
- 1 drop pink gel food coloring
- 14 grams (1 tablespoon) whole milk
- 127 grams (¼ cup plus 2 tablespoons) raspberry preserves
- 240 grams (2 cups) fresh raspberries

1. Prepare two sheets of parchment for two baking sheets. Use a cookie cutter or glass 2½ inches (6.25 cm) wide as a guide and trace six circles on each sheet with a pencil or dark pen. Space the circles at least 2 inches (5 cm) apart.

2. Lightly coat both baking sheets with the oil and line them with the parchment guides, traced side down.

3. Into a large mixing bowl, sift the almond flour, confectioners' sugar, and salt through a fine mesh sieve. Set aside.

4. In the bowl of a stand mixer fitted with the whisk attachment, add 3 of the egg whites and the cream of tartar. Set the mixer speed to medium-high and whip until soft peaks form, 2 to 3 minutes. Reduce the speed to low and let it run while you make the syrup.

5. Make the syrup. In a small saucepan over medium-high heat, combine the sugar and water, stirring

continues

until the sugar dissolves completely. Bring it to a boil and continue cooking until the syrup reaches 245°F (118°C), 3 to 4 minutes. Remove from the heat and quickly stir in the rose water.

6. Increase the mixer speed to medium and, in a thin, steady stream, carefully pour the syrup into the whites. Aim for the side of the bowl just above the whites to avoid the syrup hitting the whisk. Beat for 30 seconds.

7. Turn off the mixer and add the food coloring. Set the mixer speed to medium-high and whip the meringue until stiff peaks form, 2 to 3 more minutes. To test the stiffness, remove the whisk attachment from the mixer and turn it upside down so the tip points up. The meringue peak should bend at 2 o'clock.

8. With a large soft spatula, transfer the meringue to the flour mixture and stir to incorporate. As you stir, turn the bowl and scrape the bottom, smearing the batter against the side just until no dry spots remain.

9. Add the remaining egg white and continue stirring until the batter loosens and flows from the spatula in a slow, thick, wide stream and reincorporates into the batter slowly, about 30 seconds. Test the consistency of the batter by placing a spoonful on a plate and letting it sit for 1 minute. If the batter spreads to a flat-topped circle, it's ready. If it remains rounded, stir again for 10 seconds and retest.

10. Transfer the batter to a pastry bag or gallon plastic bag fitted with a ½-inch (1.5-cm) round piping tip. Hold the bag perpendicular to the baking sheet and keep the tip about ½ inch (1.5 cm) above a traced circle. As the batter flows out, hold the tip steady and centered as the batter flows to the edge of the circle. Quickly flick the tip up and away from the piped batter to cut the stream. Repeat with the rest of the batter and circles.

11. To pop any interior air bubbles, gently lift and drop the pan on the counter a few times. If any surface bubbles remain, pop them with a toothpick.

12. Let the shells rest until they form a light skin that you can touch without marking the surface and they no longer jiggle, 45 minutes.

13. Arrange an oven rack in the lower third of the oven and preheat it to 300°F (149°C).

14. Bake one sheet at a time for 16 to 18 minutes. Touch the center of a shell and if it jiggles, continue baking until firm, 1 more minute.

15. Transfer the baking sheet to a wire rack and let the shells cool to room temperature. Place the sheet in the freezer or, if it won't fit, carefully slide the two pieces of parchment paper with the shells on them into the freezer for at least 30 minutes.

16. While the shells freeze, make the filling. In the bowl of a stand mixer fitted with the paddle attachment, beat the butter on medium speed until smooth, 1 minute.

17. Add the confectioners' sugar, rose water, vanilla extract, and pink food coloring. Beat again on medium speed until smooth, 2 minutes, stopping to scrape down the bowl as you go.

18. Add the milk and beat again until light and smooth, 1 more minute.

19. Transfer three-quarters of the buttercream to a pastry bag or gallon plastic bag fitted with a ½-inch (1.5-cm) round or star piping tip. Set aside the remaining buttercream.

20. Remove the shells from the freezer and carefully peel each shell from the parchment. Set them all, flat sides up, on one baking sheet.

21. Spread a thin layer of the reserved buttercream on the flat side of each macaron shell.

22. Pipe a ring of buttercream on 6 of the shells, leaving a well in the center of each for the preserves. Cover the baking sheet with plastic wrap and refrigerate it for at least 24 hours and up to 2 weeks.

23. When the shells are ready, spoon 21 grams (1 tablespoon) of preserves into each shell with a well. Top the ring of buttercream with raspberries, with the berries' open end facing down. Gently place the top shell over the raspberries.

24. Bring the macarons to room temperature before serving.

Note
Store the macarons, covered, in the refrigerator for up to 2 days.

TIPS
- It's easier to separate cold eggs. Bring the whites to room temperature after separating.
- When stirring the macaronage (macaron batter), take care not to over-stir and test the batter.

VARIATION: To make **30 SMALLER MACARONS** (2 inches, 5 cm), omit the fresh raspberries and make the following changes. In step 1, use a silicone macaron mat, or trace thirty 1½-inch (3.8-cm) circles on the pieces of parchment. In step 12, let the macarons rest for 20 minutes. In step 14, bake for 23 minutes. Omit step 21. Pipe a buttercream ring on the first half of the shells, fill the center with preserves, and top with the other half of the shells.

GLAZED ZALABIA

Like Zalabia Donuts (page 64), this zalabia also fries, but with a much different result. Glazed zalabia, or *mishabak*, meaning "lattice," sometimes goes by the name Lebanese funnel cakes. A squeeze bottle of batter forms circular spiral shapes directly in the hot oil. Like Awamet (page 126), the fried zalabia take a dip in syrup, resulting in a glazed, crunchy-fried treat perfect for the young and young at heart!

PREP: 10 MINUTES
REST: 30 MINUTES
COOK: 18 MINUTES
TOTAL: 58 MINUTES

MAKES: 22 (3-INCH, 8-CM) COOKIES
SPECIAL EQUIPMENT: PLASTIC SQUEEZE BOTTLE, ¼-INCH (6-MM) OPENING

DOUGH
- 134 grams (1 cup plus 2 tablespoons) unbleached all-purpose flour
- 70 grams (¾ cup) cornstarch
- 25 grams (2 tablespoons) granulated white sugar
- 3 grams (1 teaspoon) instant yeast
- ½ teaspoon fine sea salt
- ½ teaspoon baking powder
- ½ teaspoon baking soda
- 227 grams (1 cup) water, warm (105–110°F, 40–43°C)
- Neutral oil, for frying
- 320 grams (2 cups) Flower Water Syrup, cold (page 273)

1. In a small mixing bowl, whisk together the flour, cornstarch, sugar, yeast, salt, baking powder, and baking soda. Add the water and continue whisking until the batter becomes smooth. Cover the bowl with plastic wrap and lay a kitchen towel over that. Let the batter rise for 30 minutes.

2. Set a large saucepan over medium heat, fill it 3 inches (8 cm) deep with oil, and heat the oil to 375°F (190°C). Next to the frying station, set a baking sheet lined with paper towels, a medium bowl filled with the syrup, and a cooling rack with parchment paper underneath it.

3. Immediately before frying, transfer the batter to a squeeze bottle. Hold the squeeze bottle, tip down, about 4 inches (10 cm) from the oil. Before squeezing, swirl the bottle in a tight circular motion. Squeeze the batter into the hot oil, keeping the flow centered and forming 3 squiggled circles 3 inches (8 cm) in diameter. Fry them until they turn a deep golden brown, flipping them once or twice, 2 minutes total.

4. Transfer the zalabia to the paper towels. Let them drain and cool for 3 minutes.

5. Dunk the cooled zalabia in the syrup, turning to coat them evenly, and place them on the draining rack.

6. Repeat with the rest of the batter and serve immediately.

Note
Store leftovers at room temperature, uncovered, for up to 1 day.

TIP: Don't transfer the batter to the squeeze bottle until you're ready to fry the zalabia. Otherwise the batter may continue to rise and overflow the bottle.

APRICOT GEMS

In Michigan, the growing season for apricots—a favorite fruit at the Lebanese table—is fleeting, so we hoard them from the moment they ripen and turn them into preserves to enjoy throughout the year. This cookie provides a rich cream cheese shortbread base to hold a glistening gem of apricot preserves.

PREP: **16 MINUTES**
COOK: **44 MINUTES**
TOTAL: **1 HOUR**

MAKES: **36 (2-INCH, 5-CM) COOKIES**

170 grams (½ cup) apricot preserves
9 grams (2 teaspoons) fresh lemon juice
270 grams (2¼ cups) unbleached all-purpose flour
½ teaspoon fine sea salt
½ teaspoon baking soda
¼ teaspoon baking powder
113 grams (½ cup) unsalted butter, room temperature
133 grams (⅔ cup) granulated white sugar
141 grams (5 ounces) cream cheese, room temperature
1 large egg
4 grams (1 teaspoon) orange blossom water
½ teaspoon pure vanilla extract

1. Arrange an oven rack in the middle position and preheat the oven to 350°F (177°C). Line two baking sheets with parchment paper.

2. In a small bowl, stir together the apricot preserves and lemon juice. Set aside.

3. In a medium mixing bowl, whisk together the flour, salt, baking soda, and baking powder. Set aside.

4. In the bowl of a stand mixer fitted with the paddle attachment, cream the butter and sugar on medium speed until light and fluffy, 3 minutes.

5. Add the cream cheese, egg, orange blossom water, and vanilla extract and continue beating until smooth, 1 minute.

6. Scrape down the sides of the bowl, add the flour mixture, and beat on low speed just until the dough fully combines.

7. Divide the dough into 36 pieces, approximately 18 grams each. Between your palms, roll the pieces into balls and place them on the prepared baking sheets, 1½ inches (4 cm) apart.

8. Moisten a thumb in water and press an indentation into the center of each ball.

9. One baking sheet at a time, par-bake the cookies until they just begin to set, 8 minutes.

10. Remove the sheet from the oven but leave the oven on. Working quickly with the rounded tip of a teaspoon, make the indentation in the cookies again.

11. Use a small spoon to fill each indentation carefully with about ½ teaspoon of jam.

12. Return the sheet to the oven and bake the gems again until they turn pale golden, 10 to 12 minutes.

13. On the baking sheets, let the cookies cool for 10 minutes.

14. Transfer them to a wire rack to cool completely before serving.

Note

You can store the cookies in an airtight container at room temperature for up to 5 days.

TIP: To prep the dough ahead of time, follow the recipe through step 8. Freeze the indented dough balls on a baking sheet, then transfer them to freezer bags. Bake them from frozen for 15 minutes, reshape the indentations with your thumb or the back of a small spoon, and proceed with steps 11 through 14.

MA'AMOUL

My ma'amoul recipe includes just the right balance of flour and semolina. The dough holds together through filling and shaping to create a meltaway shortbread cookie. The different shapes look lovely and indicate the different fillings inside. Explore the many filling options, from the classic nuts and dates to my own inventions of cherry chocolate rose water and apricot cardamom.

PREP: **1 HOUR 5 MINUTES**
COOK: **18 MINUTES**
TOTAL: **1 HOUR 23 MINUTES**

MAKES: **24 (2-INCH, 5-CM) COOKIES**
SPECIAL EQUIPMENT: **MA'AMOUL MOLD(S) OR STRAWBERRY TONG HULLERS**

DOUGH

170 grams (¾ cup) Clarified Butter (page 271), cool (65–68°F, 18–20°C)
66 grams (⅓ cup) granulated white sugar
8 grams (2 teaspoons) orange blossom water, or
　4 grams (1 teaspoon) orange blossom water and
　4 grams (1 teaspoon) rose water
204 grams (1¼ cups) fine semolina flour
150 grams (1¼ cups) unbleached all-purpose flour, plus more as needed
¼ teaspoon instant yeast
6 grams (2 teaspoons) mahleb
¼ teaspoon fine sea salt
57 grams (¼ cup) whole milk, plus more as needed

FILLING OPTIONS

Walnut Orange Blossom
160 grams (1¼ cups) toasted walnuts (see page 266)
50 grams (¼ cup) granulated white sugar
9 grams (2 teaspoons) orange blossom water

Pistachio Rose Water
180 grams (1½ cups) pistachios, raw or roasted
50 grams (¼ cup) granulated white sugar
4 grams (1 teaspoon) rose water

Date Orange Blossom Cinnamon
1 recipe Date Paste with orange juice and cinnamon (page 272)

Apricot Cardamom
287 grams (10 ounces) dried apricots
50 grams (¼ cup) granulated white sugar
¼ teaspoon ground cardamom

Cherry Chocolate Rose Water
200 grams (7 ounces) dried cherries
33 grams (3 tablespoons) semi-sweet chocolate, mini chips or finely chopped chips
25 grams (1 tablespoon) granulated white sugar
½ teaspoon rose water

29 grams (¼ cup) confectioners' sugar for finishing

MAKE THE DOUGH

1. In the large bowl of a stand mixer fitted with the whisk attachment, whip the butter at medium speed until it begins to smooth out, 30 seconds. Stop to scrape down the sides of the bowl, increase the speed to high, and whip the butter until light and fluffy, 3 minutes.

2. Scrape down the sides of the bowl again, add the sugar and orange blossom water, and whip until they just combine, 30 more seconds.

3. Remove the bowl from the stand and add the semolina flour, all-purpose flour, yeast, mahleb, and salt. Use a wooden spoon to combine the ingredients into a crumbly dough.

4. Add the milk and continue stirring until the dough becomes soft and pliable.

5. Cover the bowl with plastic wrap and let it rest for 1 hour. While it rests, make your desired filling from the options on page 106.

6. Knead the dough for about 30 seconds. Incorporate an additional tablespoon of milk or flour as needed to make it soft and pliable.

continues

MAKE THE FILLING

1. To make the filling, choose from one or more of the three options described below.

   WALNUT ORANGE BLOSSOM OR PISTACHIO ROSE WATER: Finely chop the nuts and transfer them to a small bowl. Add the sugar and flower water and stir to combine.

   APRICOT CARDAMOM: Finely chop the dried apricots and transfer them to a small bowl. Add the sugar and cardamom. Stir or use your fingertips to combine them thoroughly and form a thick, uniform paste.

   CHERRY CHOCOLATE ROSE WATER: Finely chop the dried cherries and chocolate chips. Transfer both to a small bowl and add the sugar and rose water. Stir or use your fingertips to combine them thoroughly and form a thick, uniform paste.

BALL AND SHAPE THE DOUGH

1. Arrange an oven rack in the middle position and preheat the oven to 375°F (190°C). Line a baking sheet with parchment paper.

2. Roll 1 tablespoon of dough (22 grams) between your palms. Proceed with one or more of the following three shaping methods.

Shape with Molds

1. Coat the mold with flour and knock out any excess. Before shaping each cookie, coat the mold lightly with more flour to ensure that the dough releases easily.

2. Place a dough ball in the mold and press a fingertip into the center to create a small cavity. Push the dough above the edges of the mold as you go.

3. Place 1 heaping teaspoon of the walnut or pistachio filling (7 grams), date or apricot filling (10 grams), or chocolate cherry filling (8 grams) in the cavity. From around the perimeter of the mold, close the excess dough over the filling, smoothing any seams and covering the filling completely. If needed, use a bit of extra dough. Wipe any dough from the perimeter of the cavity.

4. Turn the mold upside down and firmly yet carefully tap the top corner of the mold on the counter once or twice to release the cookie.

Shape with a Fork or Tong Hullers

1. Lightly dust the counter with flour. Use your hand to flatten each dough ball into a 2-inch (5-cm) oval or circle, ¼ inch (6 mm) thick.

2. Place 1 heaping teaspoon of walnut or pistachio filling (7 grams), date paste filling or apricot filling (10 grams), or chocolate cherry rose water filling (8 grams) in the center of the dough. Draw the edges of the dough together over the filling to enclose it, smoothing any cracks.

3. Use the tines of a fork or a strawberry huller to prick deeply or pinch the dough about five times around the top and/or sides in a decorative pattern. Have fun with this step and create your own designs!

continues

Shape by Hand

1. After filling and closing the dough, squeeze the top of it between your thumb and the first knuckle of your first finger to create decorative ridges on the top of the ma'amoul.

BAKE THE COOKIES

1. Carefully transfer the shaped ma'amoul to the prepared baking sheets, placing them 1 inch (2.5 cm) apart.

2. Bake until they turn pale golden brown, 13 to 15 minutes.

3. On the pan, let the cookies cool to room temperature, at least 1 hour. Sift confectioners' sugar on them and serve.

Notes

You can store the cookies in an airtight container at room temperature for up to 2 weeks or frozen for up to 3 months. Dust them lightly with more confectioners' sugar again before serving.

TIPS

- Ma'amoul dough must be pliable enough that it won't crack when shaped, but not so soft, it won't hold its shape or release from the mold. Squeeze the dough after incorporating the ingredients, adding a touch of milk if too dry or a touch of flour if too soft, until you reach the right pliability. You can make it ahead of time, refrigerate it, and bring it back to room temperature before shaping, but it shapes best right after being made.
- If the mold clogs with dough, rinse it, dry it, and coat it with flour again.

MA'AMOUL MAD CREAM BARS

This recipe for ma'amoul mad bil ashta (ma'amoul bars with pastry cream) puts thick Lebanese pastry cream to great use. The bars layer ma'amoul cookie dough, ashta cream, and gorgeous raw pistachios in a total treat, as seen on page 112.

PREP: 15 MINUTES
REST: 1 HOUR
COOK: 38 MINUTES
TOTAL: 1 HOUR 53 MINUTES

MAKES: 16 BARS

DOUGH

123 grams (¾ cup) fine semolina flour
90 grams (¾ cup) unbleached all-purpose flour
50 grams (¼ cup) granulated white sugar
¼ teaspoon instant yeast
6 grams (2 teaspoons) mahleb
½ teaspoon fine sea salt
89 grams (⅓ cup plus 1 tablespoon) unsalted butter, room temperature, plus 5 grams (1 teaspoon) to coat the pan
26 grams (2 tablespoons) whole milk, warm (105–110°F, 40–43°C)
4 grams (1 teaspoon) orange blossom water
4 grams (1 teaspoon) rose water

FILLING

227 grams (1 cup) whole milk
227 grams (1 cup) heavy whipping cream
14 grams (2 tablespoons) cornstarch
50 grams (¼ cup) granulated white sugar
20 grams (2 tablespoons) fine semolina flour
8 grams (2 teaspoons) orange blossom water, or 4 grams (1 teaspoon) orange blossom water and 4 grams (1 teaspoon) rose water

TOPPING

60 grams (¾ cup) raw or Blanched Pistachios (page 267)
25 grams (2 tablespoons) granulated white sugar
160 grams (½ cup) Flower Water Syrup (page 273)

1. In a large bowl, combine the semolina flour, all-purpose flour, sugar, yeast, mahleb, and sea salt. Add the butter and use a soft spatula or your hands to form a sandy dough.

2. Add the milk, orange blossom water, and rose water. Knead the dough until soft and moist, 1 minute.

3. On a piece of plastic wrap, press the dough into an 8-inch (20-cm) square. Wrap the dough in the plastic wrap and let it rest for 1 hour.

4. Meanwhile, make the filling. In a medium saucepan over medium-high heat, add the milk, whipping cream, cornstarch, sugar, semolina, and flower water and whisk to combine.

5. Continue whisking until the mixture thickens and comes to a boil, reduce the heat to medium-low, and simmer, whisking constantly, for 3 minutes.

6. Remove from the heat. Place a piece of wax paper on the surface of the filling to prevent a skin from forming and set it aside.

7. In a food processor or nut grinder, finely grind the pistachios. Transfer them to a small bowl, add the sugar, and stir to combine. Set aside.

8. Arrange an oven rack in the middle position and preheat the oven to 375°F (190°C). Coat an 8-inch (20-cm) square pan with 5 grams (1 teaspoon) of butter.

9. Unwrap the rested dough and place it in the pan. With your hands, press it all the way to the edges. Pour the ashta over the dough and use an offset spatula to spread it evenly. Top the ashta evenly with the ground pistachios.

10. Bake until the edges lightly brown, 35 minutes.

11. Remove from the oven and let cool for 1 hour.

12. Serve at room temperature or refrigerate in the pan for at least 1 hour and up to 3 days. To cut, run a sharp knife around the perimeter of the pan to loosen the sides. Cut 4 rows in each direction and lift the bars from the pan with an offset spatula.

13. Before serving, drizzle each bar with flower water syrup.

> *Note*
> You can store any remaining bars in the baking pan covered with plastic wrap or in an airtight container in the refrigerator for up to 3 days.

Ma'amoul Mad
Date Bars

Ma'amoul Mad
Cream Bars

MA'AMOUL MAD DATE BARS

When baking ma'amoul, I often imagined creating an easy version: layering it in a pan to make bars with a filling sandwiched between the shortbread. It turns out that our people already thought of this (of course!) in the form of ma'amoul mad bil tamir. In Arabic, *mad* means "to spread," and that's just what happens here: flattening the cookie dough and spreading the filling. This is such an easy avenue to ma'amoul goodness, and so versatile, too. You can cut the bars to any size for cookouts, a dessert table, or just a quiet indulgence with a tall glass of Mint Lemonade (page 115).

PREP: **15 MINUTES**
REST: **1 HOUR**
COOK: **35 MINUTES**
TOTAL: **1 HOUR 50 MINUTES**

MAKES: **16 BARS**

DOUGH

- 170 grams (¾ cup) Clarified Butter (page 271), cool (65–68°F, 18–20°C)
- 66 grams (⅓ cup) granulated white sugar
- 8 grams (2 teaspoons) orange blossom water, or 4 grams (1 teaspoon) orange blossom water and 4 grams (1 teaspoon) rose water
- 204 grams (1¼ cups) fine semolina flour
- 150 grams (1¼ cups) unbleached all-purpose flour, plus more as needed
- ¼ teaspoon instant yeast
- 6 grams (2 teaspoons) mahleb
- ¼ teaspoon fine sea salt
- 57 grams (¼ cup) whole milk, plus more as needed

FILLING

- 2 recipes Date Paste with cinnamon and butter (page 272)
- 18 grams (2 tablespoons) confectioners' sugar for finishing (optional)

1. In the large bowl of a stand mixer fitted with the whisk attachment, whip the butter at medium speed until it begins to smooth out, 30 seconds.
2. Stop to scrape down the sides of the bowl, increase the speed to high, and whip the butter until light and fluffy, 3 minutes.
3. Scrape down the sides of the bowl again, add the sugar and orange blossom water, and whip until they just combine, 30 more seconds.
4. Remove the bowl from the stand. Add the semolina flour, all-purpose flour, yeast, mahleb, and salt. Use a wooden spoon to combine the ingredients into a crumbly dough.
5. Add 57 grams (¼ cup) milk and continue stirring until the dough combines.
6. Cover the bowl with plastic wrap, lay a kitchen towel over that, and let it rest for 1 hour.
7. Arrange an oven rack in the middle position and preheat the oven to 350°F (177°C). Line an 8-inch (20-cm) square pan with parchment paper, with the edges overhanging opposite sides by about 1 inch (2.5 cm).
8. After the dough has rested, knead it for about 30 seconds. Incorporate 1 tablespoon of milk or flour as needed to make it soft and pliable. When ready, halve the dough.
9. Use your hands to press half of the dough evenly into the bottom of the prepared pan. Spoon dollops of the date filling over the pressed dough and, with an offset spatula, spread it into an even layer.
10. Place the other half of the dough on a sheet of wax paper and shape it roughly into a 6-inch (15-cm) square. Place a second sheet of wax paper over the dough and roll it into an 8-inch (20-cm) square. Remove the top piece of wax paper and use

continues

the bottom sheet of paper to help flip the dough carefully onto the layer of date paste. Remove the wax paper. Dip your fingers in water to smooth any cracks in the surface of the dough.

11. Bake until the top layer turns golden brown, 30 to 35 minutes.
12. Remove it from the oven and let it cool to room temperature, about 1 hour.
13. Use the parchment flaps to lift the entire assembly carefully from the pan.
14. Use a sharp chef's knife to mark 3 cuts for 4 rows in each direction, creating 16 bars.
15. Arrange the bars on a serving platter and, if using, sift confectioners' sugar over them before serving.

> *Note*
>
> You can store the bars in an airtight container at room temperature for up to 5 days or frozen for up to 3 months.
>
> **TIP:** The date filling for this recipe must be very soft and spreadable. Commercial date paste is thick and dense, so it's best to work with homemade date paste for this application.
>
> **VARIATION:** In step 9, use any of the **MA'AMOUL FILLINGS** (page 105) to make ma'amoul mad.

Something to Drink

MINT LEMONADE

My niece Victoria, our lemon queen, finds the best ways to juice lemons and extract as much flavor as possible from them. Every summer by the lake, we drink this lemonade, which makes great use of the copious mint growing in the garden.

PREP: 6 MINUTES
COOK: 5 MINUTES
CHILL: 30 MINUTES
TOTAL: 41 MINUTES

MAKES: 8 SERVINGS

5 lemons
20 to 30 fresh mint leaves (42 grams), plus 6 small sprigs for garnish
1,250 grams (5½ cups) cold water
300 grams (1½ cups) granulated white sugar

1. Firmly roll the lemons on a hard surface to loosen them. Halve them and juice them into a large liquid measuring cup or small bowl.
2. Coarsely chop or tear the mint leaves.
3. In a medium saucepan over medium-high heat, add 170 grams (¾ cup) of the water and the sugar and bring the mixture to a boil. Reduce the heat to medium-low and simmer for 5 minutes.
4. Remove the simple syrup from the heat and add the lemon juice and fresh mint. Give the syrup a quick stir and set it aside to steep and cool for at least 30 minutes.
5. Strain the syrup into a medium bowl, liquid measuring cup, or jar. Discard the mint.
6. Fill a large pitcher with ice and add 1,080 grams (4¾ cups) of the cold water. Add the syrup and stir well.
7. Fill six glasses with ice and place a sprig of mint in each glass. Divide the lemonade equally among the glasses and serve immediately.

TIP: Use spearmint for this recipe, which has a more subtle, sweet taste than peppermint.

MILLIONAIRE MA'AMOUL MAD

Combine the decadence of Scottish millionaire shortbread with ma'amoul mad for an even more luxe experience! You'll find the original shortbread, caramel, and chocolate here with an aromatic ma'amoul shortbread crust, caramel infused with tahini and fragrant flower water, and chocolate topped with sesame seeds. My husband, Dan, says they taste so good that we should call them *billionaire* bars.

PREP: **25 MINUTES**
REST: **2 HOURS 30 MINUTES**
COOK: **45 MINUTES**
TOTAL: **3 HOURS 40 MINUTES**

MAKES: **24 (3-INCH, 2.5-CM) BARS**

DOUGH
123 grams (¾ cup) fine semolina flour
90 grams (¾ cup) unbleached all-purpose flour
50 grams (¼ cup) granulated white sugar
¼ teaspoon instant yeast
6 grams (2 teaspoons) mahleb
½ teaspoon fine sea salt
89 grams (⅓ cup plus 1 tablespoon) butter, room temperature, plus 5 grams (1 teaspoon) to coat the pan
26 grams (2 tablespoons) whole milk, warm (105–110°F, 40–43°C)
4 grams (1 teaspoon) orange blossom water
4 grams (1 teaspoon) rose water

FILLING
57 grams (¼ cup) unsalted butter
159 grams (¾ cup) light brown sugar
¼ teaspoon fine sea salt
114 grams (½ cup) heavy whipping cream
64 grams (¼ cup) tahini
9 grams (2 teaspoons) orange blossom water

TOPPING
173 grams (6 ounces) dark chocolate, 60% cacao or more, chips or coarsely chopped
3 grams (1 teaspoon) sesame seeds

1. In a large mixing bowl, combine the semolina flour, all-purpose flour, sugar, yeast, mahleb, and sea salt. Add the butter and use a soft spatula or your hands to form a sandy dough.

2. Add the milk, orange blossom water, and rose water. Knead the dough until soft and moist, 1 minute.

3. On a piece of plastic wrap, press the dough into an 8-inch (20-cm) square. Wrap the dough in the plastic wrap and let it rest for 1 hour.

4. Arrange an oven rack in the middle position and preheat the oven to 350°F (177°C). Coat an 8-inch (20-cm) square pan with 5 grams (1 teaspoon) of butter. Line the pan with parchment paper, with the edges hanging over two opposing sides to help lift the pastry from the pan.

5. Unwrap the rested dough and place it in the pan. With your hands, press it all the way to the edges.

6. Bake until it turns golden brown, 20 to 22 minutes.

7. Remove from the oven and let it cool on a cooling rack while you make the filling.

8. In a medium saucepan over medium-high heat, melt the butter. Add the brown sugar and salt, whisking until the sugar dissolves, about 3 minutes.

continues

9. Add the whipping cream, which will bubble vigorously. Continue whisking until the caramel becomes thick enough to coat a spoon and pulls away from the sides of the pan as it boils, 5 minutes.

10. Remove from the heat and whisk in the tahini and orange blossom water. Pour the caramel over the shortbread. Refrigerate until it sets, 30 to 40 minutes.

11. When the caramel has set, make the chocolate topping. In a microwave-safe bowl, melt the chocolate in the microwave in three increments of 30 seconds each, stirring between each increment.

12. Pour the chocolate over the caramel and, with an offset spatula, spread it evenly to the edges.

13. Sprinkle the sesame seeds evenly on the chocolate.

14. Chill until the chocolate becomes firm, about 1 hour.

15. Use the parchment flaps to lift the block from the pan and place it on a cutting board. Use a serrated knife to mark 24 bars: 7 cuts for 8 rows in one direction and 2 cuts for 3 rows in the other direction. Saw-cut the block into 24 bars and serve them cold.

Note
You can store the bars in an airtight container in the refrigerator for up to 5 days.

TIPS
- The caramel and chocolate layers need to be warm and fluid for easy spreading. If they're too thick, warm them briefly in the microwave on low for 30 seconds before spreading.
- To sprinkle the sesame seeds evenly, do so from 12 inches (30 cm) above the pan.

FIG CRESCENTS

Aunt Pat, my mom's sister and my godmother, is the family's cookie matriarch. On visits, she always brings a fantasia box of cookies, like a box of jewels, the cookies nestled into paper cups and arranged so artfully. After my father unexpectedly passed away, we had a huge box of chocolate candies alongside her cookies on the kitchen table to help soothe the soul. Well, I dropped it on the floor, and the candies scattered everywhere. Picking them up, Aunt Pat inhaled the aroma of the chocolate. "Have one," I said, eating the pieces too damaged to return to the box. "I no longer eat chocolate," she replied. "I have a special intention with God, and it involves fasting from chocolate." This from the daughter of a chocolatier! "Now this fig crescent is my favorite," she smiled, "and this I can eat!"

PREP: 15 MINUTES
CHILL: 1 HOUR
COOK: 12 MINUTES
TOTAL: 1 HOUR 27 MINUTES

MAKES: 32 (2½-INCH, 6.5-CM) COOKIES

CRUST
240 grams (2 cups) unbleached all-purpose flour
½ teaspoon fine sea salt
¼ teaspoon baking soda
113 grams (½ cup) unsalted butter, room temperature
50 grams (¼ cup) granulated white sugar
53 grams (¼ cup) brown sugar
1 large egg
14 grams (1 tablespoon) whole milk
4 grams (1 teaspoon) pure vanilla extract

FILLING
75 grams (½ cup) dried figs
32 grams (¼ cup) toasted walnuts (page 266)
50 grams (¼ cup) granulated white sugar
¼ teaspoon fine sea salt
14 grams (2 tablespoons) water
4 grams (1 teaspoon) fresh lemon juice
9 grams (2 teaspoons) orange blossom water
28 grams (¼ cup) confectioners' sugar

1. In a medium mixing bowl, whisk together the flour, salt, and baking soda.

2. In a stand mixer fitted with the paddle attachment, cream the butter, white sugar, and brown sugar on medium speed until light and fluffy, 3 minutes.

3. Stop to scrape down the sides of the bowl. Add the egg, milk, and vanilla extract. Beat on low to combine, then increase the speed to medium until smooth, 1 more minute.

4. Turn off the mixer and add the flour mixture. Beat on low until the flour incorporates, then on medium just until the dough forms. Wrap the dough tightly in plastic wrap and refrigerate for 1 hour.

5. Meanwhile, make the filling. Finely chop the figs and walnuts.

6. In a small saucepan over medium-high heat, combine the figs, sugar, salt, water, and lemon juice. Bring to a boil, reduce the heat to low, and simmer for 5 minutes, stirring constantly and mashing the figs with the back of the spoon until a thick paste forms.

7. Remove the fig paste from the heat and stir in the orange blossom water and walnuts.

8. Arrange an oven rack in the middle position and preheat the oven to 375°F (190°C). Line two baking sheets with parchment paper.

continues

9. Halve the chilled dough, wrap one-half in plastic wrap, and return it to the refrigerator while working with the first half.
10. Lightly dust the counter and a rolling pin with flour. Briefly knead the dough to soften it, then roll it out to ⅛ inch (3 mm) thick. Lift the dough, dust it with more flour, and keep it moving as you roll to prevent it from sticking to the counter.
11. With a 2½-inch (6.5-cm) round cookie cutter or glass, cut 12 discs from the dough. Briefly knead the scraps together, wrap them in plastic wrap, and refrigerate.
12. Spoon 6 grams (1 teaspoon) of filling in the center of a disc. Fold it in half, over the filling, and press the edges to seal it. Transfer the half-moons to the prepared baking sheet, 1 inch (2.5 cm) apart. Repeat with the remaining dough, discs, and filling.
13. One sheet at a time, bake until the cookies turn a light golden brown, 10 to 12 minutes.
14. Immediately sift the confectioners' sugar over the warm cookies. Let them cool to room temperature before serving.

> *Note*
> You can store the crescents in an airtight container at room temperature for up to 5 days or frozen for up to 3 months.
>
> **VARIATIONS**
> - Make the crescents with any of the **MA'AMOUL FILLINGS** (page 105).
> - Nut-filled crescents are called **SAMBOUSEK**; there is also a savory Sambousek (page 213).

BARAZEK SESAME COOKIES

It's so easy to make this Lebanese bakery staple at home. The small size, crisp texture, and toasty flavor combine to make it enchanting—and addictive! Cookie lovers will find it hard to resist eating several in one sitting. The cookies also make a great crunchy companion to a cool, creamy Date Ice Cream Shake (page 124).

PREP: 19 MINUTES
CHILL: 30 MINUTES
COOK: 38 MINUTES
TOTAL: 1 HOUR 27 MINUTES

MAKES: 56 (1½-INCH, 4-CM) COOKIES

---

240 grams (2 cups) unbleached all-purpose flour
7 grams (1½ teaspoons) baking powder
¼ teaspoon baking soda
⅛ teaspoon fine sea salt
150 grams (⅔ cup) unsalted butter, room temperature
53 grams (¼ cup packed) light brown sugar
38 grams (⅓ cup) confectioners' sugar
4 grams (1 teaspoon) pure vanilla extract
1 large egg, room temperature
60 grams (½ cup) pistachios, raw or roasted
72 grams (½ cup) Toasted Sesame Seeds (page 269)

1. In a medium mixing bowl, whisk together the flour, baking powder, baking soda, and sea salt. Set aside.

2. In the bowl of a stand mixer fitted with the whisk attachment, cream the butter, brown sugar, and confectioners' sugar on medium speed until light and fluffy, 2 minutes.

3. Stop to scrape down the bowl. Add the vanilla and egg and beat on medium-high speed until the egg incorporates fully and the batter becomes thick and smooth, 2 more minutes.

4. Scrape down the bowl again and add the flour mixture. With the mixer on low speed, beat just until the flour incorporates and no dry spots remain, 30 seconds. Scrape the batter onto a piece of plastic wrap, flatten and wrap the dough in the plastic wrap, and refrigerate for 30 minutes and up to 3 days.

5. Arrange an oven rack in the middle position and preheat the oven to 350°F (165°C). Line two baking sheets with parchment paper.

6. Finely chop the pistachios and place them in a small bowl. Place the sesame seeds in another small bowl.

7. Divide the dough into pieces about 9 grams each. Roll each piece into a ball between your palms, then flatten the ball slightly, about ¼ inch (6 mm) thick, in your hand.

8. Press one side of the dough disc in the sesame seeds, allowing the circle to stick to your fingers. Lift and press three to four times, coating this side of the cookie with as many sesame seeds as possible.

9. Flip over the dough disc and press it gently into the chopped pistachios, knocking off any excess.

10. On the prepared baking sheets, place the shaped cookies, pistachios down, 1 inch (2.5 cm) apart. Press gently to fix the pistachios in place. Repeat with the rest of the dough balls.

11. One sheet at a time, bake the cookies until they turn a deep golden brown, 17 to 19 minutes.

12. Transfer the cookies to a cooling rack and let them cool to room temperature, at least 15 minutes, before serving.

> *Note*
>
> You can store the cookies in an airtight container at room temperature for up to 2 weeks or frozen for up to 3 months.
>
> **VARIATION:** Make them **EXTRA LARGE!** For 3-inch (7.5-cm) cookies, make balls 2 inches (5 cm) in diameter (24 grams of dough each). Makes 24 cookies.

Something to Drink

DATE ICE CREAM SHAKE

Many versions of the California date shake function as healthy breakfast smoothies . . . but not this one! It tastes like caramel and brown sugar and instantly reminds me of culinary school in San Francisco, where I fell in love with the Golden State and her luscious dates.

PREP: **6 MINUTES**
TOTAL: **6 MINUTES**
MAKES: **2 SERVINGS**

5 pitted medjool dates (75 grams)
28 grams (2 tablespoons) whole milk, cold
226 grams (1 cup) vanilla or dulce de leche ice cream

1. Finely chop the dates.
2. In a blender or food processor, blend the dates and milk until smooth, 1 minute.
3. Add the ice cream and pulse a few times, just until blended.
4. Pour the shake evenly into two glasses and serve immediately.

> **VARIATION:** The **HUMMER**, northern Michigan's ice cream drink of choice, includes rum and Kahlúa, so I like to blend that one with mine. Add 23 grams (1 ounce) of Kahlúa and 23 grams (1 ounce) of amber rum to the blender with the dates and milk. Top each glass with whipped cream and a drizzle of chocolate sauce.

AWAMET

Known as luqaimat in the Arabian Gulf region, awamet is beloved throughout the Middle East. The Arabic word comes from the root *'am*, "to float," which the little balls do as they fry. Crispy and crunchy, they taste light as air. To achieve that texture, the batter includes cornstarch, and the ethereal little balls double-fry, an extra step essential to great results. Cut away from the tip of a piping bag, little snippets of batter go into hot frying oil, much like choux pastry dough forms churros. Then they dunk in a fragrant flower water syrup. For optimal crispness, enjoy them the same day that you make them.

PREP: **10 MINUTES**
REST: **1 HOUR**
COOK: **17 MINUTES**
TOTAL: **1 HOUR 27 MINUTES**

MAKES: **30 (1-INCH, 2.5-CM) BALLS**
SPECIAL EQUIPMENT: **PIPING BAG WITH ½-INCH (1.5-CM) ROUND PIPING TIP**

DOUGH
135 grams (1 cup plus 2 tablespoons) unbleached all-purpose flour
14 grams (2 tablespoons) cornstarch
3 grams (1 teaspoon) instant yeast
¼ teaspoon fine sea salt
170 grams (¾ cup) water, warm (105–110°F, 40–43°C)

Neutral oil for frying

GLAZE
480 grams (1½ cups) Flower Water Syrup, cold (page 273)

1. In a large mixing bowl, sift 120 grams (1 cup) of the flour and the cornstarch. Add the yeast and salt and whisk to combine. Add the water and whisk until smooth. Cover the bowl with plastic wrap and lay a kitchen towel over that. Let the mixture rise until it doubles in size, 1 hour.

2. Set a large saucepan over medium heat, fill it 3 inches (8 cm) deep with oil, and heat the oil to 375°F (190°C). Next to the frying station, set a baking sheet lined with paper towels, a medium bowl for the syrup, and a serving platter.

3. When the batter is ready, add the remaining 15 grams (2 tablespoons) flour and stir to combine. Fill a piping bag or gallon plastic zip-top bag with the batter. (If using a plastic bag, snip a bottom corner ½ inch [1.25 cm] wide). Grease your kitchen scissors with oil to prevent the dough from sticking when snipped. Hold the filled bag about 6 inches (15 cm) above the hot oil with the piping tip or trimmed corner facing down. Allow about 1 inch (2.5 cm) of batter to fall from the tip and, with the scissors, snip it off into the oil. Repeat until 10 balls are frying in the oil.

4. Stirring constantly, par-fry the awamet until they turn pale golden, about 5 minutes. Use a slotted spoon or spider skimmer to transfer the balls to the paper towel–lined baking sheet. Repeat with the rest of the dough.

5. Pour the syrup in the bowl by the frying station.

6. Bring the oil temperature back to 375°F (190°C). Fry the balls a second time in two batches, stirring constantly, until they turn a deep golden brown, about 1 minute per batch.

7. Use the slotted spoon to transfer the balls from the oil to the bowl of syrup. Using a different spoon, stir the balls to coat them with syrup for 20 seconds.

8. Transfer them to the platter and serve immediately.

TIPS
* You can par-fry the balls up to 8 hours ahead of time and keep them at room temperature before proceeding with step 6.
* For a festive look, arrange the awamet in a wreath shape on the platter and dust them with colored sprinkles.

SESAME KA'AK RINGS

When my mother came home from our friend Manya Constant's legendary dinner parties, she faithfully recounted every luscious bite at her table. I, too, have enjoyed many of Manya's glorious Cypriot treats, marveling at how each surpassed the last. She once gave me a plate of koulourakia: perfect, crunchy, little biscuit rings coated in sesame seeds, a sister to sesame ka'ak biscuits (ka'ak bil simsum). In their fabulous kitchen full of color and light, Manya and her daughter Nadina gave my sister, Peggy, and me a lesson in these cookies. The conversation and rich aromas of that baking day awakened a deep nostalgia in all of us. Manya told stories of her mother baking these cookies in Cyprus, making ash water from fragrant charred wood. She boils the cinnamon water because it reminds her of her mother making ash water. The recipe intentionally makes a lot of cookies because, like so many recipes in this book, it's about gathering and sharing with family and friends.

PREP: **30 MINUTES**
COOK: **1 HOUR 15 MINUTES**
TOTAL: **1 HOUR 45 MINUTES**

MAKES: **45 (2-INCH, 5-CM) COOKIES**

---

228 grams (8 ounces) unsalted butter, room temperature
150 grams (¾ cup) granulated white sugar
480 grams (4 cups) unbleached all-purpose flour
½ teaspoon ground cinnamon
3 grams (1 teaspoon) ground anise seed
½ teaspoon fine sea salt
128 grams (½ cup plus 1 tablespoon) water
1 cinnamon stick
¾ teaspoon baking soda
14 grams (1 tablespoon) cold water
288 grams (2 cups) sesame seeds

1. Arrange an oven rack in the middle position and preheat the oven to 350°F (177°C).
2. In the large bowl of a stand mixer fitted with the paddle attachment, beat the butter on medium speed until light and fluffy, 4 minutes.
3. Scrape down the bowl, add the sugar, and continue beating until fluffy, 3 more minutes.
4. In a medium mixing bowl, combine the flour, cinnamon, ground anise, and salt. With the mixer on low speed, slowly add the flour mixture to the butter and beat until it combines.
5. In a small saucepan over high heat, bring the water and cinnamon stick to a boil. Reduce the heat to low and simmer for 8 minutes. Discard the cinnamon stick.
6. In a small bowl, dissolve the baking soda in the 14 grams (1 tablespoon) of cold water.
7. With the mixer on low speed, add the warm cinnamon water and the baking soda mixture to the dough, mixing until soft and pliable, 2 minutes.
8. Fill a wide, shallow bowl with the sesame seeds and place two baking sheets nearby.
9. Shape a piece of dough (17 grams) into a log about 4 inches (10 cm) long by ½ inch (1.25 cm) wide.

continues

Roll it between your palms and on the countertop, working out any bubbles that may form.

10. Roll the log in the sesame seeds, pressing gently to affix the seeds to the dough.

11. Bring the ends of the log together to form a small ring, pressing them together and smoothing the seam. Place it on one of the baking sheets.

12. Repeat steps 9 through 11 with the rest of the dough, spacing the rings about ½ inch (1.25 cm) apart on the baking sheets.

13. One sheet at a time, bake until the rings turn a deep golden brown, 35 to 40 minutes. Rotate each pan after 20 minutes of baking.

14. Transfer the cookies to a cooling rack and let them cool to room temperature before serving.

Note
You can store the cookies in an airtight container at room temperature for 3 weeks or frozen for up to 5 months.

MOCHA BROWNIES
with Olive Oil and Tahini Swirl

Experimenting with nonessential butter in recipes, I tried using olive oil in homemade brownies. My mother made such deep, dark, chewy treats that it didn't seem possible to achieve something similar without butter—but, habibi, the olive oil! A mild extra virgin olive oil beautifully enhances the chocolate flavor with a coffee boost. The swirl of tahini on top adds a savory, whimsical touch to these rich brownies.

PREP: 15 MINUTES
COOK: 35 MINUTES
COOL: 1 HOUR 10 MINUTES
TOTAL: 2 HOURS

MAKES: 16 BROWNIES

- 105 grams (½ cup plus 1 teaspoon) mild extra virgin olive oil
- 200 grams (1 cup) granulated white sugar
- 106 grams (½ cup packed) light brown sugar
- 2 large eggs, cold
- 1 large egg yolk, cold
- 14 grams (1 tablespoon) pure vanilla extract
- 135 grams (1 cup plus 2 tablespoons) unbleached all-purpose flour
- 57 grams (⅔ cup) cocoa powder
- 7 grams (1 tablespoon) espresso powder
- ½ teaspoon fine sea salt
- 85 grams (½ cup) semi-sweet or dark (60% cocoa) chocolate chips

TAHINI SWIRL
- 83 grams (⅓ cup) tahini
- 22 grams (3 tablespoons) confectioners' sugar
- ⅛ teaspoon fine sea salt
- 4 grams (1 teaspoon) pure vanilla extract
- 42 grams (3 tablespoons) ice-cold water

1. Arrange an oven rack in the middle position and preheat the oven to 325°F (165°C).

2. Lightly coat an 8-inch (20-cm) metal baking pan with 5 grams (1 teaspoon) of olive oil. Line the pan with parchment paper, leaving the edges hanging over two opposing sides to help lift the brownies from the pan.

3. In a medium mixing bowl, add the white sugar, brown sugar, 100 grams (½ cup) of the olive oil, eggs and yolk, and vanilla extract. Stir vigorously to combine.

4. In a small mixing bowl, whisk together the flour, cocoa powder, espresso powder, and sea salt. Add the mocha mixture to the sugar mixture and stir to combine. Stir in the chocolate chips.

5. Make the tahini swirl. Stir the tahini until smooth.

6. In a small mixing bowl, combine the tahini, confectioners' sugar, salt, vanilla extract, and water. Stir well to combine.

7. Pour the brownie batter into the prepared pan and smooth the top with an offset spatula. Dollop the tahini mixture on the batter in 3 rows of 3 dollops (9 total).

continues

8. Drag a wooden skewer or the tip of a paring knife through the batter, first vertically and then horizontally, to create swirls.

9. Bake until a toothpick inserted in the center comes out with a few moist crumbs at the tip, 35 minutes.

10. Remove the pan from the oven and let the brownie block cool for 10 minutes.

11. Use the parchment sling to lift the brownie block from the pan. Allow the block to cool completely to room temperature to ensure that the pieces cut cleanly, at least 1 hour. The longer the brownies cool, the more cleanly they will cut.

12. Cut 3 rows in each direction to create 16 pieces.

> *Note*
> You can store the brownies in an airtight container at room temperature for up to 4 days.
>
> **TIPS**
> - When swirling the tahini atop the batter, take care not to overswirl or run the tahini too deeply into the brownie batter, so that the swirls stay larger and more distinct without disappearing into the brownies.
> - Don't overbake these! You want the brownies to taste fudgy and moist.
> - For easier and cleaner cutting, clean the knife after each cut.

WHITE CHOCOLATE PISTACHIO COOKIES

For the holidays, my sister-in-law Diane bakes the most gorgeous ginger cookies dipped in white chocolate. Pistachios pair wonderfully with white chocolate, and my version uses a thick, chewy pistachio cookie half-dipped, as Diane does, in melted white chocolate. Tuck these cookies into little clear gift bags for presents to family and friends.

PREP: **15 MINUTES**
CHILL: **1 HOUR**
COOK: **36 MINUTES**
COOL: **20 MINUTES**
TOTAL: **2 HOURS 11 MINUTES**

MAKES: **16 (3½-INCH, 9.5-CM) COOKIES**

DOUGH

- 82 grams (½ cup plus 3 tablespoons) raw or Blanched Pistachios (page 267)
- 240 grams (2 cups) unbleached all-purpose flour
- ½ teaspoon baking soda
- ½ teaspoon baking powder
- ½ teaspoon fine sea salt
- 170 grams (¾ cup) unsalted butter, room temperature
- 150 grams (¾ cup) granulated white sugar
- 9 grams (2 teaspoons) pure vanilla extract
- ¼ teaspoon pure almond extract
- 1 large egg
- 1 large egg yolk

TOPPING

- 283 grams (10 ounces) white chocolate chips

1. Line two baking sheets with parchment paper. Finely chop the pistachios and reserve 22 grams (3 tablespoons) for the topping.

2. In a medium mixing bowl, whisk together the flour, baking soda, baking powder, salt, and 60 grams (½ cup) of the chopped pistachios. Set aside.

3. In the large bowl of a stand mixer fitted with the paddle attachment, beat the butter on medium speed until light and smooth, 2 minutes. Stop to scrape down the sides of the bowl once as you go.

4. Add the sugar, vanilla extract, and almond extract and continue beating until smooth, 1 minute.

5. Stop to scrape down the sides of the bowl, add the egg and yolk, and beat on medium speed until light and fluffy, 2 more minutes.

6. Add the flour mixture and use a spoon or large soft spatula to stir it by hand, mixing just until it combines and no dry spots remain.

7. Cover the bowl with plastic wrap and refrigerate it for at least 1 hour and up to 2 days.

8. Arrange an oven rack in the middle position and preheat the oven to 350°F (177°C).

9. Divide the dough into 16 pieces, approximately 36 grams each. Roll the pieces into balls and place them 2 inches (5 cm) apart on the prepared baking sheets.

10. One sheet at a time, bake until the cookies just begin to turn golden at the base, 17 to 18 minutes.

11. Remove them from the oven and, on the baking sheets, let the cookies cool to room temperature, at least 20 minutes.

12. In a microwave-safe bowl, microwave the white chocolate in two or three increments of 30 seconds each. Stir after each increment until the chocolate just melts with some pieces still whole. Let the chocolate sit undisturbed at room temperature for 5 minutes to allow the last bits to melt slowly, then stir until smooth.

13. Dip a cookie halfway into the melted chocolate. Tilt the bowl of chocolate as needed to create depth for dipping. Immediately sprinkle the dipped cookie with a pinch of ground pistachios. Repeat with the rest of the cookies.

14. As you work, return the dipped cookies to the parchment-lined baking sheets to dry completely, about 20 minutes.

Note
You can store the cookies in an airtight container at room temperature for up to 4 days.

VARIATION: For an elegant **HOLIDAY VERSION**, dust the tops of the dipped cookies with crushed edible rose petals along with the chopped pistachios.

APRICOT WALNUT COOKIES

When I asked my cousins for handwritten recipes from their mothers or our grandmother, Alice Elum Abowd, one after another sent me their mothers' recipes for what we call Grandma's Best Cookies. But you know how family food lore goes. My sister insists that a neighbor gave this recipe to Grandma Alice and that the "Grandma" is generic. My brother Chris agrees with me that our grandmother created it and not just because it's his favorite. The recipe exists nowhere else that I've found in my extensive search. It was her best, then our best, and now it can be yours, too.

PREP: 10 MINUTES
CHILL: 2 HOURS
COOK: 24 MINUTES
TOTAL: 2 HOURS 34 MINUTES

MAKES: 36 (3-INCH, 7.5-CM) COOKIES

---

149 grams (1 cup) dried apricots
128 grams (1 cup) toasted walnuts (see page 266)
4 grams (1 teaspoon) pure vanilla extract
213 grams (1 cup) light brown sugar
200 grams (1 cup) granulated white sugar
226 grams (1 cup) unsalted butter, room temperature
480 grams (4 cups) unbleached all-purpose flour
16 grams (1 tablespoon plus 1 teaspoon) baking powder
6 grams (1 teaspoon) fine sea salt
2 grams (1 teaspoon) ground nutmeg
3 large eggs
6 grams (1 teaspoon) baking soda
14 grams (1 tablespoon) water, hot (120°F, 49°C)

1. Coarsely chop the apricots and finely chop the walnuts.
2. In the large bowl of a stand mixer fitted with the paddle attachment, add the apricots, walnuts, vanilla extract, brown sugar, white sugar, and butter. Set the mixer speed to medium and beat until the mixture fully combines.
3. In another medium mixing bowl, whisk together the flour, baking powder, sea salt, and nutmeg. Add the flour mixture to the fruit mixture and mix on low speed just until combined.
4. Lightly beat the eggs, add them to the bowl, and mix on medium speed for 1 minute to combine thoroughly.
5. In a small bowl, dissolve the baking soda in the hot water. Add the mixture to the batter and beat on medium speed for 30 seconds, forming the dough.
6. Tightly wrap the dough in plastic wrap and refrigerate it for at least 2 hours and up to 3 days.
7. Arrange an oven rack in the middle position and preheat the oven to 350°F (177°C). Line two baking sheets with parchment paper.
8. Spoon about 42 grams (2 tablespoons) of the dough, roll it into a ball, and place it on one of the prepared baking sheets. Repeat with the rest of the dough, placing the balls 2 inches (5 cm) apart.
9. One sheet at a time, bake until the cookies turn golden brown, 12 to 14 minutes.
10. On the baking sheets, let the cookies cool for 10 minutes, then transfer them to a cooling rack to cool to room temperature before serving.

> *Note*
> You can store the cookies in an airtight container at room temperature for up to 3 days or frozen for up to 3 months.
>
> **VARIATION:** My mother used dried apricots in her cookies, but my grandmother's recipe calls for chopped **DATES** and **RAISINS**. Swap the apricots for either of those or your favorite dried fruits.

GHRAYBEH

The Arabic word *ghraybeh* means "little extraordinary thing," and these simple butter cookies do taste exceptional. Every little person in our family agrees! Using a simple dough made with whipped clarified butter, these cookies redefine what it means to "melt in your mouth." The whipping time on the butter may seem long, but it lightens it without deflating it. When baked, the cookie remains uniquely white with little to no browning, and you can make it in an array of shapes. For me and my taste-tester nephews, Tommy and John, the cookies beg for a drizzle of chocolate on top—not traditional, but delicious—and kids love it.

PREP: **20 MINUTES**
COOK: **54 MINUTES**
COOL: **2 HOURS**
TOTAL: **3 HOURS 14 MINUTES**
MAKES: **22 (2-INCH, 5-CM) COOKIES**

DOUGH
- 170 grams (¾ cup) Clarified Butter (page 271), cool (60–68°F, 15–20°C)
- 85 grams (¾ cup) confectioners' sugar
- ½ teaspoon fine sea salt
- 4 grams (1 teaspoon) orange blossom water
- 4 grams (1 teaspoon) pure vanilla extract
- 233 grams (1¾ cups plus 3 tablespoons) unbleached all-purpose flour
- ½ teaspoon whole milk (optional, if needed)

NUT GARNISH
- 22 grams (3 tablespoons) raw pistachios

SUGAR GARNISH (OPTIONAL)
- 14 grams (2 tablespoons) confectioners' sugar

CHOCOLATE GLAZE (OPTIONAL)
- 85 grams (3 ounces) dark chocolate, 60% cacao
- 28 grams (2 tablespoons) evaporated milk

1. Arrange an oven rack in the middle position and preheat the oven to 325°F (165°C). Line two baking sheets with parchment paper.
2. In the large bowl of a stand mixer fitted with the whisk attachment or with a hand mixer, whip the butter on medium speed for 1 minute. Stop to scrape down the bowl.
3. Set the speed to high and beat the butter until fluffy, creamy, and pale, 5 more minutes. Scrape down the bowl again.
4. Add the sugar, salt, orange blossom water, and vanilla extract. Set the speed to low, mix for 30 seconds, and scrape down the bowl again.
5. Set the speed to medium-high and beat for 1 more minute until the mixture becomes smooth, light, and fluffy.
6. Spoon in the flour and mix until it is completely combined.
7. Shape the ghraybeh into diamonds or pillows, as described below.

Diamonds

On a lightly floured counter, shape a quarter of the dough into a log about 1 inch (2.5 cm) and 8 inches (20 cm) long. If the dough cracks, gently push it together. Use your hands, a bench scraper, or the flat side of a knife to square and smooth the top of the log. A few cracks may remain. Diagonally cut seven 1-inch (2.5-cm) diamond-shaped pieces, approximately 22 grams each. Carefully use the bench scraper or a metal spatula to lift the diamonds from the counter to the prepared baking sheets, spacing them about 1 inch (2.5 cm) apart. Repeat with the rest of the dough.

continues

Pillows

If a piece of the dough cracks when shaped into a ball, add the milk and knead to combine. Divide the dough into 22 pieces, approximately 22 grams each. Knead each piece to soften it and roll it between your palms into a smooth ball. Place the balls on the prepared baking sheets, spacing them about 1 inch (2.5 cm) apart. With your fingertips, gently tap the center of each ball to flatten just the top slightly, not the whole ball, to about ½-inch (1.25 cm) thick. Smooth any cracks that appear on the sides. Gently press 1 pistachio into the top of each pillow.

---

8. One sheet at a time, bake the ghraybeh until they cook through but still look pale, 18 to 20 minutes. They shouldn't brown except for minimally on the bottom. Cookie crumbs will stick to the tip of a finger until they cool.

9. On the baking sheets, let the cookies cool completely, about 1 hour.

10. If finishing with sugar, dust the cookies with confectioners' sugar. If using chocolate, make the glaze. In a microwave-safe bowl, add the milk and chocolate and heat on high for 20 seconds.

11. Stir and heat for 20 more seconds.

12. Transfer the chocolate glaze to a small plastic baggie and snip a bottom corner ¼ inch (6 mm) open.

13. Drizzle the chocolate over the completely cooled ghraybeh. Allow the drizzle to set for at least 2 hours.

> **Note**
>
> You can store the cookies in an airtight container at room temperature for up to 3 days or frozen for up to 3 months.
>
> **TIP:** Take care when measuring and adding the small amount of milk to the dough. The dough may need just that ½ teaspoon to help prevent cracking during shaping. More milk than that can cause the shapes to flatten and melt when they bake.
>
> **VARIATIONS**
> - In many ghraybeh recipes, butter imparts the only flavor. I include orange blossom water and vanilla extract. If you leave those out, replace them with 8 grams (2 teaspoons) of **WHOLE MILK**.
> - For **GLUTEN-FREE GHRAYBEH**, substitute King Arthur's Gluten Free Measure for Measure Flour for the unbleached all-purpose flour and use 50 grams (3½ tablespoons) of milk. Before shaping, rest the dough for 30 minutes and add more milk, 5 grams (1 teaspoon) at a time, if needed to make it soft and pliable.
> - For holidays and other celebrations, get your **SPRINKLE ON!** Immediately after drizzling the cookies with chocolate, sprinkle them with red, white, and green decorating sugar or with crushed pieces of candy cane.
> - Instead of using a pistachio, **CREATE A DESIGN** on top of the pillows. Press the tip of an eating tablespoon into the top of each pillow three times, spacing each one about ¼ inch (6 mm) apart and making each mark slightly smaller than the last.

Something to Drink

RASPBERRY BASIL ICED TEA

In the summer, the kids in the family—not kids anymore!—love picking raspberries. ("Is this a good one, Aunt Maureenie?") We've made every recipe imaginable: dipping them in chocolate, topping cakes with as many as will fit, and even (for my nephew Ricky) creating raspberry fruit leather. This tea showcases their flavor to the hilt. The basil and a whisper of rose water add a sophisticated touch.

PREP: **4 MINUTES**
COOK: **3 MINUTES**
STEEP: **1 HOUR**
TOTAL: **1 HOUR 7 MINUTES**

MAKES: **6 SERVINGS**

681 grams (3 cups) water
20 leaves (6 grams) fresh basil, plus 6 sprigs for garnish
127 grams (1 cup) raspberries, fresh or thawed from frozen
24 grams (2 tablespoons) granulated white sugar
9 grams (2 teaspoons) fresh lemon juice
2 grams (1 tablespoon) loose-leaf black tea
227 grams (1 cup) ice water
4 grams (1 teaspoon) rose water

1. In a kettle or the microwave, heat the 681 grams (3 cups) water until boiling.
2. Meanwhile, coarsely chop or tear the basil leaves.
3. In a medium mixing bowl, add the raspberries, chopped basil, sugar, and lemon juice and mash with a masher, muddler, or wooden spoon.
4. In another medium mixing bowl, add the tea and the boiling water. Let it steep for 3 minutes.
5. Add the 227 grams (1 cup) ice water and the raspberry mixture. Stir and let it steep for 1 hour.
6. Through a fine mesh strainer, strain the tea into another bowl or a large pitcher. Add the rose water and stir to combine.
7. Refrigerate for at least 1 hour or up to 4 days.
8. To serve, fill six glasses with ice and divide the tea evenly among the glasses.
9. Garnish each glass with a sprig of fresh basil and serve.

GLAZED KA'AK SHORTBREAD

Why can't I leave good enough alone? Maybe it's impatience, maybe it's restlessness. Classic ka'ak uses a beautiful yeasted dough that takes a few hours to prepare. But drawing on the tradition of German and other beautifully molded shortbread cookies, I present a shortbread version of ka'ak. The dough holds the shape of the mold so well. The buttery, brown sugar goodness of the cookie features an amazing, harmonious cast of supporting spices and flavors. Baking the cookies to a deep golden brown achieves a great crunchy-crumbly texture and enhances the toasty flavor. The glaze coats thickly but still reveals the pattern underneath.

PREP: **25 MINUTES**
COOK: **30 MINUTES**
REST: **3 HOURS**
TOTAL: **3 HOURS 55 MINUTES**

MAKES: **10 (5-INCH, 13-CM) COOKIES**
SPECIAL EQUIPMENT: **KA'AK MOLD**

DOUGH
341 grams (1½ cups) unsalted butter, room temperature
159 grams (¾ cup, packed) light brown sugar
12.5 grams (1 tablespoon) granulated white sugar
2 large eggs
9 grams (2 teaspoons) orange blossom water
4 grams (1 teaspoon) pure vanilla extract
4 grams (1 teaspoon) pure anise extract
570 grams (4¾ cups) unbleached, all-purpose flour, plus more as needed
½ teaspoon fine sea salt
18 grams (2 tablespoons) mahleb
27 grams (3 tablespoons) ground anise seed
½ teaspoon ground nutmeg

GLAZE
342 grams (3 cups) confectioners' sugar
39 grams (2 tablespoons) light corn syrup
9 grams (2 teaspoons) orange blossom water
57 to 71 grams (4 to 5 tablespoons) water

1. Arrange an oven rack in the middle position and preheat the oven to 400°F (200°C). Line two baking sheets with parchment paper.

2. In the large mixing bowl of a stand mixer fitted with the paddle attachment, cream the butter, brown sugar, and white sugar on medium speed until light and fluffy, 2 minutes.

3. Stop to scrape down the bowl. Add the eggs, orange blossom water, vanilla extract, and anise extract and beat on medium speed until well incorporated, 2 minutes.

4. In a medium mixing bowl, combine the flour, salt, mahleb, anise seed, and nutmeg.

5. With the mixer on low speed, add half of the flour mixture. Once moistened, add the remaining half of the flour mixture and continue to mix until fully combined. When squeezed, the dough should hold together without adhering to your fingers. If needed, add more flour, 7 grams (1 tablespoon) at a time, to create a cohesive but not dry dough.

6. Dust the mold lightly with flour, knocking out any excess. Repeat for each cookie to ensure easier release.

7. Divide the dough into 10 pieces, approximately 120 grams each. Roll each piece into a ball, then flatten each ball into a 3-inch (7.5-cm) disc on the counter. Smooth any cracks in the discs.

8. Gently and evenly press a dough disc into the prepared mold. Smooth the edges. To unmold the dough, use your hands to loosen it gently around the perimeter, slowly working your way to center as you loosen. Hold the mold face down and gently release the shaped dough with your hands.

9. Repeat with the rest of the dough, placing the cookies on the prepared baking sheets with the design facing up, 2 inches (5 cm) apart, 5 cookies per pan.

10. One baking sheet at a time, bake the cookies until they turn completely golden brown, not just at the edges, 15 to 17 minutes.

11. Transfer the cookies to a cooling rack and let them cool completely before glazing.

12. While the cookies are cooling, make the glaze. In a wide, shallow bowl, combine the confectioners' sugar, corn syrup, orange blossom water, and 43 grams (3 tablespoons) of the water. Stir until the glaze falls in a thick ribbon from the spoon. Add drops of water if needed. If not glazing immediately, place a piece of plastic wrap directly on the surface of the glaze to prevent a skin from forming.

13. Place a sheet of parchment paper underneath the cooling rack to catch any drips.

14. Spoon 20 grams (1 tablespoon) of glaze in the center of a cookie and, with the back of the spoon or a pastry brush, spread the glaze evenly to the edges. Make sure you can see the mold pattern.

15. Allow the glazed cookies to set for at least 3 hours and up to overnight.

Note

You can store the cookies in an airtight container, separated by layers of wax paper, at room temperature for up to 1 week or frozen for up to 3 months.

TIP: If anise, which tastes like black licorice, doesn't do it for you—as is the case with my brother Chris and editor James—use only vanilla extract or vanilla extract and orange blossom water. In that case, replace the dry spice ingredients with the same amount (46 grams, 1½ tablespoons) of flour.

Cakes

In daydreams of "what I would do if I could do anything," a brick-and-mortar bakery comes to mind: a sweet, cozy confection of a shop with every manner of cakes on offer. My grandmother Alice, who mastered many crafts to which she set her hands, including cake decorating, inspired my cake dreams. My mother was cut from the same cloth, baking every special occasion cake in *Betty Crocker's Cookbook* to fulfill each of her five children's cake desires. I'm next in the line of generational cake crafting, and these cakes represent my dreams made into delicious reality.

ORANGE BLOSSOM CAKE

This white cake resembles the one my niece Maria Belén and I baked for my friend Kelsey's wedding (my first and only wedding cake!). It's not about piped shell borders or icing roses, though. In cake form, with a tender crumb, it sweetly expresses how I'd like my cake bakery to be. Oranges, orange blossom water, and orange blossom syrup delicately infuse every bite, and the garnish adds charming detail.

PREP: **20 MINUTES**
COOK: **20 MINUTES**
COOL: **40 MINUTES**
TOTAL: **1 HOUR 20 MINUTES**
MAKES: **14 SERVINGS**

CAKE
170 grams (¾ cup) unsalted butter, cold, plus more for greasing
360 grams (3 cups) cake flour, plus more for dusting
5 large egg whites, room temperature
1 large egg, room temperature
9 grams (2 teaspoons) pure vanilla extract
75 grams (⅓ cup) fresh orange juice from 1 orange
12 grams (2 tablespoons) orange zest from 2 oranges
400 grams (2 cups) granulated white sugar
20 grams (1 tablespoon plus 1 teaspoon) baking powder
½ teaspoon fine sea salt
171 grams (¾ cup) whole milk, room temperature
84 grams (¼ cup) Flower Water Syrup (page 273) using orange blossom water

BUTTERCREAM
684 grams (3 cups) unsalted butter, room temperature
113 grams (½ cup) block cream cheese, room temperature
908 grams (8 cups) confectioners' sugar
9 grams (2 teaspoons) orange blossom water
28 to 56 grams (2 to 4 tablespoons) whole milk, room temperature

GARNISH
3 candied orange slices
3 fresh mint sprig tops or fresh bay leaves

1. Arrange an oven rack in the middle position and preheat the oven to 350°F (177°C). Coat the bottom of three 8-inch (20-cm) cake pans with butter and line them with parchment paper circles. Coat the parchment and sides of the pans with butter, then dust with flour, and knock out any excess.

2. Make the cake. In a medium mixing bowl, whisk together the egg whites, egg, vanilla extract, orange juice, and orange zest. Set aside.

3. Cut the cold butter into 1-inch (2.5-cm) pieces.

4. In the large bowl of a stand mixer fitted with the paddle attachment, whisk together the flour, sugar, baking powder, and sea salt. Set the mixer speed to low and add the butter one piece at a time. After adding the last piece of butter, continue mixing until the mixture develops a fine, crumbly texture, 3 minutes.

5. Add the milk and continue mixing for 1 minute. Stop to scrape down the sides of the bowl.

6. With the mixer speed on low, add the egg mixture in three batches. Stop to scrape down the bowl again.

7. Increase the speed to medium and beat the batter until light and fluffy, 3 more minutes.

8. Divide the batter equally among the prepared pans, about 400 grams (1¾ cups) into each.

9. Bake until the cake bounces back when touched in the center and a toothpick inserted in the center comes out with only a few crumbs, 18 to 20 minutes.

10. Remove the cakes from the oven and, still in the pans, transfer them to a cooling rack to cool for 10 minutes.

continues

11. To remove the cakes from the pans, run a knife around the perimeter of each cake and shake the pans from side to side to loosen the cakes. Place a plate over a pan and invert both, carefully flipping the cake onto the plate. Repeat with the other two cakes, flipping each onto its own plate.

12. Brush the top and sides of each cake with 28 grams (⅓ cup) of the orange blossom syrup. Let the cakes cool completely, at least 30 minutes.

13. Meanwhile, make the buttercream. In the bowl of a stand mixer fitted with the paddle attachment or with a hand mixer, mix the butter and cream cheese on low speed until smooth, 30 seconds.

14. In several batches, add the confectioners' sugar and continue mixing to incorporate.

15. Add the orange blossom water and 14 grams (1 tablespoon) of the milk. Continue mixing until the buttercream becomes light and smooth. Add more milk, 14 grams (1 tablespoon) at a time as needed (up to 56 grams, 4 tablespoons), to create a thick, spreadable frosting.

16. On a cake stand or serving platter, place a cake layer with the flattest side down so everything will sit evenly.

17. Use an offset spatula to spread a third of the buttercream (about 580 grams, 2⅔ cups) evenly on the top of the cake. Place the second layer of cake on the first and frost the same. Repeat with the third layer, leaving the sides of the cake unfrosted.

18. Garnish the top of the cake with the candied orange slices, off-center. Just before serving, garnish with the mint sprigs.

Note

You can store leftover cake in an airtight container at room temperature for up to 3 days or frozen for up to 1 month.

TIPS

- To minimize air bubbles forming in the buttercream, mix it on low speed.
- To make ahead of time and minimize crumbs in the buttercream when frosting, freeze the cake layers before assembling the cake. Wrap them tightly in plastic wrap and freeze for at least 1 hour and up to 1 month.

ATAYEF

Atayef (qataif, katayef, qatayef) are darling little pancakes with fillings. They date at least to the 900s in the earliest known cookbook written in Arabic. Atayef pancakes serve as the base for the following recipes, Walnut Atayef (page 154) and Pistachio Cream Atayef (page 153), both traditional desserts during Ramadan and for other celebrations. But you can enjoy them anytime for a special take on finger food for brunch or a dessert buffet.

PREP: **5 MINUTES**
REST: **20 MINUTES**
COOK: **30 MINUTES**
TOTAL: **55 MINUTES**

MAKES: **18 ATAYEF (9 SERVINGS)**

- 90 grams (¾ cup) unbleached all-purpose flour, more as needed
- 41 grams (¼ cup) fine semolina flour
- ¼ teaspoon instant yeast
- ½ teaspoon baking powder
- 25 grams (2 tablespoons) granulated white sugar
- ¼ teaspoon fine sea salt
- 57 grams (¼ cup) whole milk, warm (105–110°F, 40–43°C), more as needed
- 185 grams (¾ cup plus 1 tablespoon) water
- 9 grams (2 teaspoons) pure vanilla extract

1. In a medium mixing bowl, whisk together the flour, semolina, yeast, baking powder, sugar, and salt. Add the milk, water, and vanilla and whisk to combine until no lumps remain.

2. Cover the bowl with plastic wrap and let it rest at room temperature for no more than 20 minutes.

3. Line a baking sheet with paper towels. To prevent the pancakes from drying as you make them, keep a clean kitchen towel nearby to cover them. Coat a metal spatula with oil.

4. Heat a nonstick griddle or 12-inch (30-cm) sauté pan over medium heat. Test the heat and the batter by pouring 1 tablespoon of batter on the dry, hot skillet. The entire surface of the pancake should bubble. If it doesn't, wait a few more minutes for the pan to heat and adjust the batter by adding more water, 1 teaspoon at a time, to thin it. The proper consistency of the batter may seem too thin, so test it to make sure many tiny bubbles form on the pancake (success!). If not, add more water or more flour, 1 teaspoon at a time, to thin or thicken it, as needed.

5. Onto the hot pan, spoon 20 grams (½ ounce) of batter per pancake (3 pancakes in a sauté pan, 4 on a griddle). Cook until the top looks bubbly and no longer shiny and the bottom has turned golden brown, 5 to 6 minutes. Don't flip the pancakes; the soft side needs to stick together when folded and sealed.

6. Use the oiled spatula to transfer the pancakes to the baking sheet. Repeat with the rest of the batter, covering the finished pancakes with the kitchen towel as you go.

PISTACHIO CREAM ATAYEF

These soft, splendid bites contain fragrant ashta cream, giving them their Arabic name of atayef bil ashta. Fold the pancakes while still warm so the edges stick together.

PREP: **15 MINUTES**
CHILL: **1 HOUR**
COOK: **4 MINUTES**
TOTAL: **1 HOUR 19 MINUTES**

MAKES: **18 ATAYEF (9 SERVINGS)**

FILLING
227 grams (1 cup) whole milk
227 grams (1 cup) heavy whipping cream
50 grams (¼ cup) granulated white sugar
14 grams (2 tablespoons) cornstarch
10 grams (1 tablespoon) fine semolina flour
4 grams (1 teaspoon) orange blossom water
4 grams (1 teaspoon) rose water

1 recipe Atayef pancakes (page 150)
60 grams (½ cup) raw or Blanched Pistachios (page 267)
80 grams (¼ cup) Flower Water Syrup (page 273), cold

1. In a small saucepan over medium-low heat, whisk together all the filling ingredients.

2. Increase the heat to medium-high and bring the mixture to a boil, whisking constantly. As soon as the mixture begins to boil, reduce the heat to medium and continue whisking until the cream thickens and the whisk leaves a trail, 3 to 4 minutes.

3. Remove the ashta filling from the heat and let it cool for 5 minutes.

4. Transfer the cream to a bowl or airtight container and cover the surface with plastic wrap to prevent a skin from forming. Refrigerate for at least 1 hour and up to 3 days.

5. Fold the pancakes in half and pinch the edges halfway closed, leaving one end open for filling. Set them back on the lined baking sheet and keep them covered with a kitchen towel. These can rest for up to 4 hours.

6. In a nut grinder or food processor, finely grind the pistachios and place them in a small bowl.

7. Just before serving, whisk the chilled ashta until smooth. Transfer it to a piping bag fitted with a ½-inch (1.25-cm) round piping tip or a quart-sized plastic bag with a corner cut open by ½ inch (1.25 cm).

8. Fill each pancake with about 60 grams (2 tablespoons) of the ashta, dip the cream into the chopped pistachios, and press gently to affix them.

9. Arrange the atayef in a circle on a serving platter. Drizzle them lightly with the syrup and serve immediately.

> **Note**
> You can store the leftover atayef in an airtight container in the refrigerator for up to 2 days.

WALNUT ATAYEF

The pancakes contain a lot of moisture, so to achieve the crisp, deep-fried texture, you need to keep the temperature of the oil at 375°F (190°C) as you go. An instant-read thermometer makes the work of frying so much easier. Also, dip the pancakes in syrup only briefly. You can see the atayef on page 150.

PREP: **10 MINUTES**
COOK: **6 MINUTES**
TOTAL: **16 MINUTES**
MAKES: **18 ATAYEF (9 SERVINGS)**

FILLING
120 grams (½ cup) toasted walnuts (see page 266)
25 grams (2 tablespoons) granulated white sugar
½ teaspoon orange blossom water

1 recipe Atayef pancakes (page 150)
Neutral oil for frying
480 grams (1½ cups) Flower Water Syrup (page 273), cold
2 tablespoons (15 grams) raw or Blanched Pistachios (page 267)

1. In a nut grinder or food processor, finely grind the walnuts.
2. In a small bowl, combine the walnuts, sugar, and orange blossom water.
3. Add about 8 grams (½ tablespoon) of the walnut mixture to the middle of a pancake. Fold the pancake over the filling to create a half-moon and pinch the edges entirely closed. If the edges separate, dab them with water and seal them again.
4. Repeat with the remaining pancakes. Place the filled atayef on the baking sheet as you go and keep them covered with the kitchen towel.
5. Set a large saucepan over medium heat, fill it 2 inches (5 cm) deep with oil, and heat the oil to 375°F (190°C). Fill a medium bowl with the cold syrup and place it next to the baking sheet. Next to the syrup, set a cooling rack over a sheet of parchment paper.
6. With heatproof tongs or a slotted spoon, carefully lower 6 atayef into the hot oil. They will bubble vigorously. Fry them until golden brown, stirring to fry them evenly, about 2 minutes.
7. Use the tongs to transfer the fried atayef to the syrup. Don't get any syrup on the tongs so you can use it again to retrieve more atayef from the hot oil. Use a different spoon to stir them in the syrup for 15 seconds, then transfer them to the cooling rack.
8. Repeat with the remaining atayef, frying in two more batches.
9. Finely chop the pistachios. Arrange the atayef on a serving platter and garnish them with the pistachios. Serve immediately, while still warm, and for the best texture and flavor, eat them right after cooking. For this dish, you don't want leftovers!

ORANGE BLOSSOM MADELEINES
with Apricot Glaze

PREP: **10 MINUTES**
CHILL: **30 MINUTES**
COOK: **20 MINUTES**
TOTAL: **1 HOUR**

MAKES: **16 MADELEINES**
SPECIAL EQUIPMENT: **MADELEINE MOLD PAN**

The Lebanese baking repertoire enjoys some French flair, but that's not why I'm sharing this beautiful recipe. Proust's famous musing about nibbling a madeleine expresses so much of why we bake our traditions and what we hold when we do. This recipe owes a debt of inspiration to Dorie Greenspan, a great baker from whom I have learned so much, and to Nikki Law, who, Up North, owns our local Polished on Main salon, where we often talk baking while polishing. These taste incredible with Michigan Tart Cherry Limeade (page 158).

CAKE
- 101 grams (⅔ cup plus 3 tablespoons) cake flour, plus more to coat the molds
- ¾ teaspoon baking powder
- ⅛ teaspoon fine sea salt
- 100 grams (½ cup) granulated white sugar
- 6 grams (1 tablespoon) lemon zest from 1 lemon
- 2 large eggs
- 4 grams (1 teaspoon) pure vanilla extract
- 4 grams (1 teaspoon) orange blossom water
- 14 grams (1 tablespoon) whole milk
- 14 grams (1 tablespoon) neutral oil
- 89 grams (6 tablespoons plus 1 teaspoon) unsalted butter, melted

GLAZE
- 64 grams (3 tablespoons) apricot jam
- 14 grams (1 tablespoon) water

1. In a medium mixing bowl, whisk together the flour, baking powder, and salt. Set aside.
2. In a large mixing bowl, rub the sugar and lemon zest together with your fingers until the mixture becomes moist and fragrant.
3. Add the eggs and whisk until light and fluffy.
4. Add the vanilla extract, orange blossom water, milk, and oil and whisk until smooth.
5. Whisk in the flour mixture, then 85 grams (6 tablespoons) of the melted butter, until smooth.
6. Cover the surface of the batter with plastic wrap to prevent a skin from forming and refrigerate for at least 30 minutes and up to 1 hour.
7. Arrange an oven rack in the middle position and preheat the oven to 400°F (200°C). Brush the shells of the madeleine mold with some of the remaining butter, coat them with flour, and tap out any excess.
8. Place the pan on a baking sheet and spoon 1 heaping tablespoon of batter into each mold. Don't spread the batter; it will settle while baking. Cover the bowl and return the remaining batter to the refrigerator.
9. Bake until the madeleines turn pale golden brown, a bump appears in the center of each, and the tops spring back when touched, 8 to 10 minutes. Immediately release the madeleines from the pan by shaking it and gently tapping them on the counter.
10. While the madeleines bake, make the glaze. In a small bowl, whisk together the apricot jam and water.

continues

11. Brush the glaze on the shell side of each warm madeleine and set them on a cooling rack to dry and cool.

12. Clean and dry the pan, coat it with butter and flour again, and proceed at step 8 with the rest of the batter.

13. Serve at room temperature.

> **Note**
> You can store the madeleines in an airtight container at room temperature for up to 2 days or frozen for up to 3 months.

> "I carried to my lips a spoonful of the tea in which I had let soften a bit of madeleine. But at the very instant when the mouthful of tea mixed with cake crumbs touched my palate, I quivered, attentive to the extraordinary thing that was happening inside me. A delicious pleasure had invaded me, isolated me, without my having any notion as to its cause. It immediately had rendered the vicissitudes of life unimportant to me, its disasters innocuous, its brevity illusory, acting in the same way that love acts, by filling me with a precious essence: or rather this essence was not merely inside me, it was me."
> —Marcel Proust, *Swann's Way*

Something to Drink

MICHIGAN TART CHERRY LIMEADE

This showy thirst-quencher, as pictured on page 157, has as many special touches as the rolling farmland quilted with cherry trees and Little Traverse Bay breezes that inspired it. It says, "Welcome to the porch and sit a while before you go," perfectly.

PREP: **1 MINUTE**
COOK: **3 MINUTES**
TOTAL: **4 MINUTES**

MAKES: **6 SERVINGS**

175 grams (1 cup) pitted tart cherries, fresh or thawed from frozen, plus 12 cherries for garnish
160 grams (½ cup) Flower Water Syrup (page 273)
113 grams (½ cup) fresh lime juice from 3 limes, plus 1 lime for garnish
681 grams (24 ounces) crushed ice
850 grams (30 ounces) club soda, cold

1. In a blender or food processor, puree the cherries, syrup, and lime juice.
2. Thinly slice the lime into 12 wheels.
3. Strain the cherry puree into a small pitcher or liquid measuring cup.
4. Divide the cherry puree and crushed ice equally among six glasses and tuck a lime wheel and a cherry into the ice.
5. Add the club soda to each glass and stir gently. Add another lime wheel and cherry on top and serve.

MINI STICKY DATE CAKES
with Orange Blossom Caramel Sauce

Dates, or tamar, naturally have a flavor like brown sugar or caramel. Pairing them with orange blossom and vanilla creates magic. Individual cakes are lovely when served as a dessert for a dinner party or when enjoyed fresh after baking one or two at a time—and one or two more later! I challenge you to find someone who doesn't adore this cake.

PREP: 20 MINUTES
COOK: 20 MINUTES
REST: 30 MINUTES
TOTAL: 1 HOUR 10 MINUTES

MAKES: 8 MINI CAKES
SPECIAL EQUIPMENT: 8 RAMEKINS (100 GRAMS, 3½ OUNCES)

CAKE
- 71 grams (¼ cup plus 1 tablespoon) unsalted butter, room temperature
- 20 pitted medjool dates (261 grams, 1¾ cups)
- 284 grams (1¼ cups) water
- 6 grams (1 teaspoon) baking soda
- 120 grams (1 cup) unbleached all-purpose flour
- 4 grams (1 teaspoon) baking powder
- ¼ teaspoon fine sea salt
- 106 grams (½ cup) light brown sugar
- 2 large eggs
- ½ teaspoon pure vanilla extract

CARAMEL SAUCE
- 42 grams (3 tablespoons) unsalted butter
- ⅛ teaspoon fine sea salt
- 113 grams (½ cup) heavy whipping cream
- 106 grams (½ cup) light brown sugar
- ½ teaspoon orange blossom water

WHIPPED CREAM
- 113 grams (½ cup) heavy whipping cream, cold
- 12 grams (1 tablespoon) granulated white sugar

1. Arrange an oven rack in the middle position and preheat the oven to 350°F (177°C). Coat the ramekins using 14 grams (1 tablespoon) of the butter divided among them all and place them on a baking sheet. Set aside.
2. Coarsely chop the dates.
3. In a medium saucepan over high heat, bring the water to a boil. Add the dates and bring the mixture back to a boil. Reduce the heat to low and simmer, stirring occasionally, for 5 minutes.
4. Remove the cooked dates from the heat and stir in the baking soda. The mixture will foam a little. Set aside.
5. In a small mixing bowl, stir together the flour, baking powder, and salt.
6. In the large bowl of a stand mixer fitted with the paddle attachment, cream 57 grams (¼ cup) of the butter and the brown sugar on high speed until light and fluffy, about 2 minutes. Stop to scrape down the bowl halfway through beating.
7. One at a time, add the eggs. Mix thoroughly at medium speed to incorporate each one and stop to scrape the bowl as you go.
8. Add the date mixture and vanilla and continue beating on medium speed until incorporated.
9. Stop to scrape down the bowl and add the flour mixture. Mix on low speed until smooth, 1 minute.
10. Divide the batter evenly among the prepared ramekins and smooth the tops with an offset spatula.
11. Bake the cakes on the baking sheet until they turn golden brown and spring back when touched in the center, 20 minutes.

continues

12. Meanwhile, make the caramel sauce. In a small saucepan over medium heat, melt the butter.

13. Add the salt, cream, brown sugar, and orange blossom water, bring the mixture to a boil, and reduce the heat to low, whisking constantly until the mixture combines fully and thickens slightly, about 5 minutes. Reserve 118 grams (½ cup) of the caramel sauce for serving.

14. Remove the cakes from the oven and liberally poke each one with a toothpick or skewer. Spoon 15 grams (3 teaspoons) of the caramel sauce on each cake, using the back of the spoon to spread it evenly. Let the cakes rest for 15 minutes. Spread more sauce over the tops to fill any holes.

15. Meanwhile, make the whipped cream. In the large bowl of a stand mixer fitted with the whisk attachment or with a hand mixer, beat the heavy cream and sugar on medium-high speed until soft peaks form, 1 minute. Refrigerate the whipped cream until you serve the cake.

16. Before serving, microwave the reserved caramel sauce in a microwave-safe bowl for 30 seconds.

17. Top each cake with a spoonful of caramel sauce and a dollop of whipped cream and serve.

> *Note*
>
> Cover the cakes and any extra caramel sauce with plastic wrap and store them in the refrigerator for up to 3 days. Warm the caramel sauce again before serving.
>
> **TIP:** If the whipped cream becomes runny during chilling, whisk or beat it again with a mixer just before serving.

PISTACHIO CUPCAKES
with Strawberry Rose Water Buttercream

PREP: **20 MINUTES**
COOK: **20 MINUTES**
COOL: **36 MINUTES**
TOTAL: **1 HOUR 16 MINUTES**

MAKES: **22 CUPCAKES**
SPECIAL EQUIPMENT: **PIPING BAG WITH ½-INCH (1.5-CM) ROUND PIPING TIP**

Miette Bakery in San Francisco launched my obsession with cupcakes that stand tall with thick layers of buttercream. Frosting-haters will say that too much buttercream is too much, but they haven't tasted my buttercream! These cupcakes have a gorgeous combination of green and pink: pistachios and roses. In cakes and cookies, pistachios often get lost in the shuffle, but in this light cake, a whisper of almond extract enhances their flavor. Here I present my own cupcake of the highest order, Miette-inspired.

CUPCAKES
195 grams (1½ cups plus 2 tablespoons) raw or Blanched Pistachios (page 267)
207 grams (1¾ cups) cake flour
¾ teaspoon baking powder
¼ teaspoon baking soda
¼ teaspoon fine sea salt
113 grams (½ cup) unsalted butter, room temperature
212 grams (1 cup plus 1 tablespoon) granulated white sugar
3 large egg whites, room temperature
12 grams (1 tablespoon) pure vanilla extract
¾ teaspoon pure almond extract
113 grams (½ cup) whole-milk plain yogurt, room temperature
113 grams (½ cup) whole milk, room temperature

BUTTERCREAM
40 grams (1½ ounces) freeze-dried strawberries
226 grams (1 cup) unsalted butter, room temperature
85 grams (3 ounces) cream cheese, room temperature
480 grams (4 cups) confectioners' sugar
4 grams (1 teaspoon) pure vanilla extract
¼ teaspoon rose water
42 grams (3 tablespoons) whole milk

1. Arrange an oven rack in the middle position and preheat the oven to 350°F (177°C). Line the wells of one or more cupcake tins with 22 foil liners. In a nut grinder or food processor, finely grind the pistachios.

2. Make the cupcakes. In a medium mixing bowl, whisk together the cake flour, baking powder, baking soda, salt, and 180 grams (1½ cups) of the ground pistachios. Set aside.

3. In the large bowl of a stand mixer fitted with the paddle attachment, beat the butter on medium speed until smooth, 1 minute.

4. Add 200 grams (1 cup) of the sugar and beat on medium speed until light and fluffy, 1 minute.

5. Stop to scrape down the bowl with a soft spatula. Add the egg whites, vanilla extract, and almond extract. Continue beating for 1 minute.

6. Stop the mixer, add the yogurt, and continue beating until well combined, 1 minute. The batter will appear slightly separated.

7. Stop, add the dry ingredients, and mix on low speed just until everything incorporates, 30 seconds.

continues

8. Stop to scrape down the bowl again, add the milk, and continue mixing just until the batter becomes smooth, 15 seconds. Don't overmix.

9. Divide the batter evenly among the cupcake liners, filling each no more than two-thirds full (60 grams).

10. Bake until the top of the cakes bounce back when pressed and a toothpick inserted in the center comes out clean, 18 to 20 minutes.

11. In the pan, let the cupcakes cool enough to handle, about 6 minutes. Transfer them, in their liners, to a cooling rack and let them cool completely, 30 minutes.

12. Meanwhile, mix the remaining 15 grams (2 tablespoons) of ground pistachios with the remaining 12 grams (1 tablespoon) of sugar in a small mixing bowl and set aside.

13. Make the buttercream. In a food processor, pulverize the strawberries to a powder. Into the large bowl of a stand mixer fitted with the paddle attachment, sift the powder through a fine mesh strainer and discard any strained seeds.

14. Add the butter and cream cheese and beat the mixture on medium speed until smooth, 1 minute.

15. Stop to scrape down the bowl. With the mixer on low speed, add the confectioners' sugar, 120 grams (1 cup) at a time, mixing until each addition combines fully.

16. Add the vanilla and rose water and continue mixing to combine.

17. Add the milk, 14 grams (1 tablespoon) at a time, until a smooth, light buttercream forms.

18. Fill the piping bag with the buttercream. To pipe, hold the tip perpendicular to the cupcake, in the center, and ½ inch (1.5 cm) from the top. Squeeze 40 grams (2 ounces) of buttercream on each cupcake.

19. Dust each cupcake with a pinch of the reserved pistachio mixture. Serve immediately.

Notes
- Made ahead of time, the buttercream holds well refrigerated for up to 1 week or frozen for up to 3 months. To thaw from frozen, refrigerate it overnight, bring it to room temperature, and stir until smooth.
- You can store the cupcakes in an airtight container at room temperature for up to 2 days or frozen for up to 2 months.

TIPS
- It's easier to separate cold eggs. Separate cold eggs first, then bring the whites to room temperature.
- Foil cupcake liners work best here and for any cupcakes with a thick layer of buttercream. Foil liners handle the weight and hold the shape better than paper liners. Don't fill the liners past two-thirds full, otherwise the cakes may spill over when baking.
- If you don't want to pipe the frosting, spoon it or apply it with a soft spatula.

VARIATION: You can make this recipe into a **LAYER CAKE** or **LARGE ROUND CAKE**. Use two 8- or 9-inch (20- or 23- cm) round or square cake pans or one 10-inch (25-cm) cake pan coated with oil and flour and lined with parchment paper on the bottom. If using more than one pan, divide the batter evenly between them. Bake at 350°F (177°C) for 20 to 25 minutes.

MOCHA CARDAMOM SNACK CAKE

Arabic Cardamom Coffee (page 19) is a form of hospitality, a special part of a warm welcome. Some people drink it with sugar and, rarely, cream. My love for qahwa (coffee), plus an inclination to soften it with sugar and cream, inspired this recipe, which harmoniously blends chocolate, coffee, and cardamom in a simple snack cake. The swath of cardamom coffee buttercream on top makes it irresistible, as does the ease of making it.

PREP: **20 MINUTES**
COOK: **27 MINUTES**
COOL: **40 MINUTES**
TOTAL: **1 HOUR 27 MINUTES**

MAKES: **12 SERVINGS**

CAKE
54 grams (¼ cup plus 1 teaspoon) neutral oil
47 grams (½ cup plus 2 teaspoons) Dutch process cocoa powder
120 grams (1 cup) unbleached all-purpose flour
200 grams (1 cup) granulated white sugar
6 grams (1 teaspoon) baking soda
½ teaspoon baking powder
½ teaspoon fine sea salt
½ teaspoon ground cardamom
114 grams (½ cup) labneh or plain whole-milk Greek yogurt, room temperature
170 grams (¾ cup) water
11 grams (1½ tablespoons) instant espresso powder
1 large egg, room temperature
1 large egg yolk, room temperature
9 grams (2 teaspoons) pure vanilla extract

BUTTERCREAM
5 grams (2 teaspoons) instant espresso powder
28 grams (2 tablespoons) hot water
¼ teaspoon ground cardamom
9 grams (2 teaspoons) heavy whipping cream, room temperature
9 grams (2 teaspoons) pure vanilla extract
170 grams (¾ cup) unsalted butter, room temperature
342 grams (3 cups) confectioners' sugar

1. Arrange an oven rack in the middle position and preheat the oven to 350°F (177°C).
2. Coat an 8-inch (20-cm) square pan lightly with oil. Line the bottom of it with parchment paper overhanging two sides and coat the parchment with more oil. Dust the parchment and the sides of the pan with 4 grams (2 teaspoons) of the cocoa powder, knocking out any excess.
3. Make the cake. In a large mixing bowl, whisk together the flour, sugar, 43 grams (½ cup) cocoa powder, baking soda, baking powder, salt, and cardamom. Set aside.
4. In a medium mixing bowl, whisk together the labneh, 170 grams (¾ cup) water, espresso powder, 50 grams (¼ cup) of the oil, egg, egg yolk, and vanilla.
5. Pour the wet ingredients into the dry ingredients and whisk thoroughly until a smooth batter forms and no lumps remain.
6. Pour the batter into the prepared pan and bake until the top of the cake springs back when touched and a toothpick inserted in the center comes out clean, 25 to 27 minutes.
7. Let the cake cool in the pan for 10 minutes. Loosen the cake from the pan by running a knife around the perimeter and gently shaking it from side to side. Use the parchment sling to lift the cake and transfer it to a cooling rack. Let it cool to room temperature, 30 minutes.

continues

8. Transfer the cake to a cake stand or serving platter.

9. While the cake is cooling, make the buttercream. In a small mixing bowl, dissolve the espresso powder in 28 grams (2 tablespoons) hot water. Add the cardamom, heavy cream, and vanilla extract and stir to combine.

10. In another large mixing bowl, use a large soft spatula to stir and smooth the butter. Add the espresso mixture and stir well to combine. Add the confectioners' sugar, 114 grams (1 cup) at a time, mixing well to incorporate after each addition.

11. Dollop the buttercream evenly on the cake. Use an offset spatula to spread the buttercream decoratively, creating deep waves. Leave the sides bare.

12. Slice and serve immediately.

> **Notes**
> - Coating the pan with cocoa powder adds richness, and it disappears when baked, unlike flour, which can streak a dark cake.
> - Mixing the buttercream by hand helps prevent air bubbles from forming, creating a smooth texture.
> - You can store leftovers in an airtight container at room temperature for up to 2 days or frozen for up to 2 months.

APRICOT UPSIDE-DOWN CAKE

PREP: 25 MINUTES
COOK: 50 MINUTES
COOL: 15 MINUTES
TOTAL: 1 HOUR 30 MINUTES

MAKES: 12 SLICES

Michigan summers gift us with an abundance of fresh apricots bursting with flavor. In this generous but short season, we try to make as many interesting dishes with them as possible: jam, Apricot Gems (page 102), and Orange Blossom Madeleines with Apricot Glaze (page 155). My sister, Peggy, a fan of pineapple upside-down cake, brought this incredible dessert to a family cookout overlooking the bay. Kissed by the wide, pink-orange sunset, the cake captivated everyone.

TOPPING

60 grams (¼ cup plus 1 teaspoon) unsalted butter, room temperature
213 grams (1 cup, packed) dark brown sugar
½ teaspoon orange blossom water
½ teaspoon pure vanilla extract
¼ teaspoon fine sea salt
8 apricots

CAKE

240 grams (2 cups) unbleached all-purpose flour
8 grams (2 teaspoons) baking powder
¼ teaspoon fine sea salt
113 grams (½ cup) unsalted butter, room temperature
300 grams (1½ cups) granulated white sugar
2 large eggs, separated, room temperature
227 grams (1 cup) whole milk, room temperature
½ teaspoon pure vanilla extract
½ teaspoon orange blossom water

WHIPPED CREAM

227 grams (1 cup) heavy whipping cream
8 grams (2 teaspoons) granulated white sugar
½ teaspoon pure vanilla extract

1. Arrange an oven rack in the middle position and preheat the oven to 350°F (177°F).
2. Coat a 9-by-13-by-2-inch (23-by-33-by-5-cm) cake pan with ½ teaspoon of the butter. Line the bottom of the pan with parchment and butter the parchment with another ½ teaspoon.
3. Make the topping. In a small saucepan over medium heat, melt 56 grams (¼ cup) of butter until it foams and the solids turn brown, 5 to 7 minutes. Don't let the butter burn.
4. Remove it from the heat, add the brown sugar, orange blossom water, vanilla extract, and salt and stir until the mixture becomes sandy.
5. Sprinkle the sugar mixture evenly over the parchment in the pan.
6. Halve the apricots, discard the pits, and cut each half into four wedges. Nestle the apricots close together in rows or decoratively in the pan. Set aside.
7. Make the cake. In a medium mixing bowl, sift the flour, baking powder, and salt. Set aside.
8. In the large bowl of a stand mixer fitted with the paddle attachment, cream the butter and sugar on medium-high speed until light and fluffy, 2 minutes.
9. One at a time, add the egg yolks, beating well after each addition. Stop to scrape down the bowl after each one.
10. With the mixer speed set to medium, add a third of the flour mixture and 76 grams (⅓ cup) of milk and beat just until combined, then stop and

continues

scrape down the bowl. Repeat twice more with the remaining flour mixture and milk.

11. Add the vanilla extract and orange blossom water and continue beating until smooth.

12. If you don't have another bowl for the stand mixer, transfer the batter to another large mixing bowl and clean the bowl and whisk attachment. Beat the egg whites on medium speed until they hold stiff but not dry peaks, about 2 minutes. When lifted, the beaten whites should hold a curved peak on the end of the whisk.

13. Use a soft spatula to fold the egg whites gently into the batter just until they incorporate. Don't overmix.

14. Spread the batter evenly over the apricots in the cake pan.

15. Bake until the cake turns golden brown and the top bounces back when touched in the center, 45 to 50 minutes.

16. Let the cake cool in the pan for 15 minutes. To remove it, place a large serving platter or baking sheet upside down over the pan and flip both over together. Remove the pan. The apricots are now the top of the cake.

17. While the cake cools, make the whipped cream. In the bowl of the stand mixer fitted with the whisk attachment, beat the heavy cream, sugar, and vanilla extract on medium-high speed until stiff peaks form, 2 to 3 minutes.

18. To serve, cut the cake into 12 squares. Place each slice on a dessert plate and top it with a dollop of whipped cream.

Notes

- Three techniques can break this cake. When browning the butter, to prevent it from burning remove the pan from the heat as soon as the butter browns. Don't overbeat egg whites, which will dry them out and make them difficult to incorporate into the batter. When adding the beaten whites into the batter, gently fold them just until they're no longer visible, otherwise the batter will lose its air and not bake as tall.
- I like to use an oval baking dish similar in size to the 9-by-13-by-2-inch (23-by-33-by-5-cm) cake pan, arranging the apricots around the oval accordingly.
- Store leftovers, covered with plastic wrap, at room temperature for up to 2 days. You can store any leftover whipped cream in an airtight container in the refrigerator for up to 2 days.

LEMON YOGURT CAKE
with Strawberry Rose Water Sauce and Labneh

PREP: **26 MINUTES**
COOK: **60 MINUTES**
COOL: **10 MINUTES**
TOTAL: **1 HOUR 36 MINUTES**

MAKES: **8 SERVINGS**

Yogurt cakes represent a great tradition among the Lebanese, and the French, too. Examples include Mocha Cardamom Snack Cake (page 165), Coconut Semolina Cake (page 185), and of course this cake. Baking this one creates an adventure for the senses, from the texture of lemon sugar to the aroma of rose water strawberries. Olive oil adds elegant depth to the fruit flavors of this bright, fragrant confection, and the labneh topping makes it one of the best versions of strawberry shortcake you can make, eat, or share.

CAKE
104 grams (½ cup plus 1 teaspoon) extra virgin olive oil
180 grams (1½ cups) unbleached all-purpose flour, plus more to coat the pan
8 grams (2 teaspoons) baking powder
½ teaspoon fine sea salt
200 grams (1 cup) granulated white sugar
12 grams (2 tablespoons) lemon zest from 2 lemons
3 large eggs, room temperature
171 grams (¾ cup) whole-milk yogurt

SAUCE
500 grams (1 pound) strawberries
100 grams (½ cup) granulated sugar
56 grams (¼ cup) fresh lemon juice from 2 lemons
9 grams (2 teaspoons) rose water

TOPPING
227 grams (1 cup) labneh or whole-milk Greek yogurt

1. Arrange an oven rack in the middle position and preheat the oven to 350°F (177°C). Coat an 8-inch (20-cm) loaf pan lightly with 4 grams (1 teaspoon) of the olive oil, then flour, and knock out any excess.
2. Make the cake. In a small mixing bowl, whisk together the flour, baking powder, and salt.
3. In another small bowl, rub the sugar and lemon zest together with your fingers until the mixture becomes moist and fragrant.
4. In the large bowl of a stand mixer fitted with the whisk attachment, mix the eggs and lemon sugar on medium-high speed until thick and pale yellow, 2 minutes.
5. Add the 100 grams (½ cup) of olive oil and beat on medium speed until smooth, 30 seconds.
6. Add the yogurt and continue beating until it combines, 1 more minute.
7. With a soft spatula, gently fold in the flour mixture just until it combines. Spread the batter evenly in the prepared loaf pan.
8. Bake until the cake turns a deep golden brown, 45 to 50 minutes.
9. Transfer the cake, still in the pan, to a cooling rack to cool for 10 minutes, then remove the cake to cool completely on the rack.
10. Meanwhile, make the strawberry sauce. Hull and halve 4 strawberries; set aside. Hull and coarsely chop the remaining strawberries.

continues

11. In a large, heavy saucepan over medium-high heat, add the strawberries, sugar, and lemon juice. Bring the mixture to a boil, then reduce the heat to medium.

12. Mash the berries with a masher. Simmer until the mixture thickens, stirring occasionally, 15 to 20 minutes.

13. Remove the strawberry sauce from the heat and stir in the rose water. Let it cool before serving.

14. To serve, spoon 42 grams (2 tablespoons) of the strawberry sauce on eight dessert plates or in eight bowls. Slice the cake into eight pieces, each 1 inch (2.5 cm) thick, and lay the slices on the sauce on the plates. Garnish with more sauce and the reserved halved strawberries.

15. Stir the labneh until smooth. Top each piece of cake with a dollop of labneh and serve immediately.

> **Notes**
> - Use fresh strawberries for the garnish. If the berries are red all the way to a pretty green stem, don't hull the garnish berries and simply halve them.
> - You can make the strawberry-rose water sauce up to 3 weeks ahead of time and store it in an airtight container in the refrigerator.
> - You can store leftover cake in an airtight container at room temperature for up to 2 days or frozen for up to 3 months.
>
> **TIP:** You will be using the zest of the 2 lemons for the cake and their juice for the sauce. It's easier to zest a lemon before juicing, so zest first, then juice.

TURMERIC TEA CAKE

Sfouf, a tall, yellow snack cake, has a soft texture, a sweet flavor reminiscent of ka'ak (page 76), and a timeless simplicity. This version ramps it up nicely with turmeric powder and anise seed, and tahini on the bottom adds the lightest, savory touch of sesame. Enjoy it with a cold glass of milk or Matcha Orange Blossom Latte (page 176).

PREP: **5 MINUTES**
COOK: **36 MINUTES**
COOL: **1 HOUR**
TOTAL: **1 HOUR 41 MINUTES**

MAKES: **24 PIECES**

16 grams (1 tablespoon) tahini
360 grams (3 cups) unbleached all-purpose flour
500 grams (2½ cups) granulated white sugar
163 grams (1 cup) fine semolina flour
18 grams (1½ tablespoons) baking powder
18 grams (2 tablespoons) turmeric powder
9 grams (1 tablespoon) ground anise seed
¼ teaspoon fine sea salt
454 grams (2 cups) whole milk, room temperature
198 grams (1 cup) neutral oil
228 grams (1 cup) water
30 grams (¼ cup) pine nuts

1. Arrange an oven rack in the middle position and preheat the oven to 350°F (177°C). Coat the bottom of a 9-by-13-by-2-inch (23-by-33-by-5 cm) baking pan with the tahini.

2. In a large mixing bowl, whisk together the flour, sugar, semolina, baking powder, turmeric, anise seed, and sea salt. Add the milk, oil, and water and whisk until smooth.

3. Pour the batter into the prepared pan. Scatter the pine nuts on the batter.

4. Bake until the cake turns golden brown, 34 to 36 minutes. Broil (on high if your broiler has levels) until the top turns a deep golden brown, 2 minutes. Watch closely to ensure that it doesn't burn.

5. In the pan, let it cool completely, at least 1 hour. Cut it into 2-inch (5-cm) squares to serve from the pan.

> *Note*
> To store the cake, cover the pan with plastic wrap or keep pieces in an airtight container at room temperature for up to 3 days.

Something to Drink

MATCHA ORANGE BLOSSOM LATTE

My handsome, sweet, bonus son, Steven, makes iced matcha lattes with religious precision. The Zen-like ceremony, with the tin of bright green tea powder and the little bamboo whisk, helps achieve a calming tranquility. Like baking, the process delights as much as the results (see the latte pictured on page 174), which taste earthy, creamy, slightly sweet, and, with orange blossom added, slightly floral.

PREP: 5 MINUTES

MAKES: 1 LATTE

2 grams (1 teaspoon) ceremonial matcha
57 grams (¼ cup) water, hot (110°F, 38°C)
13 grams (2 teaspoons) Flower Water Syrup (page 273), using orange blossom water
170 grams (¾ cup) milk of choice

> *Note*
> Matcha comes in various grades. Ceremonial has the most vibrant color and balanced flavor. Culinary has a stronger flavor and more bitterness, which works great for baking.

1. Sift the matcha powder into a small bowl. Add the hot water and whisk vigorously until smooth, light, and frothy, 1 minute.

2. Fill a glass with ice. Add the matcha mixture and syrup and stir.

3. Add the milk, stir, and serve.

MICHIGAN TART CHERRY BUNDT CAKE

Tart cherries, the pride of the Great Lakes State, take the cake! Jammy and juicy, they stud the batter of this light, almond-scented treat. The cake's texture perfectly suits a pretty Bundt pan, making it an excellent gift cake. It also keeps nicely on the counter, under glass, so that anyone passing through the kitchen can sneak a slice. My brother Dick, who loves this cake, gave me a glass cloche for just this purpose.

PREP: **15 MINUTES**
COOK: **44 MINUTES**
COOL: **1 HOUR 10 MINUTES**
TOTAL: **2 HOURS 9 MINUTES**

MAKES: **9 SERVINGS**
SPECIAL EQUIPMENT: **BUNDT PAN**

CAKE

Baking spray with flour
247 grams (2 cups plus 1 tablespoon) unbleached all-purpose flour, plus more to coat the pan
72 grams (¾ cup) almond flour
8 grams (2 teaspoons) baking powder
9 grams (1 tablespoon) mahleb
½ teaspoon fine sea salt
170 grams (¾ cup) unsalted butter, room temperature
250 grams (1¼ cups) granulated white sugar
3 large eggs
4 grams (1 teaspoon) pure almond extract
227 grams (1 cup) plain whole-milk yogurt
227 grams (2 cups) pitted tart cherries, fresh or thawed from frozen

GLAZE

84 grams (¾ cup) pitted tart cherries, fresh or thawed from frozen
228 grams (2 cups) confectioners' sugar
28 grams (2 tablespoons) plain whole-milk yogurt

1. Arrange an oven rack in the middle position and preheat the oven to 350°F (177°C). Generously coat a 6-cup Bundt pan with baking spray, then also flour the pan.

2. Make the cake. In a large mixing bowl, sift 240 grams (2 cups) of the flour, almond flour, baking powder, mahleb, and salt. Set aside.

3. In the large bowl of a stand mixer fitted with the paddle attachment, cream the butter and sugar on medium speed until pale and fluffy, 5 minutes.

4. Reduce the speed to low and add the eggs, 1 at a time, mixing until each incorporates fully before adding the next.

5. With the mixer off, add half of the dry ingredients. Mix on low speed until they incorporate fully, turn the mixer off again, scrape down the bowl, and add the remaining dry ingredients. Continue mixing for 30 seconds.

6. Add the almond extract and yogurt. Mix until smooth, 1 more minute.

7. In a small bowl, stir together the cherries and 7 grams (1 tablespoon) of the flour.

8. Pour half of the batter into the prepared pan. Press half of the floured cherries into the batter, distributing them evenly. Add the rest of the batter to the pan and press the rest of the cherries evenly into the batter.

9. Bake until the cake turns golden brown, the top springs back when touched, and a toothpick inserted in the center comes out clean, 44 to 46 minutes.

continues

10. Place the pan on a cooling rack to cool for 10 minutes.

11. Loosen the cake from the pan by gently shaking it several times. Turn the cake out on the cooling rack to cool completely to room temperature, about 1 hour.

12. Meanwhile, make the glaze. In a food processor or blender, puree the cherries, confectioners' sugar, and yogurt.

13. Place a piece of parchment paper or a plate under the cake on the cooling rack. Pour the glaze evenly over the cooled cake. Use a pastry brush to brush the glaze evenly over the cake, using the drippings from beneath, as well. Serve the cake the same day you bake it.

> **Notes**
> - Bundt pans can prove notoriously tricky to coat evenly with butter and flour, an essential step for releasing the finished cake. Baking spray with flour makes easy work of the task.
> - Store leftover cake, covered, at room temperature for 2 days or frozen for up to 3 months.

LEBANESE BAKING

Michigan Cherries

Many harvests encapsulate Michigan: morels, whitefish, red haven peaches, but nothing—move over, Motor City!—expresses us better than our cherries. Yes, we produce a mother lode of the sweet fruit for commercial yogurt and other dishes, but our tart cherries—the Montmorency and Balaton cultivars—reign supreme.

Our universities dive deep in to tart cherry research, sharing their findings with growers and the rest of us. That may sound over the top, but around here, it's not surprising. After all, if you fly into Traverse City, you glide over rich farmland dotted with cherry trees as far as the eye can see and land at Cherry Capital Airport. Traverse City, called Cherryland, also hosts the National Cherry Festival. We supply the nation with the lion's share of its tart cherries, so when you eat one, you likely have had a taste of the Water Wonderland.

Unless you live near orchards in season, you typically can find tart cherries, also called sour cherries, in the freezer section. Freezing preserves their delicate nature (they're so delicate, they must be shaken from the trees). They go into cherry pie, cherry cake, cherry drinks, and so much more. My love affair with Michigan cherries no doubt connects to mahleb, a special Lebanese spice ground from the pit of the St. Lucie cherry. The gentle almond fragrance of this damp spice always transports me both to Lebanon and my home state.

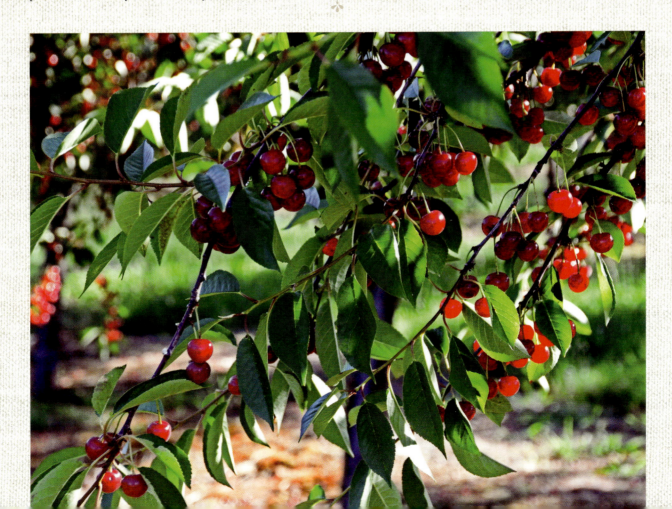

LEBANESE NIGHTS CREAM CAKE
with Berry Compote

Famous among the many pudding treats of Lebanon and the Middle East, layali Lubnan ("Lebanese nights") cream cake features three creamy layers, each lighter than the one below. It starts with a base of thick semolina pudding with an aromatic, piny flavor from ground mastic. The middle layer consists of rich ashta pastry cream, followed by a light layer of whipped cream crowned with ground pistachios. A bright, tart berry compote beautifully balances the creamy cake.

PREP: **20 MINUTES**
CHILL: **3 HOURS**
COOK: **20 MINUTES**
TOTAL: **3 HOURS 40 MINUTES**

MAKES: **9 SERVINGS**
SPECIAL EQUIPMENT: **MORTAR AND PESTLE**

SEMOLINA BASE
568 grams (2½ cups) whole milk
82 grams (½ cup) fine semolina flour
25 grams (2 tablespoons) granulated white sugar
½ teaspoon orange blossom water
1 small mastic pebble

ASHTA LAYER
227 grams (1 cup) whole milk
227 grams (1 cup) heavy whipping cream
50 grams (¼ cup) granulated white sugar
16 grams (2 tablespoons) cornstarch
10 grams (1 tablespoon) fine semolina flour
4 grams (1 teaspoon) orange blossom water
4 grams (1 teaspoon) rose water

BERRY COMPOTE
167 grams (1 cup) strawberries
170 grams (1 cup) blueberries
50 grams (½ cup) granulated white sugar
½ teaspoon ground cinnamon
28 grams (2 tablespoons) water

WHIPPED CREAM LAYER
30 grams (¼ cup) raw or Blanched Pistachios (page 267)
227 grams (1 cup) heavy whipping cream, cold
8 grams (2 teaspoons) granulated white sugar

1. Make the semolina base. In a small saucepan over medium heat, whisk together the milk, semolina, and sugar. Continue cooking, whisking constantly, until the mixture thickens, 3 minutes.

2. Remove the saucepan from the heat, add the orange blossom water, and whisk to combine.

3. In a mortar and pestle, crush the mastic pebble, add it to the pudding, and whisk to combine.

4. Into an 8-inch (20-cm) square cake pan, pour the semolina pudding and spread it evenly with an offset spatula. Press wax paper or plastic wrap against the surface of the pudding to prevent a skin from forming and refrigerate until it sets and chills through, at least 1 hour and up to 1 day.

5. When the semolina base has chilled fully, make the ashta layer. Remove the cake pan from the refrigerator, remove the plastic wrap, and set aside.

6. In a small saucepan over medium heat, whisk together the milk, whipping cream, sugar, cornstarch, and semolina. Cook, whisking constantly, until the mixture thickens, 3 minutes.

continues

7. Remove the saucepan from the heat, add the orange blossom water and rose water, and whisk to combine.

8. Pour the cream layer on the chilled semolina layer and spread it evenly with an offset spatula. Press wax paper or plastic wrap against the surface of the ashta to prevent a skin from forming and refrigerate until it sets and chills through, at least 1 hour and up to 1 day.

9. Meanwhile, make the berry compote. Hull the strawberries and, depending on their size, halve or quarter them.

10. In a small saucepan over low heat, cook the strawberries, blueberries, sugar, cinnamon, and water until the berries soften and the juices slightly thicken, 15 to 20 minutes.

11. In the pan, let the compote cool to room temperature, transfer it to an airtight container, and refrigerate it until you're ready to serve the cake, at least 1 hour and up to 1 day.

12. Remove the pan from the refrigerator and remove the plastic wrap. In a nut grinder or food processor, finely grind the pistachios. Set both aside.

13. Make the whipped cream. In the large bowl of a stand mixer fitted with the whisk attachment, beat the heavy cream and sugar on medium-high speed until stiff peaks form, 2 to 3 minutes.

14. Spread the whipped cream evenly on the ashta layer, smoothing it with an offset spatula. Sprinkle the ground pistachios evenly on the whipped cream.

15. Cut the cake into 9 squares and serve each with a heaping spoonful of berry compote on the side.

> *Notes*
> You can store leftover slices of cake, covered, in the refrigerator for up to 5 days. You can store the compote in the refrigerator in an airtight container for up to 3 days.

COCONUT SEMOLINA CAKE

The light texture of this cake, namoura, the hero cake of the Middle East, tastes so tender, so buttery—a feat achieved with yogurt and baking soda. Some versions of namoura, also called basbousa and harissa, don't include coconut, but many do. This recipe takes that fabulous flavor further with a splash of coconut extract. That addition has made it the hero cake of my kitchen now, too.

PREP: 10 MINUTES
REST: 2 HOURS
COOK: 21 MINUTES
COOL: 2 HOURS
TOTAL: 4 HOURS 31 MINUTES
MAKES: 24 SERVINGS

---

127 grams (½ cup plus 1 tablespoon) Clarified Butter (page 271), melted
352 grams (2 cups) coarse semolina (Cream of Wheat)
85 grams (1 cup) desiccated coconut
341 grams (1½ cups) whole-milk yogurt
200 grams (1 cup) granulated white sugar
4 grams (1 teaspoon) pure coconut extract
4 grams (1 teaspoon) baking powder
½ teaspoon baking soda
½ teaspoon fine sea salt
18 grams (2 tablespoons) slivered almonds or pine nuts for topping
480 grams (1½ cups) Flower Water Syrup (page 273), cold

1. Coat the bottom of a 9-by-13-by-2-inch (23-by-33-by-5 cm) metal baking pan with 14 grams (1 tablespoon) of the clarified butter.

2. In a medium mixing bowl, combine the semolina, coconut, and remaining 113 grams (½ cup) of clarified butter by hand until the mixture becomes sandy, 1 minute.

3. In another medium mixing bowl, whisk together the yogurt, sugar, coconut extract, baking powder, baking soda, and salt. Pour the yogurt mixture into the semolina mixture and stir well with a wooden spoon until a thick, smooth batter forms.

4. Pour the batter into the prepared pan. Use an offset spatula to spread it evenly and smooth the top. Let the batter rest, uncovered, for 2 hours, which will enable the semolina to absorb the liquid ingredients and thicken enough to hold cut lines before baking.

5. When the batter has rested, arrange an oven rack in the middle position and preheat the oven to 400°F (200°C).

6. With the tip of a sharp chef's knife, cut the raw cake, making 3 cuts for 4 columns lengthwise and 5 cuts for 6 rows crosswise.

7. Place the nuts decoratively in the center of each square.

8. Bake the cake until the edges turn golden brown, 20 to 25 minutes.

9. If needed, broil the cake (on high if your broiler has levels), until the top turns a deep golden brown, 1 to 2 minutes. Watch closely to ensure that it doesn't burn.

10. Remove the cake from the oven and immediately pour the cold syrup evenly over the hot cake. Allow the cake to cool completely and absorb the syrup before serving, at least 2 hours.

Notes
- Coarse semolina (Cream of Wheat) is also known as farina.
- In an airtight container, store the cake at room temperature for up to 1 week or frozen for up to 3 months.

BAKLAWA CHEESECAKE

Among the family, our holiday buffets are legendary, and especially the dessert buffet. We fuss over those desserts like you wouldn't believe! Dan's sister, Carol, always says, "I'll come up with something," and brings an incredible surprise. Years ago (before this cake's trend)—inspired by her mother's famous, tall, luscious cheesecakes—she brought a baklawa cheesecake, and the family, as Aunt Hilda would say, "went crazy for it, honey!" This showstopper is loads of fun to bake.

PREP: 30 MINUTES
COOK: 1 HOUR 8 MINUTES
CHILL: 6 HOURS
TOTAL: 7 HOURS 38 MINUTES

MAKES: 10 SERVINGS
SPECIAL EQUIPMENT: 9-INCH (23-CM) SPRINGFORM PAN

TOP CRUST

32 grams (2 tablespoons plus 1 teaspoon) Clarified Butter (page 271), melted

6 sheets phyllo dough (76 grams, ¼ pound) from 1 sleeve of a 9-by-14 inch (23-by-35.5-cm) package, room temperature

42 grams (2 tablespoons) Flower Water Syrup (page 273), cold, plus more for serving

BOTTOM CRUST

12 sheets phyllo dough (151 grams, ⅓ pound) from 1 sleeve of a 9-by-14 inch (23-by-35.5-cm) package, room temperature

57 grams (¼ cup) Clarified Butter (page 271), melted, plus 14 grams (1 tablespoon) to coat the pan

240 grams (2 cups) raw or Blanched Pistachios (page 267)

100 grams (½ cup) granulated white sugar

9 grams (2 teaspoons) rose water

CHEESECAKE FILLING

908 grams (32 ounces) plain cream cheese, room temperature

228 grams (1 cup) labneh or plain whole-milk Greek yogurt, room temperature

3 large eggs, room temperature

400 grams (2 cups) granulated white sugar

30 grams (¼ cup) unbleached all-purpose flour

37 grams (⅓ cup) cornstarch

28 grams (2 tablespoons) orange blossom water

9 grams (2 teaspoons) rose water

1. Arrange an oven rack in the middle position and preheat the oven to 425°F (220°F). Line two baking sheets with parchment paper.

2. Coat a 9-inch (23-cm) springform pan with ½ teaspoon of the melted butter, line the pan with a 9-inch (23-cm) circle of parchment paper, and grease the top of the parchment circle with the same amount of butter.

3. Make the top crust. Unroll the sleeve of phyllo and cover the stack with a kitchen towel. Select 6 sheets of phyllo to trim to the size of the pan. If the top sheet shows any damage, such as tears or folding, pull a sheet from the middle and place it on top. Gently place the springform pan on the stack and use it as a guide to cut all 6 layers into 9-inch (23-cm) circles with kitchen scissors. Discard the scraps and place another kitchen towel over the circle stack to prevent it from drying.

4. Lay one circle in the center of one of the parchment-lined baking sheets. Brush the top of the circle evenly with melted clarified butter. Repeat with the rest of the circles.

5. Use a sharp knife or kitchen scissors to cut the stack into 10 equal wedges. Halve the stack, mark 4 cuts, spaced just under 3 inches (8 cm) apart, for 5 wedges, and cut, keeping the wedges in place. Repeat with the other semicircle stack.

6. Bake until the wedges turn golden brown, 8 minutes.

7. Remove them from the oven and immediately drizzle them evenly with the cold syrup. Set aside, uncovered, at room temperature until you're ready to serve the cheesecake, up to 1 day.

continues

8. Next, make the bottom crust. From the covered stack of phyllo, lay 1 sheet in the springform pan covering half of the pan, gently nudging it into the bottom but with the short ends hanging over the top edge. Brush the sheet generously with butter.

9. Lay another sheet of phyllo perpendicular over the first, tucking it into the pan with ends overhanging. Brush it generously with butter. Repeat with 10 more sheets of phyllo for a total of 12 sheets. Rotate the placement of each sheet to cover all sides of the pan evenly.

10. In a nut grinder or food processor, finely grind the pistachios, transfer them to a small bowl, add the sugar and rose water, and stir to combine. Reserve 19 grams (2 tablespoons) of the mixture for garnish.

11. Spread the unreserved nuts evenly in the raw phyllo crust.

12. Par-bake the crust just until it turns pale golden brown, 5 minutes.

13. Transfer it, still in the pan, to a cooling rack set over a piece of parchment paper. Use a knife or kitchen scissors to trim the phyllo hanging over the rim of the pan. Discard the trimmings. Reduce the oven to 375°F (190°C).

14. Next, make the filling. In the large bowl of a stand mixer fitted with the paddle attachment, beat the cream cheese on medium speed until smooth, 2 minutes.

15. Stop and scrape down the bowl. Add the labneh and beat on medium speed until smooth, 1 more minute.

16. Meanwhile, in a small bowl, lightly beat the eggs.

17. Add the eggs, sugar, flour, cornstarch, orange blossom water, and rose water and continue beating until smooth, 2 minutes. Pour the filling into the baked crust.

18. Place the second parchment-lined baking sheet on the middle rack of the oven. It will catch any melted butter that may seep from the cheesecake as it bakes.

19. Place the raw cheesecake on the baking sheet in the oven and bake until the center nearly sets and still jiggles slightly, 45 to 55 minutes.

20. Transfer the cheesecake, still in the pan, to a cooling rack to cool to room temperature. Refrigerate it, still in the pan, for at least 6 hours and up to 1 day.

21. To serve, remove the band from the springform pan. Use a long metal spatula to lift the cheesecake from the base of the pan, leaving the parchment behind, and carefully transfer it to a cake stand or serving platter.

22. Onto the cheesecake, arrange the 10 sets of phyllo wedges that you baked earlier, reassembling them in a circle. Dust each wedge with the reserved sugared pistachios.

23. Slice the cheesecake into 10 pieces using the wedges as a guide. Serve with a drizzle of flower water syrup over each piece.

> *Note*
>
> Store leftover cheesecake, covered with plastic wrap, in the refrigerator for up to 2 days.
>
> **VARIATION:** Carol likes to use what she calls a "lazy" garnish rather than phyllo wedges. For a **SIMPLE GARNISH**, increase the amount of sugared pistachios when making them for the bottom of the cake, and set them aside: combine 120 grams (1 cup) pistachios, 50 grams (¼ cup) granulated white sugar, and 4 grams (1 teaspoon) orange blossom water. Just before serving, sprinkle these reserved pistachios evenly on the cheesecake.

POMEGRANATE MOUSSE CAKE
with Lime Icing

PREP: **15 MINUTES**
CHILL: **7 HOURS 30 MINUTES**
TOTAL: **7 HOURS 45 MINUTES**

MAKES: **8 SERVINGS**
SPECIAL EQUIPMENT: **9-INCH (23-CM) SPRINGFORM PAN**

Pomegranates hold a high place of honor in Lebanese cuisine. The skin of the fruit glows with a gorgeous intensity and the seeds glisten, capturing that sweet-tart flavor we love. This cake, dramatic as the fruit itself, works so well for gatherings because you need to make it in advance and chill it. The cake also displays one of my favorite color combinations: pink and green, with a white topping. Bursting with the splendor of pomegranates, lime, and pistachios, it looks like eye candy, smells like lime-zest heaven, and tastes cool, light, and airy—a sweet feast for all the senses.

PISTACHIO CRUST

4 grams (1 teaspoon) neutral oil
14 grams (2 tablespoons) confectioners' sugar
180 grams (1½ cups) raw or Blanched Pistachios (page 267)
56 grams (¼ cup) unsalted butter, cold
62 grams (⅓ cup) coarse semolina (Cream of Wheat)
¼ teaspoon fine sea salt
80 grams (¼ cup) Flower Water Syrup (page 273), cold

POMEGRANATE MOUSSE

340 grams (1½ cups) POM-brand pomegranate juice
42 grams (3 tablespoons) fresh lime juice
4 grams (1 teaspoon) rose water
5 drops pink food coloring (optional)
18 grams (2 tablespoons) unflavored gelatin powder
5 large egg whites
⅛ teaspoon cream of tartar
150 grams (¾ cup) granulated white sugar
57 grams (¼ cup) water
284 grams (1¼ cups) heavy whipping cream

LIME ICING

151 grams (⅔ cup) sour cream
28 grams (2 tablespoons) fresh lime juice
24 grams (2 tablespoons) granulated white sugar
2 grams (1 teaspoon) lime zest for finishing

1. Coat the bottom and sides of a 9-inch (23-cm) springform pan with some of the oil and line the bottom with a circle of parchment paper. Coat the top of the parchment with oil, coat the entire interior of the pan with the confectioners' sugar, and knock out any excess.

2. In a nut grinder or food processor, finely grind the pistachios. Set aside.

3. In a medium saucepan over medium heat, melt the butter. Add the semolina and cook, stirring constantly, until the mixture combines, 1 minute.

4. Remove the saucepan from the heat, add the pistachios and fine sea salt, and stir to combine.

5. Add the flower water syrup, 20 grams (1 tablespoon) at a time, stirring well after each addition.

6. Transfer the dough to a small bowl and refrigerate it, uncovered, for 30 minutes.

7. Crumble the cold crust mixture into the prepared springform pan. Coat your palms with water and press the crust mixture evenly into the base of the pan and up the sides by 1 inch (2.5 cm). Set aside.

continues

8. Next, make the pomegranate mousse. In another small saucepan, add the pomegranate juice, lime juice, rose water, and pink food coloring, if using. In a thin layer, sprinkle some of the gelatin very slowly and evenly over the surface of the juice mixture, allowing it to absorb. No white should remain before you add more.

9. Warm the mixture on medium-low heat until the gelatin dissolves, 5 minutes.

10. Transfer the mixture to a bowl, cover, and refrigerate for 30 minutes.

11. In the large bowl of a stand mixer fitted with the whisk attachment, add the egg whites and cream of tartar and beat on medium-high speed just until soft peaks form, 1 minute. Turn the mixer to low and let it run while you make the syrup.

12. In a small saucepan over medium-high heat, dissolve the sugar in the water. Cook until the syrup reaches 245°F (118°C), 2 to 3 minutes.

13. Remove the syrup from the heat, increase the mixer speed to medium, and in a thin, steady stream, carefully pour the hot syrup into the whites. Aim for the side of the bowl just above the whites to prevent the syrup from hitting the whisk. Increase the speed to medium-high and whip the meringue until stiff peaks form, 1 to 2 minutes. Set aside.

14. If you don't have another bowl for the stand mixer, transfer the meringue to another large mixing bowl and clean the bowl and whisk attachment. In the bowl of the stand mixer fitted with the cleaned whisk attachment, beat the whipping cream on medium speed until soft peaks form, 1 to 2 minutes. Set aside.

15. Remove the pomegranate mixture from the refrigerator and whisk it until smooth. With a soft spatula, gently fold the pomegranate mixture into the meringue just until it combines and no streaks remain.

16. Use the same spatula to add a third of the pomegranate meringue to the whipped cream, mixing well. Gently fold all the whipped cream mixture back into the rest of the pomegranate meringue, just until no whites remain visible.

17. Pour the mousse into the prepared crust, smoothing the top with an offset spatula. Refrigerate, uncovered, for 30 minutes.

18. Meanwhile, make the lime icing. In a small bowl, whisk together the sour cream, lime juice, and sugar.

19. Spread the icing evenly on the chilled mousse and refrigerate the cake for least 6 hours and up to 1 day.

20. To serve, remove the band of the springform pan. Warm a thin knife in hot water for 15 or 20 seconds. Run the knife around the perimeter of the mousse and release the sides of the pan. Run a long metal spatula under the cake, between the crust and the pan, and carefully transfer the cake to a cake stand or serving platter. Discard the parchment circle.

21. Evenly dust the top of the cake with the lime zest, slice it into 10 pieces, and serve.

Notes
- In my experience, POM-brand pomegranate juice imparts better color than other brands.
- You can store leftover cake, covered, in the refrigerator for up to 2 days.

TIPS
- It's easier to zest a lime before juicing, so zest first, then juice.
- In step 15, don't stir the meringue mixture too much, or it will lose its air.
- To make clean slices, dip a long, sharp knife in warm water, dry it, and slice. Wipe the knife and repeat for each cut.

VARIATION: For a **VEGETARIAN VERSION**, substitute 4 grams (2 teaspoons) agar powder for the gelatin.

Fatayer

The world of savory Lebanese pies has caused such joy—and such frustration!—in my kitchen. The little pies always seem to open at the seams, willy-nilly. Solving that problem required PhD-level research in books, consultation with other bakers, and extensive recipe testing (along with curses that I didn't know I had in me!). That research took me not only to family kitchens but to Ba'albek in Lebanon and Dearborn in Michigan, where I have seen and eaten the very finest fatayer, all resulting in a treasure trove of ideas to put into practice. Turn the page to learn the secrets to making perfect fatayer.

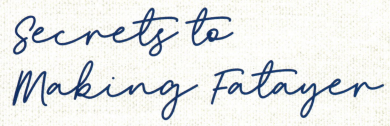

Secrets to Making Fatayer

For fatayer, sfeha, and cheese pies that look beautiful and taste even better, the dough can't run too thick, it must hold together at the seams, and it should bake to golden-brown goodness while remaining tender. Here's how to achieve these qualities for a baking tradition worth trying, keeping, and sharing.

USE A STICKY DOUGH

You need a high water-to-flour ratio for the right level of stickiness, which, in this case, means a damp dough that doesn't leave residue on your fingers. A generous amount of oil in the dough also contributes to the required stickiness, which helps keep the seams closed when the pies bake. Use a stand mixer to achieve the right consistency.

NO SECOND RISE

Many bread doughs require a second rise to reinflate the dough, relax the gluten, and create the desired crumb. But for thin, tender pockets, dispense with the second rise. Fatayer dough needs to stay flat and thin. With one short rise, swiftly filling and shaping the pies help prevent the dough from puffing, which can cause the seams to reopen.

ROLL AND CUT THE DOUGH

Sitto didn't do this, the aunts didn't, and Mom didn't either—but I do. Embrace the efficiency of cutting multiple discs, all with an even thickness. To prevent the dough from shrinking after cutting, lift the dough gently off the counter and lay it back down in sections. Mark as many circles as possible by aligning the cutter with the edges of previous cuts and don't worry about boundaries. Allow the rough outer edges of the rolled dough to form part of a disc. Let one circle overlap another slightly. It's better to get more discs from the first rollout.

Rolling has one downside: the scraps. They don't roll well a second time. Dough rolled a second time becomes less sticky, pliable, and obedient; and it doesn't yield the same tenderness when baked. In my recipe, the scrap dough yields about four more fatayer. Sometimes I use the scraps, and—don't tell Sitto!—sometimes I don't. Scrap dough requires kneading back into a ball and another rest, 30 minutes, for the gluten to relax before rerolling.

You can divide the dough into small balls, 28 grams each, and roll them out individually to avoid scraps altogether. But the dough will continue to rise as you work, one piece at a time, and many of the fatayer won't end up thin and lovely.

USE DRY FILLINGS

During baking, wet fillings emit steam and can force open the seams of the pastry. Wet fillings also find their way on the edges of the dough, making for slippery seams. Blending lemon juice and extra virgin olive oil to a spinach filling, for example, and squeezing out the liquid adds flavor but keeps the spinach dry.

TAKE CONTROL OF THE SEAMS AND SHAPE

Tell the dough who's in charge! To provide just the right amount of dampness, mist water on the edges of the dough just before firmly pressing the seams in

FATAYER

place. Use your hands to press hard on the seams, making them stand nice and tall. If the triangles, squares, or little boats don't hold their shape, don't take no for an answer. Push them into place again. Hands of any size can do it.

BAKE AT HIGH HEAT

If your oven has a convection setting, use it! The fan circulates the heat and allows the fatayer to bake and turn golden in less time. Without convection, turn up the heat to 425°F (220°C). The higher temperature results in softer, more tender fatayer in the faster bake time.

EAT IT OFTEN

Fully baked fatayer freeze perfectly, which means more fatayer more often! Pull out a few, heat them up, and there you go. To reheat them, bring the fatayer to room temperature, place them on a baking sheet, and bake at 275°F (140°C) for 5 minutes. They taste great at room temperature, too, and their compactness makes them excellent picnic and travel food.

FATAYER DOUGH

My sister, Peg, and I ate our way through every bakery in Dearborn to discover who makes the best of the best. Lebon Sweets bakery sets the gold standard. So I asked (begged) the owner to show me. "We start early," he said. On the coldest day of the year—which is saying a lot for Michigan!—their fatayer expert, Iyleen, generously taught me her shaping techniques and tricks of the trade. We begin with making the dough, which we'll use in recipes that follow.

PREP: **5 MINUTES**
REST: **30 MINUTES**
TOTAL: **35 MINUTES**
MAKES: **DOUGH FOR 20 TO 24 PIES**

390 grams (3 cups) bread flour
6 grams (2 teaspoons) instant yeast
12 grams (1 tablespoon) granulated white sugar
6 grams (1 teaspoon) fine sea salt
198 grams (¾ cup plus 2 tablespoons) water, warm (105–110°F, 40–43°C)
66 grams (⅓ cup) neutral oil

1. In the large bowl of a stand mixer fitted with the dough hook attachment, add the flour, yeast, sugar, and salt and stir to combine. Add the water and mix on low speed until the water incorporates fully, 30 seconds.
2. Add the oil, increase the speed to medium, and beat until the dough forms, 30 more seconds.
3. Increase the speed to medium-high and knead until the dough becomes soft and smooth, 3 minutes.
4. Cover the bowl with plastic wrap and lay a kitchen towel over that. Let the dough rise for no more than 30 minutes.
5. Use where indicated in the recipes that follow.

CHEESE FATAYER

Known as fatayer bil jibneh, these special cheese pies use techniques that keep the filling in place without it running over the edges and ends of the boats that don't puff and open. Sesame seeds on the edges of the fatayer bil jibneh add even more flavor and beauty. This dish tastes great with a salad of romaine lettuce, tomato, and onion dressed with good extra virgin olive oil, lemon, garlic, and mint. The perfect Lebanese lunch!

PREP: 25 MINUTES
COOK: 18 MINUTES
TOTAL: 43 MINUTES

MAKES: 20 TO 24 PIES
SPECIAL EQUIPMENT: MISTING BOTTLE

50 grams (¼ cup) neutral oil for brushing
3 grams (1 tablespoon) fresh mint
1 clove garlic
226 grams (8 ounces) block mozzarella cheese
28 grams (2 tablespoons) labneh
½ teaspoon fine sea salt
2 grams (1 teaspoon) Dried Mint (page 270)
1 recipe Fatayer Dough (page 199)
18 grams (2 tablespoons) sesame seeds

1. Arrange an oven rack in the upper third of the oven and preheat it on the convection setting to 400°F (200°C) or 425°F (220°C) without convection. Line two baking sheets with parchment paper and generously brush them with some of the oil.

2. Finely chop the fresh mint and mince or grate the garlic. Cut the cheese into large chunks and, in a food processor, grind the chunks until they resemble coarse bread crumbs.

3. In a small mixing bowl, use a soft spatula to stir together the cheese, labneh, salt, dried mint, fresh mint, and garlic. Set aside.

4. Pat the fatayer dough into a rough square and roll it into an 18-inch (46-cm) square, ⅛ inch (3 mm) thick. As you roll, lift the dough off the counter a few times to allow it to spring back before rolling again. Lift the dough before cutting.

5. Use a 3½-inch (10-cm) round cookie cutter or glass to mark 20 discs in the dough, marking the cuts as close together as possible. If you can't get to 20, roll and lift the dough again.

6. Remove the scraps, knead them into a cohesive ball for 1 minute, place the ball in a bowl, and cover it with plastic wrap.

7. Lightly knead the cheese filling into a cohesive ball so that you can pull pieces from it.

8. Fill the center of each dough disc with 7 grams (1 heaping teaspoon) of the filling. Don't let the filling touch the perimeter of the dough.

9. Lightly mist the edges of 3 or 4 discs with water. Pinch together two opposing sides of the dough. Pinch the discs into a boat shape as shown in the photos. Firmly press the filling into the base of the boat so the middle of the pie looks flat and wide. Transfer the raw fatayer to the prepared baking sheets, arranging them, angled, about ½ inch (1.25 cm) apart. Repeat with the rest of the discs, 3 or 4 at a time.

10. Fill a small bowl with the sesame seeds. Mist the ends of a few cheese pies with water. Moisten your fingertips, dip them in the seeds, and press the seeds on the ends of the pies. Repeat with the rest of the fatayer.

11. Generously brush the remaining edges of the pies with oil.
12. Bake until the pies turn golden brown, 9 to 10 minutes with convection or 12 to 14 minutes without.
13. Meanwhile, roll out, fill, shape, and bake the scrap dough as above.
14. Remove the fatayer from the oven, immediately brush the edges again lightly with oil, and serve warm.

Note

Immediately store any leftovers in an airtight container, where they will keep in the refrigerator for up to 5 days or in the freezer for up to 3 months. If frozen, thaw them to room temperature and reheat in a 275°F (140°C) oven for 5 minutes.

TIP: Don't mist all the dough discs at once, otherwise the dough will get soggy. Mist just a few at a time, shape those, then mist the next few.

VARIATION: You can substitute **GREEK YOGURT** for the labneh, but not plain yogurt, which contains too much liquid and runs too thin.

CHEESE FATAYER XL

If you like cheese fatayer (fatayer bil jibneh), this recipe allows you to enjoy even more of it! The filling tastes spicy, but you can adjust the level to your preference. The topping opportunities are endless. Whatever you love on your pizza will taste great here, too. You can cut the pie into wedges, which is perfect for mezze (an appetizer course of small dishes) or a cocktail hour featuring a Mulberry Manhattan (page 215). The recipe makes two pies, so you can invite friends or eat one now and freeze one for later.

PREP: 20 MINUTES
COOK: 18 MINUTES
TOTAL: 38 MINUTES

MAKES: 2 (16-INCH, 43-CM) PIES (8 SERVINGS)
SPECIAL EQUIPMENT: MISTING BOTTLE

---

25 grams (2 tablespoons) neutral oil for brushing
1 clove garlic
282 grams (10 ounces) block mozzarella cheese
42 grams (3 tablespoons) labneh
½ teaspoon fine sea salt
1 recipe Fatayer Dough (page 199)
6 grams (2 teaspoons) nigella seeds
9 grams (1 tablespoon) sesame seeds
¼ teaspoon red pepper flakes

1. Arrange an oven rack in the middle position and preheat it on the convection setting to 400°F (200°C) or 425°F (220°C) without convection. Line two baking sheets with parchment paper and lightly brush them with oil.

2. Mince or grate the garlic. Set aside. Cut the cheese into large chunks and, in a food processor, grind the chunks until they resemble coarse bread crumbs.

3. In a small mixing bowl, use a soft spatula to stir together the cheese, labneh, salt, and garlic. Set aside.

4. Halve the fatayer dough. Pat one of the halves into a rough oval and roll it into a 17-by-6-inch (43-by-15-cm) oval. As you roll, lift the dough off the counter a few times to allow it to spring back before rolling again. Transfer to one of the prepared baking sheets.

5. Evenly spread half of the filling on the dough, leaving a 1-inch (2.5-cm) border around the perimeter.

6. In a small bowl, combine the nigella seeds and sesame seeds.

7. Onto the filling, sprinkle ⅛ teaspoon of the red pepper flakes and 3 grams (1 teaspoon) of the nigella–sesame seed mixture.

8. Mist the edges of the two short ends of the dough with water. At one short end, lift the sides of the dough over the filling and firmly pinch them together to make a 3-inch (8-cm) seam. Repeat at the opposite end.

9. Fold the long sides of the dough over the filling by 1 inch (2.5 cm). Every few inches, pinch and crimp the edges all the way around.

10. Mist the two pinched ends of the fatayer with water. Moisten your fingertips, dip them in the seeds, and press the seeds on the ends of the pie.

11. Generously brush the remaining edges of the pie with oil.

12. Bake until the pie turns golden brown, 9 to 10 minutes with convection or 14 to 16 minutes without.

13. While the first fatayer bakes, repeat steps 4 through 11 with the remaining half of dough.

14. Remove the fatayer from the oven, immediately brush the edges lightly with oil, cut it into wedges, and serve hot. Follow step 12 for the second fatayer.

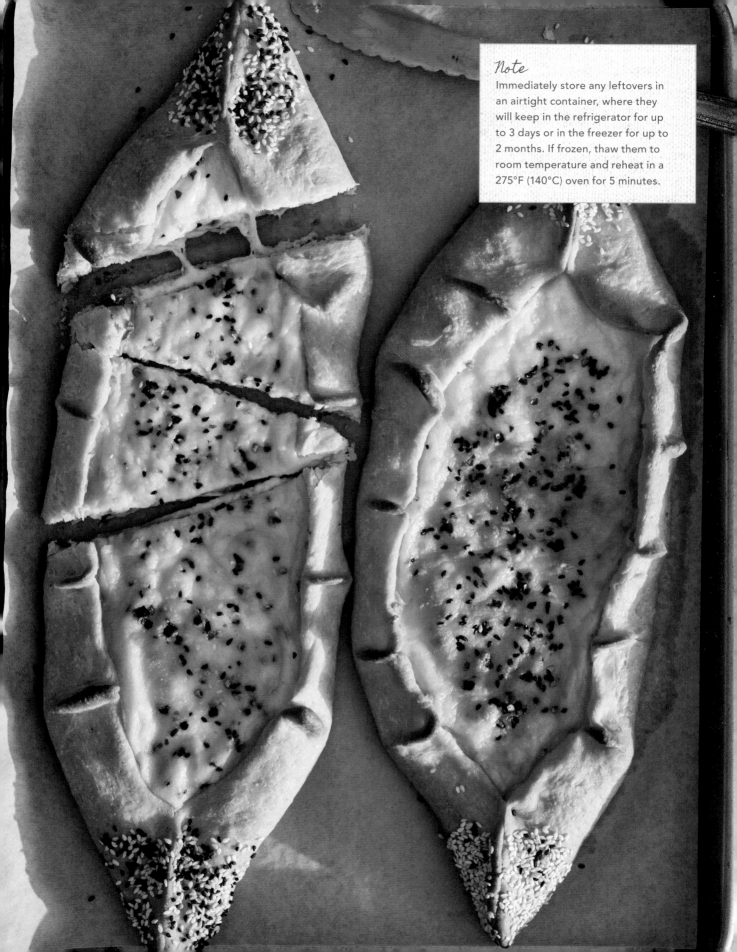

Note
Immediately store any leftovers in an airtight container, where they will keep in the refrigerator for up to 3 days or in the freezer for up to 2 months. If frozen, thaw them to room temperature and reheat in a 275°F (140°C) oven for 5 minutes.

SFEHA

At a lunch in Ba'albek, Lebanon, our host placed four of these pies, called Ba'albek sfeha, next to my plate. My hand instinctively shot up to say, *Whoa, too many.* She nodded to reply, *You'll eat them*—and I did, every last one, plus more! The dough absorbs so much flavor from the filling that you probably won't be able to stop at two . . . or four.

PREP: 25 MINUTES
COOK: 21 MINUTES
TOTAL: 46 MINUTES

MAKES: 24 PIES (12 SERVINGS)
SPECIAL EQUIPMENT: MISTING BOTTLE

25 grams (2 tablespoons) neutral oil
339 grams (¾ pound) ground lamb or beef (90% lean)
21 grams (1 tablespoon) pomegranate molasses
5 grams (2 teaspoons) tahini
¼ teaspoon ground cinnamon
6 grams (1 teaspoon) fine sea salt
⅛ teaspoon ground black pepper
47 grams (⅓ cup) sweet onion
1 recipe Fatayer Dough (page 199)
15 grams (2 tablespoons) toasted pine nuts

1. Arrange an oven rack in the upper third of the oven and preheat it on the convection setting to 400°F (200°C) or 425°F (220°C) without convection. Line two baking sheets with parchment paper and brush them with some of the oil.

2. In a medium sauté pan over medium heat, use a wooden spoon to break up the meat. Add the pomegranate molasses, tahini, cinnamon, salt, and pepper and stir to combine. Cook just until the meat lightly browns, 3 minutes.

3. Meanwhile, finely chop the onion.

4. Drain the liquid from the pan, transfer the meat mixture to a medium mixing bowl, and stir in the onion.

5. Pat the dough into a rough square and roll it into an 18-inch (46-cm) square, ⅛ inch (3 mm) thick. As you roll, lift the dough off the counter a few times to allow it to spring back before rolling again. Lift the dough before cutting.

6. Use a 3½-inch (9-cm) round cookie cutter or glass to mark 20 discs in the dough, marking the cuts as close together as possible. If you can't get to 20, roll and lift the dough again.

7. Remove the scraps, knead them into a cohesive ball for 1 minute, place the ball in a bowl, and cover it with plastic wrap.

8. Fill the center of each dough circle with 14 grams (1 scant tablespoon) of the filling. Don't let the filling touch the perimeter of the dough. Top the meat mixture with a few pine nuts.

9. Lightly mist the edges of 3 or 4 discs with water. Pinch together two opposing sides of the dough, followed by the other two opposing sides, to form a small square packet, as in the photos. Leave a small opening (½-inch, 1.25-cm) in the center of the four seams. Transfer the raw fatayer to the prepared baking sheet, placing them ½ inch (1.25 cm) apart. Repeat this process with the rest of the dough.

10. Lightly brush all the sfeha with oil.

11. Bake until the pies turn golden brown, 9 to 10 minutes with convection or 12 to 14 minutes without.

12. Meanwhile, roll out, fill, shape, and bake the scrap dough as above.

13. Remove the sfeha from the oven, immediately brush them lightly with oil, and serve warm.

FATAYER

Note

Immediately store any leftovers in an airtight container, where they will keep in the refrigerator for up to 5 days or in the freezer for up to 2 months. If frozen, thaw them to room temperature and reheat in a 275°F (140°C) oven for 5 minutes.

TIP: Don't mist all the dough discs at once, otherwise the dough will get soggy. Mist just a few at a time, shape those, then mist the next few.

VARIATIONS: Sfeha filling typically achieves balance with an acidic or tart element. Try substituting **TOMATO PASTE** for the pomegranate molasses, and **ALLSPICE** or **BAHARAT** (Lebanese seven spice) for the ground cinnamon.

SPINACH FATAYER

This fatayer holds a special place in Lebanese baking and in our family, too. My aunt Peggy Shaker makes the finest spinach fatayer that I ever have eaten. As a teenager, I asked for her recipe, which had an extensive ingredients list: lots of fresh herbs and spices along with (surprise!) toasted walnuts in lieu of the typical pine nuts. It doesn't surprise me that Aunt Peg—the quintessential methodical, talented craftswoman—never minded all that chopping. On a recent visit, Aunt Peg at age 94 presented a stash of her spinach fatayer ready for us to eat. My heroine.

PREP: 25 MINUTES
COOK: 18 MINUTES
TOTAL: 43 MINUTES

MAKES: 20 TO 24 PIES
SPECIAL EQUIPMENT: MISTING BOTTLE

25 grams (2 tablespoons) neutral oil
42 grams (⅓ cup) toasted walnuts (see page 266)
5 grams (2 tablespoons) fresh mint leaves
5 grams (2 tablespoons) flat leaf parsley
2 scallions (16 grams)
35 grams (¼ cup) yellow onion
226 grams (8 ounces) frozen chopped spinach, thawed
28 grams (2 tablespoons) fresh lemon juice from 1 lemon
25 grams (2 tablespoons) extra virgin olive oil
6 grams (1 teaspoon) fine sea salt
¼ teaspoon black pepper
¼ teaspoon allspice
¼ teaspoon sumac
1 recipe Fatayer Dough (page 199)

1. Arrange an oven rack in the upper third of the oven and preheat it on the convection setting to 400°F (200°C) or 425°F (220°C) without convection. Line a baking sheet with parchment paper and generously brush it with some of the neutral oil.

2. Coarsely chop the walnuts and finely chop the mint, parsley, scallions, and onion.

3. In a fine mesh colander set in the sink, drain the spinach. Squeeze it hard to remove as much liquid as possible. Add the lemon juice and olive oil, rubbing by hand to combine them. Squeeze the spinach again.

4. In a medium mixing bowl, fluff the spinach with a fork. Add the walnuts, mint, parsley, scallions, onion, salt, pepper, allspice, and sumac. Stir to combine.

5. Pat the dough into a rough square and roll it into an 18-inch (51-cm) square, ⅛ inch (3 mm) thick. As you roll, lift the dough off the counter a few times to allow it to spring back before rolling again. Lift the dough before cutting.

6. Use a 3½-inch (9-cm) round cookie cutter or glass to mark 20 discs in the dough, marking the cuts as close together as possible. If you can't get to 20, roll and lift the dough again.

7. Remove the scraps, knead them into a cohesive ball for 1 minute, place the ball in a bowl, and cover it with plastic wrap.

8. Fill the center of each dough disc with 8 grams (1 heaping tablespoon) of the filling. Pack the filling into the spoon to ball it together and to keep the filling from touching the perimeter of the dough.

9. Lightly mist the edges of 3 or 4 discs with water. Pinch the discs into a triangle by bringing together three opposing sides of the disc and pinching three seams closed, as shown in the photos on page 209. Transfer the raw fatayer to the prepared baking

sheet, arranging them about ½ inch (1.25 cm) apart. Repeat with the rest of the discs, 3 or 4 at a time.

10. Generously brush all the fatayer with neutral oil.
11. Bake until the pies turn golden brown, 9 to 10 minutes with convection or 12 to 14 minutes without.
12. Meanwhile, roll out, fill, shape, and bake the scrap dough as above.
13. Remove the fatayer from the oven, immediately brush them again lightly with neutral oil, and serve warm.

Notes
- Adding lemon juice and olive oil to the spinach and then squeezing them out adds flavor and richness while keeping the fatayer as dry as possible.
- Immediately store any leftovers in an airtight container, where they will keep in the refrigerator for up to 5 days or in the freezer for up to 3 months. If frozen, thaw them to room temperature and reheat in a 275°F (140°C) oven for 5 minutes.

TIPS
- The spinach filling can adhere to the dough, your hands, and the countertop. Keep a kitchen towel or paper towels nearby to wipe hands and surfaces as you work.
- Don't mist all the dough discs at once, otherwise the dough will get soggy. Mist just a few at a time, shape those, then mist the next few.

VARIATION: The bakers in my extended family make **FATAYER TRIANGLES** with meat filling rather than as sfeha squares. To do that, use the meat filling for Sfeha (page 204) and follow the shaping method for fatayer.

KALE AND FETA FATAYER

The wonderful complex flavor of kale with briny feta cheese gives the original Spinach Fatayer (page 206) a run for its money! Use baby kale for its softer texture and flavor rather than curly kale or dinosaur kale. Most Middle Eastern markets sell Bulgarian feta cheese, which tastes irresistibly creamy and rich and pairs excellently with the kale.

PREP: 25 MINUTES
COOK: 18 MINUTES
TOTAL: 43 MINUTES

MAKES: 20 TO 24 PIES
SPECIAL EQUIPMENT: MISTING BOTTLE

25 grams (2 tablespoons) neutral oil
142 grams (5 ounces) baby kale
2 scallions (16 grams)
5 grams (2 tablespoons) fresh mint leaves
200 grams (7 ounces) block feta cheese
5 grams (2 teaspoons) sumac
½ teaspoon fine sea salt, if needed
1 recipe Fatayer Dough (page 199)

1. Arrange an oven rack in the upper third of the oven and preheat it on the convection setting to 400°F (200°C) or 425°F (220°C) without convection. Line a baking sheet with parchment paper and generously brush it with some of the oil.

2. Finely chop the kale, scallions, and mint. Crumble the feta cheese.

3. In a medium mixing bowl, fluff the kale and feta with a fork. Add the scallions, mint, and sumac. Stir to combine. Taste, add the salt if needed, and stir to combine.

4. Pat the dough into a rough square and roll it into an 18-inch (46-cm) square, ⅛ inch (3 mm) thick. As you roll, lift the dough off the counter a few times to allow it to spring back before rolling again. Lift the dough before cutting.

5. Use a 3½-inch (9-cm) round cookie cutter or glass to mark 20 discs in the dough, marking the cuts as close together as possible. If you can't get to 20, roll and lift the dough again.

6. Remove the scraps, knead them into a cohesive ball for 1 minute, place the ball in a bowl, and cover it with plastic wrap.

7. Fill the center of each dough disc with 8 grams (1 heaping tablespoon) of the filling. Pack the filling into the spoon to ball it together and to keep the filling from touching the perimeter of the dough.

8. Lightly mist the edges of 3 or 4 discs with water. Pinch the discs into a triangle by bringing together three opposing sides of the disc and pinching three seams closed, as shown on the opposite page. Transfer the raw fatayer to the prepared baking sheet, arranging them about ½ inch (1.25 cm) apart. Repeat with the rest of the discs, 3 or 4 at a time.

9. Generously brush all the fatayer with oil.

10. Bake until the pies turn golden brown, 9 to 10 minutes with convection or 14 to 16 minutes without.

11. Meanwhile, roll out, fill, shape, and bake the scrap dough as above.

12. Remove the fatayer from the oven, immediately brush them again lightly with oil, and serve warm.

FATAYER

Note
Immediately store any leftovers in an airtight container in the refrigerator, where they will keep for up to 5 days or in the freezer for up to 3 months. If frozen, thaw them to room temperature and reheat in a 275°F (140°C) oven for 5 minutes.

TIP: Don't mist all the dough discs at once, otherwise the dough will get soggy. Mist just a few at a time, shape those, then mist the next few.

KOUSA FATAYER

We Lebanese love to hollow kousa—a pale green summer squash sometimes called gray squash or Mexican squash—stuff it with rice and meat, and cook it in tomato sauce. Similar to zucchini, kousa makes a delicious filling for fatayer. With a characteristic Lebanese entrepreneurial spirit, Kameel Chamelly, owner of Martha's Vineyard market in Grand Rapids, Michigan, has created a mecca for gourmet food and wine while putting a distinctly Lebanese spin on some of the foods prepared there. That's where I first tasted this delectable version of fatayer.

PREP: 30 MINUTES
COOK: 18 MINUTES
TOTAL: 48 MINUTES

MAKES: 20 TO 24 FATAYER
SPECIAL EQUIPMENT: MISTING BOTTLE

25 grams (2 tablespoons) neutral oil
3 medium (140 grams) kousa
6 grams (1 teaspoon) fine sea salt
14 grams (1 tablespoon) fresh lemon juice
35 grams (¼ cup) yellow onion
8 grams (1 tablespoon) sumac
¼ teaspoon black pepper
1 recipe Fatayer Dough (page 199)

1. Arrange an oven rack in the upper third of the oven and preheat it on the convection setting to 400°F (200°C) or standard 425°F (220°C). Line a baking sheet with parchment paper and brush it generously with some of the oil.

2. Roughly chop the kousa and, in a food processor, pulse the pieces until finely shredded.

3. In a fine mesh colander set in the sink, combine the kousa, salt, and lemon juice. Let the mixture sit for 5 minutes, then squeeze it several times to remove as much liquid as possible.

4. Finely chop the onion.

5. In a medium mixing bowl, combine the kousa, onion, sumac, and black pepper.

6. Pat the dough into a rough square and roll it into an 18-inch (46-cm) square, ⅛ inch (3 mm) thick. As you roll, lift the dough off the counter a few times to allow it to spring back before rolling again. Lift the dough before cutting.

7. Use a 3.5-inch (9-cm) round cookie cutter or glass to mark 20 discs in the dough, marking the cuts as close together as possible. If you can't get to 20, roll and lift the dough again.

8. Remove the scraps, knead them into a cohesive ball for 1 minute, place the ball in a bowl, and cover it with plastic wrap.

9. Fill the center of each dough disc with 8 grams (1 heaping tablespoon) of the filling. Pack the filling into the spoon to ball it together and to keep the filling from touching the perimeter of the dough.

10. Lightly mist the edges of 3 or 4 discs with water. Pinch the discs into a triangle by bringing together three opposing sides of the disc and pinching three seams closed, as shown in the Kale and Feta Fatayer photos (page 209). Transfer the raw fatayer to the prepared baking sheet, arranging them about ½ inch (1.25 cm) apart. Repeat with the rest of the discs, 3 or 4 at a time.

11. Generously brush all the fatayer with oil.

12. Bake until the pies turn golden brown, 9 to 10 minutes with convection or 14 to 16 minutes without.

13. Meanwhile, roll out, fill, shape, and bake the scrap dough as above.

14. Remove the fatayer from the oven, immediately brush them again lightly with oil, and serve warm.

Note

Immediately store any leftovers in an airtight container in the refrigerator, where they will keep for up to 5 days or in the freezer for up to 3 months. If frozen, thaw to room temperature and reheat in a 275°F (140°C) oven for 5 minutes.

TIP: Don't mist all the dough discs at once, otherwise the dough will get soggy. Mist just a few at a time, shape those, then mist the next few.

VARIATION: GREEN or **YELLOW ZUCCHINI** makes a fine substitute for kousa.

SAMBOUSEK

The dough of this fried fatayer resembles that of piecrust, with no yeast. You can crimp it in lots of fancy ways, but any seal that keeps the shape closed during frying will do. These turnovers have a crispy crust that gives way to a moist, tender, seasoned meat filling studded with pine nuts. These make a delicious appetizer with a cocktail, especially a Mulberry Manhattan (page 215).

PREP: **35 MINUTES**
COOK: **25 MINUTES**
TOTAL: **1 HOUR**

MAKES: **20 PIES**
SPECIAL EQUIPMENT: **MISTING BOTTLE**

FILLING
35 grams (¼ cup) sweet onion
226 grams (½ pound) ground beef or lamb (90% lean)
28 grams (2 tablespoons) labneh or Greek yogurt
21 grams (1 tablespoon) pomegranate molasses
5 grams (2 teaspoons) tahini
¼ teaspoon ground cinnamon
½ teaspoon fine sea salt
⅛ teaspoon ground black pepper
15 grams (2 tablespoons) toasted pine nuts

DOUGH
2 grams (1 teaspoon) cornstarch
113 grams (½ cup) water, warm (105–110°F, 40–43°C)
240 grams (2 cups) unbleached all-purpose flour
6 grams (1 teaspoon) fine sea salt
66 grams (⅓ cup) neutral oil
Neutral oil for frying

1. Make the filling. Finely chop the onion.
2. In a medium mixing bowl, use a large spoon to break up the meat. Add the labneh, onion, pomegranate molasses, tahini, cinnamon, salt, and pepper and stir to combine thoroughly. Set aside.
3. Make the dough. In a liquid measuring cup or small mixing bowl, dissolve the cornstarch in the water.
4. In a medium mixing bowl, whisk together the flour and salt. Add the cornstarch water and stir until fully incorporated, 30 seconds.
5. Add the oil and, with your hands, work the mixture until shaggy, 30 more seconds.
6. Ball the dough and knead it until soft and smooth, 2 minutes. Cover the dough with plastic wrap and let it rest for 10 minutes.
7. Halve the dough.
8. On a lightly floured surface, roll one of the halves to ⅛ inch (3 mm) thick, lifting the dough and dusting it with more flour to prevent it from sticking to the counter when rolling.
9. With a 3-inch (7.5-cm) round cookie cutter or glass, cut 10 discs from the dough.
10. Remove the scraps and knead them until cohesive, 1 minute. Cover them with plastic wrap and set them aside to rest while you shape the sambousek.
11. Into the center of each disc, spoon 14 grams (1 tablespoon) of the meat mixture. Don't let the meat touch the perimeter of the dough. Top the meat mixture with a few pine nuts.
12. Lightly mist the edges of the dough with water. Fold the discs in half to form half-moons. Rope-crimp the edges or use the tines of a fork to seal the dough. Transfer the raw sambousek to an unlined baking sheet.
13. Repeat steps 8 to 12 with the rest of the dough and filling.
14. Line another baking sheet with paper towels and set it next to the stove. Set a large saucepan over medium heat, fill it 2 inches (5 cm) deep with oil, and heat it to 350°F (177°C).

continues

15. Use a spider skimmer or slotted spoon to lower 3 or 4 sambousek carefully into the hot oil. To ensure even frying, don't fry more than that many at a time. Fry until the bottoms turn golden brown, about 3 minutes.

16. Use heatproof tongs to flip them over and continue frying until they turn golden all over, 2 more minutes.

17. Use the tongs or the slotted spoon to transfer the fried sambousek to the paper towel–lined baking sheet. Wait until the oil returns to 350°F (177°C) and repeat with the rest of the sambousek.

18. Let the sambousek cool for 3 minutes and serve hot.

> *Notes*
> - Sambousek taste best immediately after frying.
> - You can store leftovers in an airtight container in the refrigerator for up to 3 days or in the freezer for up to 3 months. If frozen, thaw them to room temperature and reheat in a 275°F (140°C) oven for 5 minutes.
>
> **VARIATIONS**
> - For an excellent **VEGETARIAN VERSION**, use the filling from Cheese Fatayer (page 200) and omit the sesame seeds.
> - **FIG CRESCENTS** (page 119), when filled with nuts, are a cookie version of sambousek.

Something to Drink

MULBERRY MANHATTAN

It's worth ordering mulberry syrup—made from the abundant crop in Lebanon and available widely there, at specialty markets, or online—to make this rich, royal beauty of a cocktail designed by my sister, as pictured on page 212. You *can* substitute muddled blackberries, but then you won't have a Mulberry Manhattan!

PREP: **30 SECONDS**
TOTAL: **30 SECONDS**
MAKES: **1 COCKTAIL**

44 grams (2 ounces) bourbon or rye
11 grams (1 ounce) sweet vermouth
4 grams (1 barspoon) mulberry syrup
2 dashes orange bitters
Lemon or orange peel (7.5 cm, 3 inches) for garnish

1. In a mixing glass filled halfway with ice, combine all the ingredients except the citrus peel and stir vigorously with the barspoon or another long-handled spoon for 30 seconds.
2. Strain the cocktail into a chilled coupe or rocks glass.
3. Express the citrus peel, skin side down, on the cocktail, run the skin around the rim of the glass to distribute the citrus oils, and add the peel, skin side up, to the glass and serve.

Savory Yeast Breads

This chapter presents an exciting array of traditional and inventive yeast breads. We begin with manakeesh, flatbreads made with various toppings. The Lebanese breakfast table often features za'atar manakeesh plus fresh tomato, sweet onion, fresh mint, cucumber, and labneh to enjoy with every bite. Manakeesh may remind us of pizza, but let's not call them that! In this chapter, you also will learn how to make pita and how to put it to delicious use. At the end of the chapter lies a triumphant trifecta of savory baking projects: talami bread, saj bread, and za'atar croissants. The results will dazzle you!

Secrets to Making Manakeesh

USE A STICKY DOUGH
Flatbreads like this call for plenty of hydration in the dough to allow for a thin, chewy crust. Use a stand mixer to achieve the right consistency.

KEEP IT MOVING
Lightly dust the dough with flour, underneath and on top, as you roll. Every few rolls, lift the dough from the counter, flip it over, and continue rolling to achieve an even circle.

ROLL IT THIN
You want dough less than 1/8 inch (3 mm) thick, consistently from the center to the edges, in a 9-inch (23-cm) circle. When baked, the dough will shrink by about 1 inch (2.5 cm) to make 8-inch (20-cm) manakeesh.

DOCK THE DOUGH
Poking small holes in the rolled dough allows air to flow through the bread as it bakes, preventing large bubbles or a pita pocket from forming. Use a docker or fork to prick the top of the rolled dough liberally with tiny holes.

BAKE ON A STEEL OR STONE
Sitto used a baking steel fitted to her oven. It's my favorite option because one of those usually fits the full size of the oven rack, allowing for more wiggle room and for baking more than one man'oushe at a time. It also imparts exceptional heat distribution. A pizza stone also performs well for manakeesh (man'oushe = singular; manakeesh = plural), holding lots of heat to bake the flatbreads quickly without drying them out. As a workable alternative, use a dark, heavy-gauge baking sheet flipped upside down.

USE A BREAD PEEL DUSTED WITH FLOUR
The peel makes baking manakeesh a breeze. A light dusting of flour allows the dough to slide into the hot oven with ease. Once the dough is on the peel, work quickly to top it, though. The longer the dough rests, the more it will stick to the peel.

WATCH THE SHOW!
Turn on the oven light so you can watch the manakeesh bake to a bubbling, golden brown.

DRESS THEM UP
Trimmings make the meal. Scatter sliced cucumbers, labneh, freshly torn mint leaves, sliced sweet onion, sliced tomatoes, toum (garlic aioli), or your favorite toppings on your baked man'oushe. Fold it in half and enjoy!

MANAKEESH DOUGH

Manakeesh anchor the Lebanese breakfast experience and elevate appetizers and snacking to a new level of greatness. You can enjoy a man'oushe with any of the toppings listed in the following recipes, cut in slices or wrapped in a piece of paper, on the run. It tastes chewy and soft, often with charred edges from a traditional wood-fired oven, an effect you can achieve with a baking stone or steel in a standard oven at high temperatures.

PREP: 15 MINUTES
REST: 1 HOUR 30 MINUTES
TOTAL: 1 HOUR 45 MINUTES

MAKES: DOUGH FOR 4 FLATBREADS

- 248 grams (2 cups plus 1 tablespoon) bread flour, plus more as needed
- 5 grams (1½ teaspoons) instant yeast
- 4 grams (1 teaspoon) granulated white sugar
- 12 grams (2 teaspoons) fine sea salt
- 170 grams (¾ cup) water, warm (105–110°F, 40–43°C)
- 4 grams (1 teaspoon) extra virgin olive oil

1. In the large bowl of a stand mixer, add the flour, yeast, sugar, and salt and stir to combine with a wooden spoon or the dough hook (not attached). Slowly add the water and mix until a shaggy dough forms, 1 minute.
2. Attach the dough hook, set the mixer speed to medium-high, and knead the dough until smooth and slightly sticky, 3 minutes.
3. Coat a medium mixing bowl with the oil. Ball the dough, transfer it to the prepared bowl, and flip the dough to coat it completely with oil. Cover the bowl with plastic wrap and lay a kitchen towel over that. Let the dough rise until it almost doubles in size, 45 minutes.
4. Quarter the dough and ball the quarters (as pictured on page 219).
5. On the counter, place the balls 3 inches (7.5 cm) apart, cover them with plastic wrap, and lay a kitchen towel over that. Let them rise again until they almost double in size, 45 more minutes.
6. Use where indicated in the recipes that follow.

> *Note*
> To store the dough, wrap the balls individually in plastic wrap and refrigerate them for up to 8 hours or freeze them for up to 1 month. When ready to use, thaw them for about 4 hours in the refrigerator, bring them to room temperature, and use as indicated.

ZA'ATAR MANAKEESH

This dish, also known simply as za'atar, reigns as the king of manakeesh, delivering an herby za'atar blend of thyme, sumac, and sesame seeds in robust olive oil atop the thin crust. When each man'oushe first exits the oven, the za'atar topping may seem too oily, but within minutes it will set to look and taste just right. If your za'atar blend contains salt, omit the additional salt.

PREP: 23 MINUTES
COOK: 12 MINUTES
TOTAL: 35 MINUTES

MAKES: 4 (8-INCH, 20-CM) FLATBREADS
SPECIAL EQUIPMENT: PIZZA STONE OR BAKING STEEL, BREAD PEEL

TOPPING
24 grams (4 tablespoons) za'atar
63 grams (¼ cup plus 1 tablespoon) extra virgin olive oil
¼ teaspoon fine sea salt (optional)

DOUGH
30 grams (¼ cup) bread flour or unbleached all-purpose flour for shaping
1 recipe Manakeesh Dough (page 221)

1. Arrange an oven rack in the lowest position and remove any other racks. Place the baking steel, baking stone, or an overturned dark, heavy baking sheet on the rack. Preheat the oven to 550°F (288°C) or its highest temperature.
2. In a small mixing bowl, combine the za'atar, olive oil, and salt, if using. Set aside.
3. Lightly dust the center of the bread peel with a pinch of flour and place it next to your work area.
4. Dust the counter with the flour, place a dough ball on it, and dust the top with flour. Pat down the dough and roll it into a 9-inch (23-cm) circle, maintaining an even thickness. As you roll, stop to lift the dough and rotate it to roll an even circle and to prevent it from sticking to the counter. Dock the dough with a fork or docker, pricking the top all over.
5. Transfer the dough to the prepared peel. Spoon a quarter (22 grams) of the za'atar oil on the center of the dough. Use the back of the spoon or an offset spatula to coat the dough evenly, leaving a ⅛-inch (3-mm) border around the perimeter. Some spots will have more za'atar than others.
6. Shake the peel to ensure that the dough moves easily. If any spot sticks to the peel, lift the dough and dust more flour underneath it.
7. Transfer the dough from the peel to the baking surface in the oven. Bake until the edges turn golden brown and slightly char in spots, 3 to 4 minutes. If needed, use heatproof tongs to turn the bread for even browning.
8. Use tongs to transfer the bread back to the peel. Let the bread cool on a cutting board for at least 3 minutes.
9. Repeat with the remaining dough balls.
10. To serve, quarter each man'oushe with a pizza wheel or chef's knife or fold it in half and wrap it in wax paper to eat on the go.

Note

In a sealable plastic storage bag, store the manakeesh in the refrigerator for up to 2 days or frozen for up to 3 months. To reheat, thaw if frozen and warm in a 250°F (120°C) oven for 10 minutes.

TIP: Enjoy this man'oushe with cool, creamy labneh and fresh mint for one of the finest flavor and texture pairings you can imagine.

VARIATION: For equally traditional ZA'ATAR CHEESE MANAKEESH, use a quarter of the topping from the recipe for Cheese Manakeesh (page 226) for each man'oushe, adding it halfway through baking.

LABNEH MINT MANAKEESH

The combination of labneh and mint creates a harmonious, cuisine-defining flavor. When stirred into the creamy, thick labneh, dried mint packs more punch than fresh. Add the labneh mixture *after* baking the manakeesh for the freshest flavor and creamiest texture. (See page 224.)

PREP: **30 MINUTES**
COOK: **12 MINUTES**
TOTAL: **42 MINUTES**

MAKES: **4 (8-INCH, 20-CM) FLATBREADS**
SPECIAL EQUIPMENT: **PIZZA STONE OR BAKING STEEL, BREAD PEEL**

TOPPING
1 clove garlic
¼ small sweet onion (9 grams, 1 tablespoon)
114 grams (½ cup) labneh
2 grams (2 teaspoons) Dried Mint, crushed (page 270)
¼ teaspoon fine sea salt
10 fresh mint leaves (3 grams)
12 grams (1 tablespoon) extra virgin olive oil, plus more for finishing

DOUGH
30 grams (¼ cup) bread flour or unbleached all-purpose flour for shaping
1 recipe Manakeesh Dough (page 221)

1. Arrange an oven rack in the lowest position and remove any other racks. Place the baking steel, baking stone, or an overturned dark, heavy baking sheet on the rack. Preheat the oven to 550°F (288°C) or its highest temperature.

2. Into a medium mixing bowl, grate the garlic and onion. Add the labneh, dried mint, and salt and stir until smooth.

3. Finely chop the fresh mint and set aside.

4. Lightly dust the center of the bread peel with a pinch of the flour.

5. Dust the counter with the flour, place a dough ball on it, and dust the top with flour. Pat down the dough and roll it into a 9-inch (23-cm) circle, maintaining an even thickness. As you roll, lift the dough and rotate it to prevent it from sticking. Prick the dough with a fork or docker all over.

6. Transfer the dough to the prepared peel. Lightly brush the top of the dough with 3 grams (1 teaspoon) of the oil.

7. Shake the peel to ensure that the dough moves easily. If any spot sticks to the peel, lift the dough and dust more flour underneath it.

8. Transfer the dough from the peel to the hot baking surface in the oven. Bake until the edges turn golden brown and slightly char in spots, 3 to 4 minutes. If needed, use heatproof tongs to turn the bread for even browning.

9. Use tongs to transfer the bread back to the peel. Let the bread cool on a cutting board for at least 3 minutes.

10. Spread a quarter (30 grams, 2 tablespoons) of the labneh mixture evenly over the bread. Sprinkle it with a quarter of the chopped mint and lightly drizzle it with olive oil.

11. Repeat with the remaining dough balls.

12. To serve, quarter each man'oushe with a pizza wheel or chef's knife or fold it in half and wrap it in wax paper to eat on the go.

Note
In a sealable plastic storage bag, store the manakeesh in the refrigerator for up to 2 days or frozen for up to 3 months. To reheat, thaw if frozen and warm in a 250°F (120°C) oven for 10 minutes.

CHEESE MANAKEESH

The cheese mixture in this mouthwatering bread, as seen on page 224, comes together so easily and tastes so deliciously seasoned. Consider adding it to your Za'atar Manakeesh (page 222) for two great tastes in one fantastic man'oushe.

PREP: 25 MINUTES
COOK: 12 MINUTES
TOTAL: 37 MINUTES

MAKES: 4 (8-INCH, 20-CM) FLATBREADS
SPECIAL EQUIPMENT: PIZZA STONE OR BAKING STEEL, BREAD PEEL

TOPPING

2 cloves garlic
9 grams (1 tablespoon) sweet onion
226 grams (1 cup) shredded mozzarella cheese
25 grams (2 tablespoons) extra virgin olive oil
3 grams (1 tablespoon) Dried Mint, crushed (page 270)
10 fresh mint leaves (3 grams)

DOUGH

30 grams (¼ cup) bread flour or unbleached all-purpose flour for shaping
1 recipe Manakeesh Dough (page 221)

1. Arrange an oven rack in the lowest position and remove any other racks. Place the baking steel, baking stone, or an overturned dark, heavy baking sheet on the rack. Preheat the oven to 550°F (288°C) or its highest temperature.
2. Into a medium mixing bowl, grate the garlic and onion. Add the cheese, olive oil, and dried mint.
3. Finely chop the fresh mint and set aside for garnishing.
4. Lightly dust the center of the bread peel with a pinch of the flour and place it next to your work area.
5. Dust the counter with the flour, place a dough ball on it, and dust the top with flour. Pat down the dough and roll it into a 9-inch (23-cm) circle, maintaining an even thickness. As you roll, stop to lift the dough and rotate it to roll an even circle and to prevent it from sticking to the counter. Dock the dough with a fork or docker, pricking the top all over.
6. Transfer the dough to the prepared peel. Evenly scatter a quarter (65 grams, ¼ cup) of the cheese mixture on the dough, leaving a ⅛-inch (3-mm) border around the perimeter. Use the back of the spoon or an offset spatula to coat the dough evenly and press the mixture into it.
7. Shake the peel to ensure that the dough moves easily. If any spot sticks to the peel, lift the dough and dust more flour underneath it.
8. Transfer the dough from the peel to the hot baking surface in the oven. Bake until the edges turn golden brown and slightly char in spots, 3 to 4 minutes. If needed, use heatproof tongs to turn the bread for even browning.
9. Use tongs to transfer the bread back to the peel. Let the bread cool on a cutting board for at least 3 minutes. Sprinkle it with a quarter of the chopped mint.
10. Repeat with the remaining dough balls.
11. To serve, quarter each man'oushe with a pizza wheel or chef's knife or fold it in half and wrap it in wax paper to eat on the go.

Note
In a sealable plastic storage bag, store the manakeesh in the refrigerator for up to 2 days or frozen for up to 3 months. To reheat, thaw if frozen and warm in a 250°F (120°C) oven for 10 minutes.

MUHAMMARA MANAKEESH

Scooped up in torn pieces of bread, the much-loved red bell pepper dip made with walnuts and pomegranate molasses serves as a staple of Lebanese mezze. This dish fuses that must-have combo to the bread, and the muhammara's juicy flavors penetrate the dough, so soft and so good. In Dearborn, my sister handed me a man'oushe topped with muhammara. Neither of us had eaten manakeesh this way, and after one bite, there was no going back. "You've got to figure this one out," she said. "Immediately," I replied. (See page 224.)

PREP: 26 MINUTES
COOK: 12 MINUTES
TOTAL: 38 MINUTES

MAKES: 4 (8-INCH, 20-CM) FLATBREADS
SPECIAL EQUIPMENT: PIZZA STONE OR BAKING STEEL, BREAD PEEL

TOPPING
1 roasted red bell pepper (85 grams)
32 grams (¼ cup) toasted walnuts (see page 266)
7 grams (1 teaspoon) pomegranate molasses
6 grams (2 tablespoons) panko bread crumbs
12 grams (1 tablespoon) extra virgin olive oil
9 grams (2 teaspoons) fresh lemon juice
1 clove garlic
¼ teaspoon fine sea salt
¼ teaspoon paprika
¼ teaspoon cumin
¼ teaspoon red pepper flakes
⅛ teaspoon black pepper
10 fresh mint leaves (3 grams)

DOUGH
30 grams (¼ cup) bread flour or unbleached all-purpose flour for shaping
1 recipe Manakeesh Dough (page 221)

1. Arrange an oven rack in the lowest position and remove any other racks. Place the baking steel, baking stone, or an overturned dark, heavy baking sheet on the rack. Preheat the oven to 550°F (288°C) or its highest temperature.

2. In a small food processor, puree the red bell pepper and walnuts until smooth. Add the pomegranate molasses, panko, olive oil, lemon juice, garlic, salt, paprika, cumin, red pepper flakes, and pepper and process until smooth. Turn off the processor and scrape down the sides of the bowl once as you puree. Transfer the muhammara to a small bowl.

3. Finely chop the fresh mint and set aside.

4. Lightly dust the center of the bread peel with a pinch of the flour and place it next to your work area.

5. Dust the counter with the flour, place a dough ball on it, and dust the top with flour. Pat down the dough and roll it into a 9-inch (23-cm) circle, maintaining an even thickness. As you roll, stop to lift the dough and rotate it to prevent it from sticking to the counter. Dock the dough with a fork or docker, pricking the top all over.

6. Transfer the dough to the prepared peel. In several spots, dollop a quarter (30 grams, ¼ cup) of the muhammara on the dough. Use the back of the spoon or an offset spatula to coat the dough evenly, leaving a ⅛-inch (3-mm) border around the perimeter.

7. Shake the peel to ensure that the dough moves easily. If any spot sticks to the peel, lift the dough and dust more flour underneath it.

continues

8. Transfer the dough from the peel to the hot baking surface in the oven. Bake until the edges turn golden brown and slightly char in spots, 3 to 4 minutes. If needed, use heatproof tongs to turn the bread for even browning.

9. Use tongs to transfer the bread back to the peel. Let the bread cool on a cutting board for at least 3 minutes. Sprinkle it with a quarter of the chopped mint.

10. Repeat with the remaining dough balls.

11. To serve, quarter each man'oushe with a pizza wheel or chef's knife or fold it in half and wrap it in wax paper to eat on the go.

> **Note**
>
> In a sealable plastic storage bag, store the manakeesh in the refrigerator for up to 2 days or frozen for up to 3 months. To reheat, thaw if frozen and warm in a 250°F (120°C) oven for 10 minutes.
>
> **TIP:** You can roast your own red bell peppers, but it's easier to buy a jar of them from the grocery store.

LAMB AND TOMATO MANAKEESH

Lahm bi ajeen, "lamb with bread," packs a fantastic punch of flavor. My friend Reem owns a bakery in Lansing that makes manakeesh goodness every day. We hovered over her counter, discussing a problem with the meat-topped flatbreads that I had been testing (and testing). We mapped out the best way to keep the topping in place, landing deliciously here. A simple meat spread will shrink and create an uneven topping, so the additional ingredients in this recipe help the spread stay put and taste phenomenal. (See page 224.)

PREP: **26 MINUTES**
COOK: **12 MINUTES**
TOTAL: **38 MINUTES**

MAKES: **4 (8-INCH, 20-CM) FLATBREADS**
SPECIAL EQUIPMENT: **PIZZA STONE OR BAKING STEEL, BREAD PEEL**

TOPPING
150 grams (¼ pound) ground lamb (90% lean)
90 grams (½ cup plus 2 tablespoons) white onion
84 grams (½ cup plus 1 tablespoon) grape tomatoes
10 grams (2 teaspoons) tomato paste
2 cloves garlic
7 grams (1 teaspoon) pomegranate molasses
½ teaspoon fine sea salt
1 gram (1 teaspoon) paprika
⅛ teaspoon black pepper
10 fresh mint leaves (3 grams)
1 lemon

DOUGH
30 grams (¼ cup) bread flour or unbleached all-purpose flour for shaping
1 recipe Manakeesh Dough (page 221)

1. Arrange an oven rack in the lowest position and remove any other racks. Place the baking steel, baking stone, or an overturned dark, heavy baking sheet on the rack. Preheat the oven to 550°F (288°C) or its highest temperature.
2. Break up the lamb and quarter the onion.
3. In a food processor, puree the lamb, onion, tomatoes, tomato paste, garlic, pomegranate molasses, salt, paprika, and black pepper. Transfer the mixture to a medium bowl.
4. Finely chop the fresh mint and set aside for garnishing.
5. Lightly dust the center of the bread peel with a pinch of the flour and place it next to your work area.
6. Dust the counter with the flour, place a dough ball on it, and dust the top with flour. Pat down the dough and roll it into a 9-inch (23-cm) circle, maintaining an even thickness. As you roll, stop to lift the dough and rotate it to roll an even circle and to prevent it from sticking to the counter. Dock the dough with a fork or docker, pricking the top all over.
7. Transfer the dough to the prepared peel. Spoon a quarter (about 83 grams, ¼ cup plus 3 tablespoons) of the meat mixture on the dough. Use the back of the spoon or an offset spatula to spread it evenly, all the way to the edges.
8. Shake the peel to ensure that the dough moves easily. If any spot sticks to the peel, lift the dough and dust more flour underneath it.
9. Transfer the dough from the peel to the hot baking surface in the oven. Bake until the edges turn golden brown and slightly char in spots, 3 to 4 minutes. If needed, use heatproof tongs to turn the bread for even browning.

10. Use tongs to transfer the bread back to the peel. Let the bread cool on a cutting board for at least 3 minutes. Sprinkle it with a quarter of the freshly chopped mint.

11. Repeat with the remaining dough balls.

12. To serve, quarter the lemon and squeeze each quarter on each man'oushe. Quarter each man'oushe with a pizza wheel or chef's knife or fold it in half and wrap it in wax paper to eat on the go.

> **Notes**
> - Unlike the other toppings here for manakeesh, lamb and tomato tend to shrink when baked. That's why you spread the topping to the edge of the dough.
> - In a sealable plastic storage bag, store the manakeesh in the refrigerator for up to 2 days or frozen for up to 3 months. To reheat, thaw if frozen and warm in a 250°F (120°C) oven for 10 minutes.
>
> **VARIATION:** Substitute an equal amount of **LEAN GROUND BEEF** for the ground lamb.

…

TALAMI BREAD

No other bread from my oven has elicited the same intensity of response from baker and eater alike than this talami. On any visit, every member of the next generation in our family needs this talami—*needs*, not wants. Megan named it, hands-down, her last-supper food. She's not a crier, but she's so touched she sheds tears when we give her a loaf. My sister-in-law Amara says this recipe "nails it!" At my behest, my lifelong friend Geralyn bought a stand mixer for the sole purpose of making talami. Imagine her face when I told her that I make it by hand now! In times of trouble, when nothing can give comfort, talami has that power. The crumb is open, airy, and incredibly soft, with an equally soft crust that absorbs the garlic-butter glaze like a dream. Talami of this order misses nothing when eaten on its own. With some labneh and olives or a silky bowl of hummus with olive oil, it sings. Consider this bread the ultimate bread love language.

PREP: 1 HOUR 35 MINUTES
REST: 2 HOURS
COOK: 25 MINUTES
TOTAL: 4 HOURS

MAKES: MAKES 1 (10-BY-14-INCH, 25.5-BY-35.5-CM) LOAF (12 SERVINGS)
SPECIAL EQUIPMENT: QUARTER BAKING SHEET OR 12-INCH (30-CM) CAST-IRON SKILLET

DOUGH
397 grams (1¾ cups) water, warm (105–110°F, 40–43°C)
50 grams (¼ cup) granulated white sugar
12 grams (1 tablespoon) instant yeast
480 grams (4 cups) unbleached all-purpose flour
36 grams (2 tablespoons) fine sea salt
49 grams (4 tablespoons) neutral oil

GLAZE
1 clove garlic
28 grams (2 tablespoons) unsalted butter, room temperature
6 grams (1 teaspoon) fine sea salt

1. In a large mixing bowl, combine the water, sugar, and yeast.
2. Add the flour, 120 grams (1 cup) at a time, and use a Danish whisk or wooden spoon to create a shaggy dough. Add the salt with the last cup of flour.
3. Let the dough rest, uncovered, for 10 minutes.
4. Use an oiled bench scraper or soft spatula to lift an edge of the dough and fold it over to the opposite side of the bowl. Make these folds around the "clock" of the bowl at 12, 3, 6, and 9 o'clock. Repeat twice more, 10 minutes apart.
5. Use a pastry brush to coat the dough and the bowl with 14 grams (1 tablespoon) of the oil. Brush the underside of the dough by lifting it with the bench scraper.
6. Cover the bowl with plastic wrap, lay a kitchen towel over that, and let the dough rise in a warm part of your kitchen or proofing oven not hotter than 100°F (38°C) until it doubles in size, 2 hours.
7. Repeat step 4 but fold just one time around the clock.
8. Line the quarter baking sheet, if using, with non-stick foil. Brush the base and sides of the foil-lined sheet or skillet with the rest of the oil.
9. With the oiled bench scraper, gently transfer the dough onto the sheet. Use a pastry brush to coat the dough with the oil that settles around it. Gently nudge the dough to the center, if needed.
10. Let the dough rise, uncovered, until it doubles in size and nearly fills the sheet, 1 to 2 hours.
11. Meanwhile, make the glaze. Grate or mince the garlic.

continues

12. In a small mixing bowl, combine the butter, garlic, and salt. Stir well.

13. Arrange an oven rack in the lower position and preheat the oven to 400°F (200°C).

14. Bake until the bread turns a deep golden brown, 20 to 25 minutes. Rotate the pan halfway through.

15. Remove the bread from the oven and immediately coat the surface evenly with the garlic-butter glaze.

16. Let the bread cool in the pan for at least 1 hour before slicing and serving.

Notes

You can store leftover bread wrapped in plastic wrap and in an airtight container or foil at room temperature for up to 2 days. Reheat the bread, wrapped in foil, in a 250°F (120°C) oven for 15 minutes.

TIP: In step 6, proofing time depends on the warmth of your kitchen and freshness of the yeast. Check the dough after 1 hour, and every 15 minutes after that.

ZA'ATAR CHEESE DOME

With this glorious bread, more is more! Two layers of dough hold a flavorful, melty cheese within, and a za'atar oil finishes the top. When it bakes, the loaf puffs like pita, creating an impressive dome. Serve it for breakfast or brunch as a play on the Za'atar Manakeesh (page 222), a Lebanese breakfast favorite, with the traditional accompaniments for za'atar bread: labneh, olives, fresh mint, and wedges of tomatoes and onion. It also makes an impressive appetizer to pull from the oven when friends arrive. If your za'atar blend contains salt, omit the additional salt.

PREP: 2 HOURS 15 MINUTES
COOK: 12 MINUTES
TOTAL: 2 HOURS 27 MINUTES

MAKES: MAKES 1 (10-INCH, 25-CM) PIE (8 TO 10 SERVINGS)
SPECIAL EQUIPMENT: MISTING BOTTLE

DOUGH
240 grams (2 cups) bread flour, plus more for kneading
5 grams (1½ teaspoons) instant yeast
4 grams (1 teaspoon) granulated white sugar
6 grams (2 teaspoons) fine sea salt
170 grams (¾ cup) water, warm (105–110°F, 40–43°C)
4 grams (1 teaspoon) extra virgin olive oil

FILLING
170 grams (1½ cups) block mozzarella cheese
3 cloves garlic
¼ teaspoon fine sea salt
57 grams (½ cup) block feta cheese

TOPPING
18 grams (3 tablespoons) za'atar
33 grams (2 tablespoons plus 1 teaspoon) extra virgin olive oil
¼ teaspoon fine sea salt (optional)

1. In the large bowl of a stand mixer, add the flour, yeast, sugar, and salt and stir to combine with a wooden spoon or the dough hook (not attached). Slowly add the water and mix until a shaggy dough forms, 1 minute.

2. Attach the dough hook, set the mixer speed to medium-high, and knead the dough until smooth and slightly sticky, 3 minutes.

3. Lightly coat a medium mixing bowl with the olive oil. Ball the dough, transfer it to the prepared bowl, and flip the dough to coat it completely with oil. Cover the bowl with plastic wrap and lay a kitchen towel over that. Let the dough rise until it doubles in size, 1 to 2 hours.

4. On a lightly floured counter, halve the dough. Ball each half (as pictured on page 219).

5. On the lightly floured counter, lightly dust the balls with more flour. Cover them with plastic wrap and lay a kitchen towel over that. Let them rise until puffy and nearly doubled in size, 1 hour.

6. Meanwhile, make the filling. Chop the cheese into chunks.

7. Add the cheese, garlic, and salt to the food processor and process it to the texture of bread crumbs.

8. In a small mixing bowl, crumble the feta. Add the mozzarella mixture and stir to combine thoroughly. Set aside.

9. Make the topping. In another small bowl, whisk together the za'atar, olive oil, and salt. Set aside.

10. Arrange an oven rack in the lowest position and remove any other racks. Preheat the oven to 500°F (260°C) and line a baking sheet with parchment paper.

11. On a lightly floured counter, roll one dough ball into a 10-inch (25-cm) circle, ¼ inch (6 mm) thick. As you roll, stop to lift the dough and rotate it to roll an even circle and to prevent it from sticking to

continues

the counter. Dock the dough with a fork or docker, pricking the top all over. By hand, gently transfer the dough to the prepared baking sheet.

12. Spoon the cheese filling on the dough. Use the back of the spoon or an offset spatula to coat the dough evenly, leaving a 1-inch (2.5-cm) border around the perimeter. Mist or brush the edges lightly with water.

13. Roll out the second dough ball as in step 11, also docking it.

14. By hand, gently lay the second circle over the cheese filling. Adjust it to fit precisely.

15. Pinch the edges to form a 1-inch-(2.5-cm) high rim to seal the pie and prevent the za'atar oil from running off the pie as it bakes.

16. Spoon the za'atar oil on the top circle. Use the back of the spoon or an offset spatula to coat the dough evenly. Some spots will have more za'atar than others.

17. Bake until the pie turns golden brown and the top puffs into a dome, 12 to 13 minutes.

18. Transfer the pie to a cutting board and let it rest for 5 minutes before serving.

19. Use a bread knife to cut it in half and slice the halves into wedges. Serve warm.

> **Notes**
> - In a sealable plastic storage bag, store the wedges in the refrigerator for up to 2 days or frozen for up to 3 months. To reheat, thaw if frozen and warm in a 250°F (120°C) oven for 10 minutes.
> - The wedges make a light meal alongside a salad dressed, Lebanese-style, with lemon, olive oil, garlic, and mint.

SESAME PURSE BREAD

Vendors hang this Beirut street bread, a sesame-coated savory version of ka'ak, by the distinctive hole that forms a kind of handle, making the finished dish resemble a purse. It bakes and eats puffy, like pita. You can fill it with a slice of cheesy, syrup-laden knafeh (page 45) for a traditional breakfast, load it with other fillings, or tear it to pieces to pick up bites from your plate. Adorable, hearty, and versatile!

PREP: **15 MINUTES**
REST: **2 HOURS 30 MINUTES**
COOK: **15 MINUTES**
TOTAL: **3 HOURS**

MAKES: **4 (8-INCH, 20-CM) LOAVES**
SPECIAL EQUIPMENT: **PIZZA STONE OR BAKING STEEL**

DOUGH
- 240 grams (2 cups) bread flour
- 5 grams (1½ teaspoons) instant yeast
- 8 grams (2 teaspoons) granulated white sugar
- 6 grams (1 teaspoon) fine sea salt
- 57 grams (¼ cup) whole-milk plain yogurt
- 113 grams (½ cup) water, warm (105–110°F, 40–43°C)
- 13 grams (1 tablespoon) extra virgin olive oil, plus more to coat the bowl
- 48 grams (⅓ cup) sesame seeds

1. In the large bowl of a stand mixer, add the flour, yeast, sugar, and salt and stir to combine with a wooden spoon or the dough hook (not attached). Add the yogurt, then slowly add the water and mix until a shaggy dough forms, 1 minute.

2. Attach the dough hook, set the mixer speed to medium-high, and knead the dough until smooth and slightly sticky, 3 minutes.

3. Coat a medium mixing bowl with 1 teaspoon (4 grams) of the olive oil. Ball the dough, transfer it to the prepared bowl, and flip the dough to coat it completely with oil. Cover the bowl with plastic wrap and lay a kitchen towel over that. Let the dough rise until it doubles in size, 1 to 2 hours.

4. Quarter the dough and ball the quarters (as pictured on page 219).

5. On the counter, place the balls 2 inches (5 cm) apart, lightly cover them with plastic wrap, and let them rise for 30 minutes.

6. Arrange an oven rack in the lowest position and remove any other racks. Place the baking steel, baking stone, or an overturned dark, heavy baking sheet on the rack. Preheat the oven to 500°F (260°C) with convection or 525°F (274°C) without.

7. Pour the sesame seeds into a wide, shallow bowl or dish.

8. On the counter, pat a dough ball flat. Dip the slightly damp bottom side into the sesame seeds, pressing firmly. With the seed side up, roll the dough into an 8-by-6-by-¼-inch (20-by-15-cm-by-6-mm) oval. As you roll, stop to lift the dough to prevent it from sticking to the counter. Repeat with one more dough ball. Use a 1½-inch (4-cm) round cutter to cut a hole, offset on one half of the oval. Remove the cutout and gently stretch the oval lengthwise.

9. By hand, transfer the 2 raw purse breads to the hot baking surface in the oven, sesame side up.

10. Bake until the bread puffs and turns a light golden, 4 to 8 minutes.

11. Use a metal spatula to transfer the purse breads to a cooling rack. Cover them with a kitchen towel while they cool.

12. Repeat steps 8 through 11 with the remaining dough balls.

13. Serve immediately or place the still-warm purse breads in a plastic storage bag, sealed, to soften.

Note
In a sealable plastic storage bag, store the bread in the refrigerator for up to 5 days or frozen for up to 2 months. To reheat, thaw if frozen, wrap in foil, and warm in a 300°F (150°C) oven for 10 minutes.

PITA

You *can* make this Arabic bread (kubiz Arabi or khimaj)! It's surprisingly simple, puffing like magic to create the pocket with no special technique. Soft and fresh, homemade pita generates the deep satisfaction of eating the work of your hands. A very hot oven set on convection, if you have it, and a hot baking surface make the magic happen. Pita represents the ultimate ancient eating utensil and flavor-maker. Tear off pieces to scoop up bites from your plate; open the pocket for fillings, such as Arayes (page 247); or transform it into crunchy, delicious Pita Chips (page 243). Warm, soft pita is comfort food at its best!

PREP: **15 MINUTES**
REST: **2 HOURS 45 MINUTES**
COOK: **12 MINUTES**
TOTAL: **3 HOURS 12 MINUTES**

MAKES: **6 (6-INCH, 15-CM) PITAS**
SPECIAL EQUIPMENT: **PIZZA STONE OR BAKING STEEL, BREAD PEEL**

240 grams (2 cups) bread flour
5 grams (1½ teaspoons) instant yeast
8 grams (2 teaspoons) granulated white sugar
6 grams (1 teaspoon) fine sea salt
113 grams (½ cup) water, warm (105–110°F, 40–43°C)
57 grams (¼ cup) whole-milk plain yogurt
17 grams (1 tablespoon plus 1 teaspoon) extra virgin olive oil

1. In the large bowl of a stand mixer, add the flour, yeast, sugar, and salt and stir to combine with a wooden spoon or the dough hook (not attached). Slowly add the water and yogurt and mix until a shaggy dough forms, 1 minute.

2. Attach the dough hook, set the mixer speed to medium-high, and knead the dough until smooth and slightly sticky, 3 minutes.

3. Coat a medium mixing bowl with (4 grams) 1 teaspoon of the olive oil. Ball the dough, transfer it to the prepared bowl, and flip the dough to coat it completely with oil. Cover the bowl with plastic wrap and lay a kitchen towel over that. Let the dough rise until it doubles in size, 1 to 2 hours.

4. Divide the dough into 6 pieces, approximately 74 grams (½ cup) each. Ball the pieces (as pictured on page 219).

5. On the counter, place the balls 2 inches (5 cm) apart, lightly cover them with plastic wrap, and let them rise for 45 minutes.

6. Arrange an oven rack in the lowest position and remove any other racks. Place the baking stone, baking steel, or an overturned dark, heavy baking sheet on the rack. Preheat the oven to 500°F (260°C) with convection or 525°F (274°C) without.

7. On the lightly floured counter, pat a dough ball flat. Gently and evenly roll it into a circle 7 or 8 inches (18 or 20 cm) in diameter and ¼ inch (6 mm) thick. As you roll, stop to lift the dough and rotate it to roll an even circle and to prevent it from sticking to the counter. Repeat with 2 more dough balls.

8. By hand, transfer the raw pitas to the hot baking surface in the oven.

9. Bake until the pitas puff and turn a light golden, 3 to 8 minutes.

continues

10. Use a metal spatula to transfer the pitas to a cooling rack. Cover them with a kitchen towel while they cool.

11. Repeat steps 7 through 10 with the remaining dough balls.

12. Serve immediately or place the still-warm pitas in a plastic storage bag, sealed, to soften.

Note

In a sealable plastic storage bag, store the pitas in the refrigerator for up to 5 days or frozen for up to 2 months. To reheat, thaw if frozen, wrap in foil, and warm in a 300°F (150°C) oven for 10 minutes.

TIPS

- If you haven't invested in a baking steel or pizza stone, consider buying one. An overturned dark, heavy baking sheet can work, too.
- Baking time depends on the stone or steel you use. Keep an eye on it, and when puffed and pale golden, it's ready.
- Also, make lots! Pita stores so well in the freezer that I often make a double batch so we can enjoy it for a couple of weeks.

FILL 'EM UP

Pita makes an excellent edible vessel for just about anything. Follow this outline for superb homemade pita pockets.

- Spread or sauce: tahini, hummus, toum (garlic aioli), or labneh
- Fresh herbs: chopped fresh mint, parsley, cilantro, or chives
- Veggies of choice: fresh or roasted, sliced
- Pickles: pink pickled turnips, dill spears or chips
- Olives: black, green, or a combo, pitted
- Protein: cooked meat, sliced or shredded, especially shawarma, or seasoned chickpeas
- Salad: fresh or leftover salad tastes so good when tucked into pita! Dress it the Lebanese way, with lemon juice, garlic, salt, pepper, and dried and fresh mint.

PITA CHIPS

These crisp, lightly salted chips surpass anything from a bag, making them such an easy (dangerous) snack. Fattoush, a Lebanese salad (from the Arabic *fatteh*, meaning "crumbs"), includes pita chips crushed into the salad and more on top. Pita chips also form the basis of fatteh, in which they pair with yogurt sauce and other trimmings such as shredded chicken. At their simplest, pita chips belong at the center of a mezze platter with dips such as hummus, baba ghanoush, muhammara, and labneh; pickles; fresh vegetables; stuffed grape leaves; and any other nibbles you crave. A bright, refreshing sip like an Orange Blossom Gin Fizz (page 245) makes the mezze cocktail hour complete (and even more fun!).

PREP: 5 MINUTES
COOK: 50 MINUTES TO BAKE, 12 MINUTES TO FRY
TOTAL: 1 HOUR 7 MINUTES

MAKES: 12 SERVINGS

---

6 loaves Pita (page 240)

36 grams (3 tablespoons) extra virgin olive oil (baked chips only)

Neutral oil for frying (fried chips only)

½ teaspoon fine sea salt

BAKED PITA CHIPS

1. Arrange an oven rack in the middle position and preheat the oven to 375°F (190°C). Line two baking sheets with parchment paper.

2. Halve the pitas widthwise and pull the halves apart along the seams. Using kitchen scissors, cut each half into 4 wedges.

3. In a large mixing bowl, toss the wedges with the olive oil and salt, using your hands to coat the bread evenly.

4. Divide the pieces between the two baking sheets, placing them in a single layer. One sheet at a time, bake until the chips turn golden brown, stirring them a few times, 20 to 25 minutes. Rotate the pan halfway through baking. Serve immediately.

FRIED PITA CHIPS

1. Set a large saucepan over medium heat, fill it 3 inches (8 cm) deep with the neutral oil, and heat the oil to 375°F (190°C). Line a baking sheet with paper towels and place it nearby.

2. Halve the pitas widthwise and pull the halves apart along the seams. Using kitchen scissors, cut each half into 4 wedges.

3. With heatproof tongs, carefully place 4 pita wedges in the hot oil. It will bubble vigorously. Fry until it turns golden, 1 to 2 minutes.

4. Use the tongs to turn the pita over. Fry until golden brown, 30 more seconds.

5. Transfer the fried pita to the prepared baking sheet. Immediately sprinkle it with a pinch of salt.

6. Repeat steps 3 through 5 with the rest of the pita wedges.

7. Serve immediately.

continues

Note

You can store pita chips in an airtight container at room temperature for up to 5 days.

VARIATION: After baking or frying, toss the still-warm chips with 6 grams (1 tablespoon) **ZA'ATAR**, **SUMAC**, or **BAHARAT** (Lebanese seven spice).

TIP: To make **FATTOUSH**, use fresh, crisp romaine and watercress, spring greens, or arugula. Add thinly sliced radish and red onion, halved cherry tomatoes, and chopped fresh mint. Crush 60 grams (1 cup) of pita chips into the salad and toss it with vinaigrette. For a vinaigrette for 6 cups of salad, combine 7 grams (1 teaspoon) pomegranate molasses, 14 grams (1 tablespoon) fresh lemon juice, 37 grams (3 tablespoons) extra virgin olive oil, 4 grams (1 teaspoon) sumac, 1.5 grams (1 teaspoon) crushed Dried Mint (page 270), 1 minced garlic clove, ½ teaspoon fine sea salt, and a few grinds of black pepper in a cruet or small jar and shake to combine, or whisk the mixture together in a small bowl. Finish the salad with more crushed pita chips, chopped mint, and a dusting of sumac.

Something to Drink

ORANGE BLOSSOM GIN FIZZ

The classic gin fizz tastes even better with a whisper of orange blossom water, and the froth makes it look so pretty, as pictured on page 244.

PREP: 5 MINUTES
TOTAL: 5 MINUTES

MAKES: 1 COCKTAIL
SPECIAL EQUIPMENT: COCKTAIL SHAKER

⅛ teaspoon orange blossom water
4 grams (1 teaspoon) granulated white sugar
14 grams (1 tablespoon) fresh lemon juice
1 large egg white, cold
59 grams (2 ounces) gin
57 grams (2 ounces) club soda, cold

1. In a cocktail shaker filled halfway with ice, add the orange blossom water, sugar, lemon juice, egg white, and gin. Seal the shaker and shake as hard as you can for 15 seconds.
2. Change hands and shake again for 15 more seconds. Strain into a large chilled coupe.
3. Top with the club soda.
4. From the shaker, spoon the foam on the drink and serve.

> **TIP:** If you're using a pasteurized egg white, take a deep breath and shake for 30 or 60 more seconds.
>
> **VARIATION:** In lieu of an egg white, use 28 grams (2 tablespoons) of **WHIPPING CREAM**.

ARAYES

Fill a pita with seasoned lamb or beef and pan-fry it for an incredibly mouthwatering, crunchy bite that's dipped in creamy labneh, and you have arayes. The pita absorbs the savory juices from the spiced meat and crisps with just a brush of olive oil. After one taste, this Lebanese street-food obsession will become your obsession, too.

PREP: 5 MINUTES
COOK: 12 MINUTES
TOTAL: 17 MINUTES

MAKES: 12 ARAYES

6 Pita (page 240), room temperature
4 grams (1 tablespoon) parsley
10 fresh mint leaves (3 grams)
71 grams (½ cup) yellow onion
2 cloves garlic
5 grams (2 teaspoons) sumac
3 grams (2 teaspoons) Dried Mint (page 270)
9 grams (1½ teaspoons) fine sea salt
¼ teaspoon black pepper
¼ teaspoon cinnamon
⅛ teaspoon cayenne pepper
448 grams (1 pound) ground lamb or beef (85% lean)
50 grams (¼ cup) extra virgin olive oil
227 grams (1 cup) labneh

1. Place a baking sheet in the oven and preheat it to 250°F (120°C). Halve the pitas crosswise into pockets.
2. Finely chop the parsley and mint.
3. In a large mixing bowl, grate the onion and garlic. Add the parsley, fresh mint, sumac, dried mint, salt, black pepper, cinnamon, and cayenne pepper and thoroughly whisk the mixture together.
4. Add the meat, break it up, and stir to combine.
5. Into a pita pocket, place 40 grams (2 heaping tablespoons) of the meat mixture and flatten it, pushing the meat evenly to the edges. Repeat with the rest of the pockets and filling.
6. In a large skillet over medium-high heat, heat 12 grams (1 tablespoon) of the olive oil. Place 2 or 3 stuffed pita pockets in the skillet. Cook, pressing each pita with the back of a metal spatula or a burger press, until the bottoms turn golden and crispy, about 2 minutes.
7. Flip the pitas over and cook, pressing again, until golden and crispy, 2 more minutes.
8. Transfer the pitas to the baking sheet in the oven to stay warm while you repeat steps 5 through 7 with the remaining pitas and filling.
9. In a small serving bowl, whisk the labneh until smooth.
10. Alongside the labneh for dipping, serve the arayes as they are or halve them first.

Note
You can store leftovers in an airtight container in the refrigerator for up to 4 days. Reheat them, over medium heat, in a skillet brushed with ½ teaspoon of oil.

TIPS
- If the pita pocket proves difficult to open, microwave it for 15 seconds and try again.
- Serve arayes cut into wedges as part of a mezze platter, eat them as a main dish with a side salad, or gobble them as a hearty late-night snack.

ZA'ATAR GARLIC KNOTS

Inspired by Za'atar Manakeesh (page 222), I always am looking for new ways to enjoy za'atar plus bread—and garlic knots were a delightful discovery. They are surprisingly easy and fun to shape. This recipe yields lovely, soft, garlicky mini-rolls that pull apart just right. These knots belong anywhere a dinner roll goes: special enough to join a celebration feast, easy enough to enjoy with a simple soup-and-salad meal.

PREP: 15 MINUTES
REST: 2 HOURS
COOK: 36 MINUTES
TOTAL: 2 HOURS 51 MINUTES
MAKES: 16 KNOTS

DOUGH
390 grams (3¼ cups) unbleached all-purpose flour, plus more for kneading
3 grams (1 teaspoon) instant yeast
12 grams (1 tablespoon) granulated white sugar
4 grams (1 teaspoon) garlic powder
6 grams (1 teaspoon) fine sea salt
227 grams (1 cup) water, warm (105–110°F, 40–43°C)
57 grams (¼ cup) plain whole-milk yogurt
4 grams (1 teaspoon) extra virgin olive oil

TOPPING
3 cloves garlic
36 grams (3 tablespoons) extra virgin olive oil
12 grams (3 tablespoons) za'atar
10 fresh mint leaves (3 grams)

1. In the large bowl of a stand mixer, add the flour, yeast, sugar, garlic powder, and salt and stir to combine with a wooden spoon or the dough hook (not attached). Slowly add the water and yogurt and mix until a shaggy dough forms, 1 minute.

2. Attach the dough hook, set the mixer speed to medium-high, and knead the dough until smooth and slightly sticky, 3 minutes.

3. Coat a medium mixing bowl with the 4 grams (1 teaspoon) of olive oil. Ball the dough, transfer it to the prepared bowl, and flip the dough to coat it completely with oil. Cover the bowl with plastic wrap and lay a kitchen towel over that. Let the dough rise until it doubles in size, 1 to 2 hours.

4. Make the topping. Grate or mince the garlic. In a small mixing bowl, stir together the olive oil, garlic, and za'atar. Set aside.

5. Line two baking sheets with parchment paper.

6. On a lightly floured counter, pat and stretch the dough into a rectangle 16 by 5 inches (40 by 12.5 cm), a long side toward you.

7. Along the length of the dough, use a sharp chef's knife or pizza wheel to score 16 strips, each 1 inch (2.5 cm) wide. Cut the strips.

8. Stretch a dough strip into a rope 8 by 1 inch (20 by 2.5 cm). Dust it lightly with flour. Tie a knot in the middle of the rope and tuck the ends under the knot to form a knotted ball. Carefully transfer the knot to a prepared baking sheet. Repeat with the rest of the strips.

9. On each baking sheet, place 8 knots, 2 to 3 inches (5 to 8 cm) apart. Lightly cover them with plastic wrap or a kitchen towel and let them rise until puffy, 30 minutes.

10. Arrange an oven rack in the middle position and preheat the oven to 400°F (200°C).

11. Stir the za'atar oil and lightly brush it on each knot. Some oil will run off, which is fine.

12. One sheet at a time, bake until the knots turn golden brown, 18 to 20 minutes.

13. Finely chop the mint.

14. Remove the knots from the oven, transfer them to a cooling rack to cool for 5 minutes, and sprinkle them with the mint. Serve warm or at room temperature.

> **Notes**
> You can store the knots in an airtight container at room temperature for up to 2 days or in the refrigerator for up to 4 days. You also can freeze them in an airtight container for up to 3 months. To reheat, thaw to room temperature, wrap the knots in foil, and warm them in a 250°F (120°C) oven for 10 minutes.

Secrets to Making Saj Bread

You can enjoy this thin flatbread in a number of ways. Tear off small pieces to scoop up food from the plate, roll it up with fillings, or simply spread it with labneh and za'atar or butter and salt (or sugar). Keep saj bread in its bag until you eat it. However inelegant a plastic bag at the table may seem, it's essential to keep the bread soft and prevent it from drying out. Here's what you need to know to make saj bread successfully.

OVEN

You can bake saj bread in three ways.

Saj Oven

In this convex griddle, a steel dome sits over coils of gas flames. The dome has no sides, making it easier to flip the thin, delicate dough onto it. If you need a saj, you can borrow one of mine (page 256)!

Baking Steel or Stone in a Standard Oven

Steel or stone holds heat well, allowing the bread to bake similar to the saj dome. Steel is better than stone because it typically covers the entire oven rack or base of the oven, giving you more wiggle room for placement.

Overturned Wok on a Gas Stovetop

The shape of the wok, when inverted, mimics the saj dome and works like a charm. If you go this route, use a wok with a smooth, rounded base. (I also have seen an overturned aluminum saucer sled on a gas stovetop. So Michigan; ingenious!) Follow the same method as baking on a saj, but the heat element comes from your stovetop gas burner.

DOUGH

Because it's a project, we always bake large batches, using 2,268 grams (5 pounds) of flour for the dough. (Aunt Hilda said that she started with 50 pounds. Fact or fiction?) My recipe calls for 540 grams (1½ pounds) of flour to yield 8 flatbreads. You can double it, triple it, or more.

The size of the balls will depend on the oven. It's easier to flip a larger, thin dough onto a saj dome. In an oven, it's easier to flip a smaller, 10-inch (25-cm) round onto a baking steel, pizza stone, or an overturned baking sheet. Use smaller balls for an overturned wok.

The size of the dough also depends on how you shape it. It takes time, study, and practice to learn how to throw the dough from hand to hand before stretching it on the kara. It's an art to keep alive, a tradition that we'll keep from fading. You also can form saj dough by rolling it and then stretching it on the kara, which works better for smaller balls.

TOOLS

Set up the work area near the oven or saj with the following tools.

Kara

After rolling or tossing the dough, this pillow shapes and transfers it to the baking surface. Place the kara in a convenient spot near where you shape the dough. I shape on the kitchen counter and keep the kara on the seat of a stool or small folding table next to me.

Tongs
Use long tongs to remove the bread from the baking element after it has baked. (My cousin and teacher Geri uses her hands, as her mother did.)

Misting Bottle
After baking, you need to mist and soften the bread for folding.

Baking Sheet
Use this or a large, flat, round pan lined with a bread towel to stack the bread after baking. Use a second bread towel and large plastic sheet, such as a large, clean trash bag, to cover the baking sheet or round pan fully to help soften the bread immediately after it bakes.

Gallon Freezer Bags
After baking, store the folded bread in these bags.

SAJ BREAD

This soft, thin, chewy bread plays an enormous role in my life and heart. For me, it drew the first distinction between what we ate at home and what other kids ate. When Sitto handed rolled pieces of saj bread with butter and salt to me and Cindy, a schoolmate, I gobbled mine, but Cindy stood, wide-eyed with fascination. Long ago, saj brought me and cousin Celine into Sitto's kitchen for lessons in Lebanese baking. The world has few saj bakers to share their wisdom anymore. Luckily, my cousin Geri throws the bread like a sitto. During my mother's last days, Geri's gift of beautiful, folded loaves inspired Celine, me, and our sisters to form a baking group to soften our grief. Every time I bake and eat them, the loaves evoke a lifetime of beloved people and memories. My parents and theirs called it Syrian bread, with the exception of one grandfather, Richard Abowd, who proudly called it Lebanese bread. It's also called mark'ouk, which often includes whole wheat flour and a semolina coating for the dough.

PREP: **1 HOUR**
REST: **2 HOURS 30 MINUTES**
COOK: **24 TO 48 MINUTES**
TOTAL: **4 HOURS 18 MINUTES**

MAKES: **14 (10-INCH, 25-CM) LOAVES OR 8 (20-INCH, 50-CM) LOAVES**
SPECIAL EQUIPMENT: **KARA (PAGE 250); SAJ DOME OVEN, BAKING STEEL, PIZZA STONE, OR WOK; TONGS; MISTING BOTTLE; TWO BREAD TOWELS; LARGE PLASTIC SHEET OR BAG (PAGE 251)**

- 540 grams (4½ cups) unbleached all-purpose flour, plus more as needed
- 12 grams (2 teaspoons) fine sea salt
- 8 grams (2 teaspoons) granulated white sugar
- 1 teaspoon instant yeast
- 340 grams (1½ cups) water, warm (105–110°F, 40–43°C)
- 25 grams (2 tablespoons) neutral oil, plus more for shaping and brushing

MAKE THE DOUGH

1. In the large bowl of a stand mixer, add the flour, salt, sugar, and yeast and stir to combine with a wooden spoon or a dough hook (not attached). Slowly add the water and oil and mix to form a moist dough, 1 minute.

2. Attach the dough hook, set the mixer speed to medium, and knead the dough until soft and smooth, 5 minutes. Touch the dough, and if it is very wet or sticking to your fingertips, add a tablespoon of flour and knead again.

3. Coat a large mixing bowl with oil. Ball the dough, transfer it to the prepared bowl, and flip the dough to coat it completely with oil. Cover the bowl with plastic wrap and lay a kitchen towel over that. Let the dough rise until it doubles in size, 1 hour 30 minutes.

4. Saj ovens typically run on propane, so if using a dome oven, set up your baking station there. On or near the work area, place the kara, tongs, misting bottle, and a baking sheet or large round pan with two bread towels. Place a large plastic sheet big enough to cover the baking sheet completely, such as a clean garbage bag, next to the bread towels. Tuck the bag under the baking sheet.

5. Once you are ready to bake, follow one of the three baking methods outlined below.

Bake on a Saj Dome Oven

1. Divide the dough into 8 pieces, approximately 116 grams each. Ball the pieces.

2. On a lightly oiled work surface, set the balls 3 inches (7.5 cm) apart. Lightly brush the balls with oil, cover them with plastic wrap, lay one or more kitchen towels over that, and let them rise for 1 hour.

continues

3. About 10 minutes before baking, turn on the saj oven and set the flame height to medium.

4. Dust the work surface with flour. Flatten a dough ball and roll it into a 6-inch (15-cm) circle. Set it aside to rest while rolling out another dough ball in the same manner.

5. After you roll out the second disc, set it aside to rest and return to the first. Roll it into a 10-inch (25-cm) circle. As you roll, stop to lift and turn the dough to roll an even circle and prevent it from sticking to the counter. Lightly dust both sides with flour as needed. Repeat with the second disc.

6. To shape by throwing, hold both hands in front of you, palms down. Use your nondominant hand to flip the dough over the back of your dominant hand. Continue flipping the dough from one hand to the other, stretching it mostly at the edges, until the dough measures about 18 inches (45 cm) in diameter. Lay the dough on the kara. Pull and stretch the edges of the dough all the way around the pillow.

7. To shape by rolling, keep rolling the dough as large as it will go, lifting and turning the dough as you roll. Transfer it to the kara. From the center out, stretch the dough from underneath with one hand holding the dough in place and the other hand palm down. Gently pull and stretch the edges of the dough all the way around the pillow.

8. Flip the dough from the kara onto the center of the hot dome. The dough will steam and bubble. Bake until golden brown spots appear, 1 minute. Use the tongs to turn the dough over. Bake for 1 more minute.

9. With the tongs, transfer the bread to the prepared sheet, placed on one of the bread towels. Immediately mist the bread all over with water. Lay the second bread towel over the bread and place the plastic bag over that, tucking it underneath the sheet.

10. Repeat steps 4 through 9 with the remaining dough balls.

Bake in the Oven

1. Divide the dough into 16 pieces, approximately 65 grams each. Ball the pieces.

2. On a lightly oiled work surface, set the balls 3 inches (7.5 cm) apart. Lightly brush the balls with oil, cover them with plastic wrap, lay one or more kitchen towels over that, and let them rise for 1 hour.

3. Arrange an oven rack in the lowest position and remove any other racks. Place the baking steel, baking stone, or an overturned dark, heavy baking sheet on the rack. Preheat the oven to 550°F (288°C) or its highest temperature.

4. Dust the counter with flour. Flatten a dough ball and roll it into a 6-inch (15-cm) circle. Set it aside to rest while rolling out another dough ball in the same manner.

5. After you roll out the second disc, set it aside to rest and return to the first. Roll it into a 10-inch (25-cm) circle. As you roll, stop to lift and turn the dough to roll an even circle and to prevent it from sticking to the counter. Lightly dust both sides with flour as needed. Repeat with the second disc.

6. Gently transfer the rolled dough to the kara. From the center out, stretch the dough from underneath with one hand holding the dough in place and the other hand palm down. Gently pull and stretch the edges of the dough all the way around the pillow.

7. Flip the dough onto the center of the baking steel. Close the oven and bake until the bread bubbles and turns golden in spots, 4 minutes. Use the tongs to turn the bread over and bake for 1 more minute.

8. With the tongs, transfer the bread to the prepared sheet, placed on one of the bread towels. Immediately mist the bread all over with water. Lay the

second bread towel over the bread and place the plastic bag over that, tucking it underneath the sheet.

9. Repeat steps 4 through 8 with the remaining dough balls.

Bake on an Overturned Wok on a Gas Stovetop

1. Divide the dough into 16 pieces, approximately 65 grams each. Ball the pieces.

2. On a lightly oiled work surface, set the balls 3 inches (7.5 cm) apart. Lightly brush the balls with oil, cover them with plastic wrap, lay one or more kitchen towels over that, and let them rise for 1 hour.

3. Turn a smooth, round-bottomed wok over the gas burner on the stovetop. Turn the burner on medium-high.

4. Dust the counter with flour. Flatten a dough ball and roll it into a 6-inch (15-cm) circle. Set it aside to rest while rolling out another dough ball in the same manner.

5. After you roll out the second disc, set it aside to rest and return to the first. Roll it into a 10-inch (25-cm) circle. As you roll, stop to lift and turn the dough to roll an even circle and to prevent it from sticking to the counter. Lightly dust both sides with flour as needed. Repeat with the second disc.

6. Gently transfer the rolled dough to the kara. From the center out, stretch the dough from underneath with one hand holding the dough in place and the other hand palm down. Gently pull and stretch the edges of the dough all the way around the pillow.

7. Flip the dough from the kara onto the center of the hot dome. The dough will steam and bubble. Bake until golden brown spots appear, 1 minute. Use the tongs to turn the dough over. Bake for 1 more minute.

8. With the tongs, transfer the bread to the prepared sheet, placed on one of the bread towels. Immediately mist the bread all over with water. Lay the second bread towel over the bread and place the plastic bag over that, tucking it underneath the sheet.

9. Repeat steps 4 through 8 with the remaining dough balls.

Fold and Store the Bread

1. To fold the bread, mist each loaf again with water and wrap them back in the bread towels and plastic bag tucked over everything.

2. Set aside to rest and hydrate for at least 30 minutes. Repeat as needed. The bread is ready when soft enough to fold easily without cracking.

3. Fold a loaf in half and in half again. Tuck 4 folded loaves in a gallon freezer bag. Repeat with the rest of the bread.

4. Press any air from the bags and seal them. Immediately freeze any bread not to be eaten on baking day.

> *Note*
> In the gallon freezer bags, freeze the bread for up to 6 months. Thaw to room temperature. Quick-thaw the bread by unfolding it and laying it over a warm or steaming pan, or a pot of goodness cooking on the stove.

A Saga of Ovens

Here's the thing about saj ovens: I have four. Before you think I've lost it, let me explain. It started in Lebanon, which for me existed for much of my life only in stories, a few photos, and imagination. I longed to go but feared going. The world stage always provided good reasons to stay away. One fall, many years ago, my sister, Peggy, threw down the gauntlet. She was traveling to London on business and was going on to visit Lebanon regardless of whether I joined. Over my dead body! At my mother's kitchen table, we jumped full-tilt into planning. Our mother quietly listened in the background. When she heard we would go to Mtein, where her father was born, she announced, "I'm going with you."

The day we arrived in Lebanon, we feasted immediately (of course) at Mir Amin Palace Terrace Restaurant in the Chouf Mountains. A woman was baking saj bread to order, handing thin loaves to the waiting line before her as she baked. She pulled dough balls from a bin of many dough balls resting in a sea of semolina. The star of the buffet, she patted a ball out with her fingertips and hands, turning the dough to flatten it. She tossed the dough from arm to arm. As if by magic, a huge, thin circle of dough grew in just seconds before she tossed it onto the saj. She was enacting my most precious memories of Sitto throwing the dough for her thin bread in our basement. I hadn't seen this incredible feat since my grandmother had passed away 20 years earlier. Lebanon knew how to welcome me with a sitto's love.

As we ventured to Mtein the next day, Hisam, our driver, kept us moving in a mad dash, but he cheerfully stopped whenever I yelled, "Wait! That bakery back there!" Then I spotted them. An open-air store displayed a selection of saj dome ovens in no fewer than 10 sizes in ascending order. "*Wait!*"

It felt like an automotive repair shop. At the back of the store sat a craftsman making ovens. My paltry Arabic was going to get me nowhere, so I simply pointed at the wall. Until that visit, I had never used a saj oven, let alone seen one in person. Sitto had thrown her dough onto a steel sheet in the base of her oven. At that point, my only encounters with saj ovens had taken place on YouTube.

We loaded one into the back of the small vehicle and spent exponentially more than it cost for the hotel to box it so we could bring it home as a "checked bag." My sister, who always offers famously priceless comments at just the right moments, said, "You'd better learn to bake a helluva lot of bread on that thing." In Chicago, the customs agent asked what was in the box. After my explanation, he shook his head. "Wow, I guess there's something for everyone."

Dan took the oven to the service center of his car dealership, which outfitted it to connect to a propane tank. For years, I had saved and protected the kara that Sitto had made for me for just this moment. We lit the gas, but I wasn't ready to use the oven properly for a good year. In that time, we visited Dearborn, always hunting for great Lebanese food. As I wandered the aisles of a kitchen supply shop, my eyes landed on a couple of small karas. I walked toward them. Lo and behold: saj ovens *galore*. Not just one or two, an entire *wall* of them in all sizes and even on stands. Arms akimbo, I must have stood there for a long time because my sister asked if everything was OK. Then she saw them. She still laughs about the antics it took to bring a saj oven home from Lebanon when, all along, they were available just 90 miles from home. That day in Dearborn, I bought one, and the next time another one, so I can bake mountains of saj bread, Sitto-style, and teach you how, too.

ZA'ATAR CROISSANTS

Traditional French pastry paired with za'atar expresses so much of the presence of French cuisine woven into Lebanese cuisine. This recipe uses techniques I learned in culinary school and the wisdom of the experts at the King Arthur Baking School and bakers such as Sarah Kieffer of the Vanilla Bean Blog, who makes "cheater" croissants, as we do, too, by spreading the butter rather than making a butter block. Breaking the lengthy process into smaller tasks performed over the course of two days takes the scariness out of this laminated dough project and leads to an exciting morning of savory homemade croissants.

PREP: **35 MINUTES**
CHILL: **11 HOURS**
REST: **2 HOURS 30 MINUTES**
COOK: **17 MINUTES**
TOTAL: **14 HOURS 22 MINUTES (OVER 2 DAYS)**

MAKES: **8 CROISSANTS**
SPECIAL EQUIPMENT: **PIZZA WHEEL**

PRE-FERMENT
60 grams (½ cup) unbleached all-purpose flour
75 grams (⅓ cup) water, warm (105–110°F, 40–43°C)
13 grams (1½ tablespoons) instant yeast

DOUGH
195 grams (1½ cups plus 2 tablespoons) unbleached all-purpose, plus more as needed
25 grams (2 tablespoons) granulated white sugar
8 grams (1½ teaspoons) fine sea salt
76 grams (⅓ cup) whole milk, warm (105–110°F, 40–43°C)
28 grams (2 tablespoons) unsalted butter, room temperature

BUTTER SPREAD
113 grams (½ cup) cultured (European) butter, 68°F (20°C)
7 grams (1 tablespoon) unbleached all-purpose flour

FILLING
24 grams (2 tablespoons) za'atar
24 grams (2 tablespoons) extra virgin olive oil

EGG WASH
1 large egg
5 grams (1 teaspoon) water

TOPPING
12 grams (1 tablespoon) za'atar

DAY 1 (3 HOURS 35 MINUTES): MAKE THE DOUGH

1. In a small mixing bowl, stir together the pre-ferment ingredients. Scrape the mixture from the sides of the bowl to the bottom. Let the poolish (fluid, yeast-cultured dough) rest, uncovered, until it triples in size, 30 minutes.

2. Make the dough. In the large bowl of a stand mixer, add the dough flour, sugar, salt, milk, and poolish. Stir to combine with the dough hook (not attached) until shaggy.

3. Attach the dough hook and mix on low speed until the dough comes together.

4. Add the butter and continue mixing until the dough becomes smooth, soft, and stretchy, 2 minutes.

5. Ball the dough and wrap it tightly in plastic wrap. Refrigerate it for 1 hour.

ROLL, FOLD, AND SHAPE THE DOUGH

1. When the dough is ready but still in the refrigerator, make the butter spread. In the large bowl of a stand mixer fitted with the paddle attachment, beat the butter and flour on low speed just until they combine, with a texture like soft cream cheese, 1 minute. Don't overbeat the butter, which will warm it.

continues

2. Roll and fold #1. Remove the dough from the refrigerator. On a very lightly floured counter, tap down the dough with the rolling pin and gently roll it into a rectangle 6 by 12 inches (15 by 30 cm), ½ inch (1.25 cm) thick.

3. With a long side of the rectangle toward you, dollop the dough with the butter mixture. Gently use an offset spatula to spread the butter evenly over the rectangle, leaving a ½-inch (1.25-cm) border around the perimeter.

4. Fold the left third of the dough halfway over the right and fold the right half over the folded left side. Stretch the corners that may have shrunk to align with the folded dough edges.

5. Wrap the dough tightly in plastic wrap and refrigerate it for 30 minutes.

6. Roll and fold #2. Remove the dough from the refrigerator and unwrap it. On a lightly floured counter, position the dough with the folded edge on your left and a short side toward you. Tap down the dough with the rolling pin and gently roll it again into a rectangle 6 by 12 inches (15 by 30 cm), ½ inch (1.25 cm) thick. As you roll it, lift the dough to prevent it from sticking to the counter.

7. From one short end, fold a third of the dough halfway over the top, then fold the other short end over the just-folded side. Stretch the corners that may have shrunk to align with the folded dough edges.

8. Wrap the dough tightly in plastic wrap and refrigerate it for 30 minutes.

9. Roll and fold #3: Repeat steps 6 to 8. At this point, the dough won't roll as easily, so take your time and use your hands to keep the rectangle shaped between rolls.

10. Wrap the dough tightly in plastic wrap and refrigerate it for 30 minutes.

SHAPE THE DOUGH

1. Make the filling. In a small mixing bowl, combine the za'atar and olive oil. Set aside.

2. Remove the dough from the refrigerator and place it on a lightly floured counter. Tap it down with the rolling pin and roll it into a rectangle, 8½ by 16½ inches (22 by 42 cm). Roll slowly and gently to ease the cold dough into shape, lifting the dough off the counter a few times and flipping it over and dusting with more flour as needed to prevent sticking and tearing.

3. Trim all the edges by ¼ inch (6 mm) for a rectangle 8 by 16 inches (20 by 40 cm).

4. Along one long edge, mark the dough at 4-inch (10-cm) intervals. Use the rolling pin as a guide and, with a pizza wheel, cut the dough into 4 strips, each 8 by 4 inches (20 by 10 cm). Halve each strip diagonally to create triangles.

continues

5. In the shortest edge of each triangle, cut a ½-inch (1.25-cm) notch. Stretch the dough by pulling from the outer edges on either side of the notch to even them out and gently stretch the entire triangle from the tip.

6. Place 8 grams (1 teaspoon) of the za'atar filling along the notched edge, leaving the other edges clean.

7. Fold the notched edge over the za'atar filling and roll it halfway. Stretch the dough point to lengthen the strip as you roll the rest of the way up to the point.

8. Repeat with the rest of the triangles.

9. Line a baking sheet with parchment paper and arrange the raw croissants on it, tip sides down, leaving at least 2 inches (5 cm) among them. Cover them lightly with plastic wrap or a kitchen towel and refrigerate overnight.

DAY 2 (2 HOURS 26 MINUTES)

1. Remove the croissants from the refrigerator. Make the egg wash. In a small bowl, whisk together the egg and water. Lightly brush each croissant all over with egg wash.

2. Let them rest, uncovered, for 2 to 3 hours.

3. Arrange an oven rack in the middle position and preheat the oven to 400°F (200°C).

4. Lightly brush each croissant again with egg wash. Sprinkle the tops liberally with za'atar.

5. Bake for 9 minutes.

6. Reduce the heat to 375°F (190°C), rotate the pan, and continue baking until the croissants turn a deep golden brown, 8 to 10 more minutes.

7. Remove the croissants from the oven and let them cool on the sheet for 5 minutes. Serve immediately.

Notes
- A pre-ferment of highly activated wet dough improves the texture (elasticity) and flavor complexity of the croissant dough.
- You can store the croissants in an airtight container in the freezer for up to 3 months. To reheat them, thaw them at room temperature and warm them in a 250°F (120°C) oven for 10 minutes.

TIPS:
- Kitchen temperature matters when working with and proofing croissant dough. If too warm, the butter will melt during the rise and run from the baked croissant. Keep it on the cooler side, about 70°F (21°C).
- When rolling the croissant dough, roll it evenly and without too much pressure, which can tear the thin layers.

VARIATION: Make **LABNEH ZA'ATAR CROISSANTS** by slicing the baked croissants horizontally and spreading a tablespoon or two of labneh in each.

Discovering Za'atar Croissants

On the first morning of my first visit to Lebanon, a beautiful platter of pastries lay spread on our table for breakfast. Seeing French pastry in Lebanon didn't surprise me. After pulling apart the ethereal pastry, what did surprise me was finding za'atar in it—subtle, unlike how we heap it on our manakeesh (page 222). The croissant's exterior had offered no hint of the brilliance inside.

Giddy, I planned to ask to spend time in the hotel kitchen to investigate this creation and their other brilliant ideas. But time was tight, and we had cousins to hug, windy monasteries to visit, and ancient ruins to admire.

The next day, in the city center, we wanted to see how Starbucks does Beirut. Instead of lemon pound cake or cheese Danish, they offered, you guessed it, za'atar croissants. It was a Starbucks croissant, but the za'atar elevated the pastry and gave me yet another iteration to absorb and the realization that za'atar croissants must be de rigueur in Lebanon. Back home, spotting them on the menu at Shatila, a bakery in Dearborn, and at Yellow, a café in Georgetown, I understood.

As I was finishing the manuscript for this cookbook, my brother Tom—among the first to cheer my change in career path to write about food—asked what I was going to do after I delivered it to the publisher. "Clean the kitchen?" I replied. But really I'd been thinking about the freedom, in that deep breath after finishing, to make za'atar croissants for fun and not recipe development.

It represents one pastry project in a long line of them that consumes me as much as I consume them. Baking projects dot my website. Many more never saw the light of blog-day because their complexity meant that I had to stay focused. I've wondered how you might feel about the Za'atar Croissants (page 257) and the homemade phyllo (page 2), not for the eating, of course, but for what the recipe requires in the kitchen. But like anything that wanders into the mind and allows the mind to wander—such as leaving a job to attend culinary school, visiting Lebanon, or writing cookbooks—the recipe was going to keep humming its little za'atar tune in my ear until I listened and shared it with you.

Baking Staples

Making the foundational recipes in this chapter and storing them can make your baking more efficient and more enjoyable. Just pull the toasted nuts from the freezer, clarified butter or flower water syrup from the fridge, or a few dried mint leaves from a jar, and you're already ahead of the game.

TOASTED NUTS

My recipes call for toasted nuts of all kinds except pistachios, which taste wonderful toasted but lose their bright green color. Buy large bags of nuts (more economical than smaller pouches), toast them right away, return them to the bag, and freeze them. Nuts hold for a long time in the freezer, and they thaw quickly, so it's a great place to store them.

PREP: **1 MINUTE**
COOK: **12 MINUTES**
COOL: **30 MINUTES**
TOTAL: **43 MINUTES**

MAKES: **3 CUPS**

426 grams (3 cups) whole unsalted walnuts, almonds, cashews, pecans, hazelnuts, or peanuts

1. Arrange an oven rack in the middle position and preheat the oven to 350°F (177°C). Line a baking sheet with parchment paper. On the baking sheet, spread the nuts in a single layer.
2. Bake until the nuts become fragrant and turn golden brown, 10 to 12 minutes.
3. Remove the nuts from the oven and let them cool to room temperature, 30 minutes.

> *Note*
> You can store the toasted nuts in an airtight container at room temperature for up to 1 month or in the freezer for up to 6 months.

BLANCHED PISTACHIOS

Not all recipes that call for pistachios require blanched pistachios, especially if you prefer your nuts with a roasted flavor. But for that bright green pop of color, you need to use raw pistachios. Blanching helps remove their papery brown skins, which brightens their color even more, especially when they are ground.

PREP: **1 MINUTE**
COOK: **30 SECONDS**
COOL: **8 HOURS**
TOTAL: **8 HOURS 1 MINUTE 30 SECONDS**

MAKES: **1 CUP**

142 grams (1 cup) shelled unsalted raw pistachios

1. Fill a small pot halfway with water, place it over high heat, and bring it to a boil. Line a baking sheet with paper towels and set aside.
2. When the water boils, add the pistachios and blanch them, undisturbed, for 30 seconds.
3. Drain the nuts and spread them on the prepared baking sheet in a single layer. Let them dry at room temperature overnight, at least 8 hours.
4. In the center of a clean kitchen towel, place the dry pistachios and rub the nuts together to remove as much of the skins as possible. (They won't come off entirely.) Discard the skins.
5. Grind or process the blanched pistachios as needed.

Note
You can store the blanched nuts in an airtight container at room temperature for up to 1 month or in the freezer for up to 6 months.

TOASTED SESAME SEEDS

Sesame seeds (simsim) appear in and on breads and cookies of all kinds. You can buy toasted sesame seeds, but they're easier to find raw. It's good to have both toasted and raw sesame seeds on hand. It's so easy to toast any amount of raw seeds you like in the oven or on the stovetop. Just keep a close eye on them to prevent burning. No multitasking during this recipe!

PREP: **1 MINUTE**
COOK: **10 MINUTES**
COOL: **15 MINUTES**
TOTAL: **26 MINUTES**

MAKES: **144 GRAMS (1 CUP)**

144 grams (1 cup) sesame seeds

STOVETOP

1. Place a 12-inch (30-cm) skillet over medium heat. Add the sesame seeds to the dry pan and stir constantly until they become fragrant and golden brown, 8 to 10 minutes.
2. Remove the pan from the heat and let the seeds cool for 15 minutes.

OVEN

1. Arrange an oven rack in the middle position, preheat it to 300°F (150°C), line a baking sheet with parchment paper, and spread the sesame seeds on it in an even layer.
2. Bake, stirring the seeds every 2 minutes, until fragrant and golden brown, 6 minutes.
3. Let them cool on the sheet for 15 minutes. Easily transfer the seeds to an airtight container by lifting the long sides of the parchment paper and letting them slide into the storage vessel.

Note
You can store the toasted seeds in an airtight container at room temperature for up to 3 months or frozen for up to 6 months.

DRIED MINT

The fresh, bright flavor of dried mint adds depth and pairs with fresh mint for double the minty goodness. If you can't find dried mint in the spice aisle, it's simple to make, especially with the microwave method. The leaves should contain no excess moisture, so if possible, don't wash the leaves before drying them. Instead, vigorously shake the sprigs to clean them.

PREP: **1 MINUTE**
COOK: **1 MINUTE 30 SECONDS**
COOL: **30 MINUTES**
TOTAL: **32 MINUTES 30 SECONDS**

MAKES: **1 TABLESPOON CRUSHED DRIED MINT**

5 sprigs mint, about 30 leaves

1. Line a microwave-safe plate with a paper towel and place just the leaves on it in a single layer.
2. Microwave the mint in three intervals of 30 seconds, until the leaves curl and start to dry but remain bright green.
3. Let the leaves cool for at least 30 minutes. They'll crisp as they dry.

Note
You can store the dried mint in an airtight container at room temperature for up to 3 months. For best flavor and color, use it within 1 month.

VARIATIONS
- If you don't have a microwave or want to do it the old-fashioned way, dry the mint at **ROOM TEMPERATURE**. Line a baking sheet with paper towels. On it, place the leaves in a single layer and let them dry for 5 to 8 days, depending on the humidity level.
- To make **GROUND MINT**, crush the dried leaves between your palms as needed for each recipe.

CLARIFIED BUTTER

The process of clarifying butter separates pure butterfat from milk solids and water. In baklawa recipes, those solids can burn as they bake. Clarified butter, or samneh, whips like a dream and goes into so many recipes in this book. American butter and cultured (European) butter can behave very differently when clarified. With standard American butter, much of the solids rise to the top of the butterfat and require skimming. With cultured butter—which is fermented and tastes extraordinarily rich and complex—the majority if not all of the solids and water sink, leaving a top layer of butterfat. It's easier to clarify butter in large quantities, so make a big batch to keep on hand for all your baking needs.

PREP: **2 MINUTES**
COOK: **30 MINUTES**
TOTAL: **32 MINUTES**

MAKES: **341 GRAMS (1½ CUPS)**

456 grams (2 cups, 1 pound) unsalted butter

1. In a medium saucepan over low heat, melt the butter, undisturbed, about 30 minutes.
2. Remove the pan from the heat and use a spoon or small strainer to skim off and discard any solids on the surface of the butterfat.
3. Into a medium bowl, slowly pour the melted butterfat. Stop pouring when you reach the solids and water at the bottom of the pan. A little melted butter will surround the solids. Discard that with the solids or reserve it for another use.

Note

Use the clarified butter either freshly melted or resolidified. You can store it in an airtight container at room temperature for 2 months or in the refrigerator for up to 6 months.

VARIATION: Instead of skimming the solids in step 2, transfer the melted butter to a large heatproof bowl. **REFRIGERATE THE MELTED BUTTER UNTIL SOLID.** Run the base of the bowl under hot water to loosen the solidified butterfat. Remove the solidified butterfat, quickly rinse it, and discard the solids and water at the base of the bowl.

DATE PASTE

Commercial versions of date paste often run quite dense. Making your own allows you to control the consistency easily and flavor it with spices and other aromatic ingredients. Most grocery stores carry medjool dates in the produce section.

PREP: **5 MINUTES**

TOTAL: **5 MINUTES**

MAKES: **254 GRAMS (1½ CUPS)**

15 pitted medjool dates (225 grams, 1½ cups)

28 grams (2 tablespoons) water, melted butter, or orange juice, plus more as needed

½ teaspoon ground cinnamon, cardamom, or both

1. In the food processor, add all the ingredients and process until the mixture forms a ball, 15 to 30 seconds. If it's too stiff to spread, add more liquid, 5 grams (1 teaspoon) at a time, until spreadable.

> *Note*
> You can store the date paste in an airtight container at room temperature for up to 2 weeks or in the refrigerator for up to 2 months. To use it, bring it to room temperature and stir to loosen it.
>
> **VARIATION:** You can use the same amount of **STORE-BOUGHT DATE PASTE**, but soften it in the microwave on low heat for 1 minute.

FLOWER WATER SYRUP

In many Lebanese pastries, flower water syrup, also known as attar, drenches less-sweet treats, baked or fried, in sweet floral flavor. Most recipes call for cold syrup, so always have a jar handy in the refrigerator. When you need cold syrup right away, my quick-chill variation works great, too. The syrup dissolves easily in cold liquid, so a spoonful imparts aroma, flavor, and sweetness to many drinks. This recipe focuses on orange blossom water and rose water, always with a squeeze of lemon juice to balance the sweetness and to prevent crystallization as the syrup chills. As a rule, my family always uses orange blossom water, but a combination of orange blossom and rose water tastes lovely. Take great care when using rose water here and anywhere. A whisper goes a long way!

PREP: 5 MINUTES
COOK: 5 MINUTES
COOL: 1 HOUR 30 MINUTES
TOTAL: 1 HOUR 40 MINUTES

MAKES: 480 GRAMS (1½ CUPS)

170 grams (¾ cup) water
300 grams (1½ cups) granulated white sugar
14 grams (1 tablespoon) fresh lemon juice from ½ lemon
9 grams (2 teaspoons) orange blossom water; ½ teaspoon rose water; or a combination of both

1. In a small saucepan over medium-high heat, combine the water, sugar, and lemon juice and bring the mixture to a boil. Reduce the heat to low and simmer for 5 minutes.

2. Remove the syrup from the heat and add the flower water, stirring to combine.

3. Let the syrup cool for 30 minutes. Transfer it to an airtight container and refrigerate until cold, at least 1 hour.

Note
You can store the syrup in the refrigerator for up to 6 months.

TIP: When dipping fried goods into the syrup, reserve any remaining glazing syrup in a jar marked fry syrup. After using it, strain the syrup through a fine mesh sieve, if needed, to remove any bits of fried dough. Store it in the refrigerator to use for any recipe that calls for a glaze after frying, including Glazed Mak'rouns (page 89) and Glazed Zalabia (page 101). It will keep for up to 6 months.

VARIATION: To **CHILL THE SYRUP MORE QUICKLY** than in step 3, pour it into a heatproof bowl or large liquid measuring cup. Fill a large mixing bowl with ice water and gently place the vessel holding the syrup in it. Don't let the ice water splash into the syrup. Frequently stir the syrup until it chills through, about 15 minutes.

Glossary and Pronunciation Guide

Here's how various Arabic words sound phonetically and what they mean.

Ahlan wa sahlan (uh-LUN wuh SUH-lun): Welcome, hello

Ajeen (ah-JHEEN): Bread

Arayes (uh-RYE-ehs): Pan-fried, meat-filled pita

Ashta (AHSH-tuh): Pastry cream or cream pudding

Atayef (ah-TIE-yef): Filled mini-pancakes

Attar (AHT-tar): Simple syrup

Awamet (AH-wuh-meh): Small, fried, syrup-soaked balls

Baklawa (bahk-LAY-wuh, bit-LAY-wuh, sometimes bit-LAY-wee): Layered phyllo pastry in many shapes and with many fillings, drenched in simple syrup

Farkeh (FAHR-kuh): Smooth knafeh crust made with ground semolina dough

Fatayer (fuh-TIE-yuhr): Savory hand pies made with yeasted dough

Ghraybeh (gri-BEE): Melt-in-your-mouth butter cookies

Habibi (huh-BEE-bee): Sweetheart, male or both male and female

Habibti (huh-BEEB-tee): Sweetheart, female

Ibrik (ee-BREEK): Meaning "water" or "to pour," referring to the small pot with a long handle and pouring lip that makes Arabic coffee on the stovetop

Jiddo (zhid-DOH): Grandfather

Ka'ak (KAH-uk): The common Arabic word for cake or biscuit, referring to several styles of cookie and sweet and savory yeasted bread

Kara (KAU-dra): The round pillow on which saj bread dough rests for shaping, then flipping onto the saj dome or into the oven

Kataifi (kuh-TIE-fee): Long thin strands of pastry dough for knafeh, bundled and purchased frozen

Khimaj (kuh-MEJH): Pita

Khubz (KHUB-iz): Any bread

Kishneh (KISH-nuh): The shredded kataifi crust for knafeh

Knafeh (kuh-NAH-fee): A traditional Arabic pastry with a buttery crust in a variety of styles, soaked in attar, and stuffed with a filling of nuts, cream, or cheese

GLOSSARY AND PRONUNCIATION GUIDE

Labneh (LUB-nuh or LUB-knee): Strained yogurt that creates a thick spread with a complex, tangy flavor

Ma'amoul (MAH-mool): Shortbread cookies molded and filled with nuts, dates, and other ingredients

Mak'roun (MAHK-droon or MAHK-uh-drown): A style of Lebanese cookie that comes in several varieties

Manakeesh (mahn-uh-EESH): Soft, foldable flatbreads covered with various toppings before or after baking

man'oushe (mahn-OO-she): The singular of manakeesh

Markouk (mahr-KOOK): Paper-thin flatbread

Muhummara (moo-HUM-udduh): Roasted red pepper dip made with walnuts, bread crumbs, and pomegranate molasses

Na'ameh (neh-EH-muh): The smooth-crust version of knafeh pastry

Nabulseyeh (neh-BULL-see-yeh): A style of knafeh crust, referring to Nablus, its origin city in Palestine

Na'na (NAH-nuh): Fresh mint

Quahwa (KUH-whey): Coffee

Qurban (OR-buhn): Sacrifice in reference to Orthodox holy bread

Saj (SAHJ): Thin flatbread and the dome oven used to bake it

Sambousek (sum-BOO-sec): Fried, filled savory pies or sweet, stuffed shortbread cookies

Samneh (SUM-nuh): Clarified butter

Sfeha (sfee-HUH): Meat-filled savory pies

Simsum (SIM-soom): Sesame seeds

Sitto (sit-TOE): Grandmother

Teta (TEH-tuh): Grandmother

Tamar (TEM-uhr): Dates

Za'atar (ZAH-tuh): A spice blend of wild thyme, sumac, and sesame seeds; or the herb hyssop

Zalabia (zuh-LAY-bee-yuh): A style of Lebanese fried dough with several varieties

Acknowledgments

> "And there are those who give and know not pain in giving, nor do they seek joy, nor give with mindfulness of virtue; They give as in yonder valley the myrtle breathes its fragrance into space. Through the hands of such as these God speaks, and from behind their eyes, He smiles upon the earth."
> —Khalil Gibran

My gratitude for all things *Lebanese Baking* runs deep.

For the loving encouragement of my hanoun (pure heart) husband, Dan Shaheen; our sons, Michael and Steven; and siblings, Tom, Amara, Chris, Dick, Silvia, Peggy (my sister who champions my every creative endeavor!), Ralph, Denise, Jim, Diane, Carol, Clay, and Trisha. Thank you to all my nieces and nephews whom I love as my own, especially my expert tasters, John, Maria, Ricky, Tommy, Victoria, Cam, Bennett, and Ford Abood, as well as Sara, Josh, Piper, Ashton, Leah, Doug, Justin, David, Ruby, Freddy, Maggie, Mitchell, Kathryn, Ben, and Savannah. You are what passing down recipes is all about. I'm counting on you to do the same!

For my agent, Jenni Ferrari-Adler of Verve, and my editor, James Jayo of Countryman Press, thank you for believing in this book and expertly guiding it every step of the way.

For the gorgeousness in these pages, I applaud and thank my new cousin-friends who came to Harbor Springs to shoot this book: photographer Kristin Teig, habibi stylist Rick Holbrook, prop and food stylist Catrine Kelty, and art director Allison Chi. You dove into this project (and the cold waters of Little Traverse Bay!) with infectious enthusiasm. I am honored by your enormous talent. Thanks to Peggy Abood, for providing excellent craft services and rooms with a view for our shoot.

For Celine Terranova, who works magic in the kitchen as my recipe tester, smile-maker, and wise friend. We went into Sitto's kitchen together long ago to bake and never stopped. Who gets to work with their gifted cousin? I do!

For my many dear cousins and aunts who sent handwritten recipes and shared your own precious secrets, thank you.

For the community of Harbor Springs, a place of inspiration where "God smiles upon the earth." This book is graced by the spectacular florals of Gayle Everest; illustrations by Brittney Banks; author photo by Stephanie Baker; props from Then and Now Antique and Consignment House, Cutler's Petoskey, and Trisha Shaheen's Woods and Waxes; nails by Nikki Law at Polished on Main; linens by 3 Pines Studio; pearls by Elizabeth Blair Fine Pearls; cookbooks from Between the Covers; team meals by Small Batch and Gurneys; and excellent ingredients from Toski Sands Market, Crooked Tree Breadworks, Harbor Market, and American Spoon.

For my talented colleagues and friends who contributed in meaningful ways, including Dianne Jacobs, Beirut Bakery in Redford, Lebon Sweets in Dearborn, Jerusalem Bakery in Lansing, Gloria Nakfoor, Geri Conklin, the Team One Chevrolet Buick GMC gang, Tom and Nancy Hunter, Esperance Hourani, Cindy Hunter Morgan, Manya and Nadina Constant, Alexis and Dennis Branoff, my lifelong friends of Waverly, Jeff and Hollye Jacobs, Paul Terranova, Sheila Abood, Sarah Abood Stump, and Kathleen Skaar (who made my kara).

For the team that makes sharing excellent ingredients and gifts with you in our online shop a joy for Peggy and me: Martha Steinhagen, Roxanne Frith, Aubrey Johnson, and Lansing's Allen Neighborhood Center.

For my parents, Maryalice and Camille Abood and Louise Shaheen, and all my grandparents (Richard Abowd, Alice Elum Abowd, Salim Abood, Nabeha Fawaz Abood, and Sarah Abood). You populated the world with a remarkable clan! May this book pay your gifts forward as you watch from heaven.

For my beloved MaureenAbood.com community. I admire you for the many ways in which you keep culinary traditions alive, passing on a legacy that values togetherness in the kitchen and at the table. Bless your hands forever!

Index

A
Akkawi cheese, in cheese knafeh, 45
Almond(s)
    Michigan tart cherry bundt cake, 177
    pistachio cupcakes with strawberry rose water buttercream, 162
    triple chocolate baklawa with toasted almonds, 33
Anise seeds
    glazed ka'ak bread, 76
    glazed mak'rouns, 89
    green tea with warm spices, 85
Apricot
    cardamom filling, 105
    gems, 102
    glaze, 155
    upside-down cake, 169
    walnut cookies, 137; variation, 137
Arabic cardamom coffee, 19
    variation, 19
Arayes, 247
Ashta filling
    cream baklawa, 29
    Lebanese nights cream cake with berry compote, 181
    ma'amoul mad cream bars, 110
    pistachio cream atayef, 153
Atayef, 150
    pistachio cream atayef, 153
    walnut atayef, 154
Attar. *See* Flower water syrup
Awamet, 126

B
Baking secrets
    baklawa, 2–4
    fatayer, 196–97
    knafeh, 38
    manakeesh, 218
    saj bread, 250
    yeasted doughs, 62–63
Baking staples, 265
    blanched pistachios, 267
    clarified butter, 271
    date paste, 272
    dried mint, 270
    flower water syrup, 273
    toasted nuts, 266
    toasted sesame seeds, 269
Baklawa, 1, 2–4
    burma baklawa, 22; variation, 23
    cream baklawa, 29
    crinkle, 26; variations, 27
    diamonds, 15; variation, 16
    diamonds with homemade phyllo, 6; variation, 9
    nests, 24
    nut-free, 31
    rolls, 20; variations, 21
    secrets to making, 2–4
    spirals with homemade phyllo, 10
    triple chocolate, 33; variations, 34
Baklawa cheesecake, 186
    variation, 188
Barazek sesame cookies, 123
    variation, 123
Basil, in raspberry basil iced tea, 141
Beef
    arayes, 247
    sambousek, 213
    sfeha, 204
Bell peppers, in muhammara manakeesh, 237
Berry(ies). *See also* Raspberry; Strawberry compote, 181
Biscuits, shredded wheat knafeh, 50
Blanched pistachios, 267
Bread, storing, 63
Bread, types of. *See* Savory yeast breads; Sweet yeast breads
Brownies, mocha, with olive oil and tahini swirl, 131
Bundt cake, Michigan tart cherry, 177
Buns, honey, 67
Burma baklawa, 22
Butter, xvii
    in baklawa, 3
    clarified, 271
Buttercream
    cardamom coffee, 165
    filling, in raspberry rose water macarons, 96
    frosting, for orange blossom cake, 146
    strawberry rose water, 162

C
Café blanc, 59
    variation, 59
Cake(s), 145
    apricot upside-down cake, 169
    atayef, 150; pistachio cream, 153; walnut, 154
    baklawa cheesecake, 186
    coconut semolina cake, 185
    date cakes, mini sticky, with orange blossom caramel sauce, 159

INDEX

Cake(s) *(continued)*
   Lebanese nights cream, with berry compote, 181
   lemon yogurt, with strawberry rose water sauce and labneh, 171
   mocha cardamom snack cake, 165
   orange blossom cake, 146
   orange blossom madeleines with apricot glaze, 155
   pistachio cupcakes with strawberry rose water buttercream, 162
   pomegranate mousse, with lime icing, 191
   tart cherry bundt cake, Michigan, 177
   turmeric tea cake, 175
Caramel
   pecan rolls, orange blossom, 79
   sauce, orange blossom, 159
Cardamom
   Arabic cardamom coffee, 19
   coffee buttercream, 165
   date rings, 70
Cheese. *See also* Cream cheese; Feta cheese; Mozzarella cheese
   fatayer, 200; variation, 201
   fatayer xl, 202
   knafeh, 45; knafeh bil ka'ak with, 46
   manakeesh, 226
Cheesecake, baklawa, 186
Cherries, maraschino, in toasted coconut mak'rouns, 95
Cherries, Michigan, 180
   Michigan tart cherry bundt cake, 177
   Michigan tart cherry limeade, 158
Chocolate. *See also* White chocolate
   chocolate pistachio knafeh bars, 54
   mocha brownies with olive oil and tahini swirl, 131
   mocha cardamom snack cake, 165
   triple chocolate baklawa, 33
Clarified butter, 271. *See also* Butter
   variation, 271
Coconut
   semolina cake, 185
   toasted coconut mak'rouns, 95

Coffee, Arabic cardamon, 19. *See also* Espresso
Combo knafeh crust, 40
   cheese knafeh with, 45
   cream knafeh with, 57
   nut-filled knafeh with, 49
Compote, berry, Lebanese nights with, 181
Cookies, 87
   apricot gems, 102
   apricot walnut cookies, 137
   awamet, 126
   barazek sesame cookies, 123
   fig crescents, 119
   ghraybeh, 138
   glazed ka'ak shortbread, 142
   glazed zalabia, 101
   ma'amoul: basic recipe for, 105; ma'amoul mad cream bars, 110; ma'amoul mad date bars, 113; millionaire ma'amoul mad, 117
   macarons, raspberry rose water, 96
   mak'rouns, 88; glazed, 89; toasted coconut, 95; walnut orange blossom mak'roun fingers, 91
   mocha brownies with olive oil and tahini swirl, 131
   sesame ka'ak rings, 129
   white chocolate pistachio cookies, 134
Cream baklawa, 29
Cream cake, Lebanese nights, with berry compote, 181
Cream cheese
   apricot gems, 102
   baklawa cheesecake, 186
   in buttercream, 146, 162
   honey buns, 67
   strawberry rose water buttercream, 162
Cream knafeh, 57
   knafeh nests with, 53
Crescents, fig, 119
Crinkle, baklawa, 26
Croissants, za'atar, 259
Crust
   combo knafeh, 40
   kataifi knafeh, 42

   pistachio, 191
   shortcut knafeh, 40
   smooth knafeh, 43
Cupcakes, pistachio, with strawberry rose water buttercream, 162
Custard filling, in baklawa crinkle, 26

D

Date paste, 272
Date(s), xviii
   ice cream shake, 124; variation, 124
   ma'amoul mad date bars, 113
   mini sticky date cakes with orange blossom caramel sauce, 159
   orange blossom cinnamon filling, 105
   orange date tea ring, 83
   rings, cardamom, 70
Diamonds, baklawa, 15
Dip
   muhammara manakeesh, 227
Donuts, zalabia, 64
Dough(s). *See also* Phyllo
   fatayer, 199
   kataifi, about, xviii
   manakeesh, 221
   yeasted, secrets to making, 62–63
Drinks
   Arabic cardamon coffee, 19
   cafe blanc, 59
   date ice cream shake, 124
   green tea with warm spices, 85
   matcha orange blossom latte, 176
   Michigan tart cherry limeade, 158
   mint lemonade, 115
   mulberry Manhattan, 215
   orange blossom gin fizz, 245
   raspberry basil iced tea, 141

E

Equipment, xv–xvi
Espresso
   cardamon coffee buttercream, 165
   mocha brownies with olive oil and tahini swirl, 131
   mocha cardamom snack cake, 165

INDEX

F

Fatayer, 195
  cheese fatayer, 200
  cheese fatayer XL, 202
  dough, 199
  kale and feta fatayer, 208
  kousa fatayer, 210
  sambousek, 213
  secrets to making, 196–97
  sfeha, 204
  spinach fatayer, 206
Feta cheese
  kale and feta fatayer, 208
  za'atar cheese dome, 235
Fig crescents, 119
  variations, 120
Fillings. *See also* Ashta filling
  in baklawa, 3–4
  buttercream, 96
  custard, 26
  ma'amoul options, 105
Flatbread. *See* Manakeesh; Pita; Saj bread; Sesame purse bread
Flavorings, xviii
Flour, xvii
Flower water syrup, 273
  variation, 273
Frosting. *See* Buttercream
Fruit. *See* Berry(ies); *specific types*

G

Garlic knots, za'atar, 248
Ghraybeh, 138
  variations, 140
Gin fizz, orange blossom, 245
Glaze. *See also* Flower water syrup
  apricot, 155
  tart cherry, 177
Glazed ka'ak bread, 76
Glazed ka'ak shortbread, 142
Glazed mak'rouns, 89
  variation, 90
Glazed zalabia, 101

Greek yogurt. *See also* Labneh; Yogurt
  in baklawa cheesecake, 186
  in mocha cardamom snack cake, 165
Green tea with warm spices, 85

H

Hand pies. *See* Fatayer
Holy bread, qurban, 73
Honey buns, 67

I

Ice cream
  date ice cream shake, 124
Iced tea, raspberry basil, 141
Icing, lime, 191
Ingredients, xvii–xviii

K

Ka'ak
  bread, glazed, 76
  rings, sesame, 129
  shortbread, glazed, 142
Kale and feta fatayer, 208
Kataifi dough, xviii
Kataifi knafeh crust, 42
  cheese knafeh with, 45
  cream knafeh with, 57
  knafeh nests with, 53
  nut-filled knafeh with, 49
Knafeh, 37, 38
  bars, chocolate pistachio, 54
  bil ka'ak, 46
  biscuits, shredded wheat, 50
  cheese knafeh, 45
  cream knafeh, 57
  crust, combo, 40
  crust, kataifi, 42
  crust, shortcut, 40
  crust, smooth, 43
  nests, 53
  nut-filled, 49
  secrets to making, 38
Kousa fatayer, 210
  variation, 211

L

Labneh. *See also* Yogurt
  in baklawa cheesecake, 186
  as dip, in arayes, 247
  labneh mint manakeesh, 225
  in lemon yogurt cake with strawberry rose water sauce and, 171
  in mocha cardamom snack cake, 165
Lamb
  arayes, 247
  sambousek, 213
  sfeha, 204
  and tomato manakeesh, 230; variation, 231
Latte, matcha orange blossom, 176
Lebanese funnel cakes. *See* Glazed zalabia
Lebanese nights cream cake with berry compote, 181
Lemonade, mint, 115
Lemon yogurt cake with strawberry rose water sauce and labneh, 171
Lime
  icing, 191
  tart cherry limeade, Michigan, 158

M

Ma'amoul
  basic recipe for, 105
  ma'amoul mad, millionaire, 117
  ma'amoul mad cream bars, 110
  ma'amoul mad date bars, 113; variation, 114
Macarons, raspberry rose water, 96
Madeleines, orange blossom, with apricot glaze, 155
Mak'rouns, 88
  glazed, 89; variation, 90
  macarons, raspberry rose water, 96
  mak'rouns fingers, walnut orange blossom, 91
  toasted coconut, 95
Manakeesh, 218
  cheese manakeesh, 226

INDEX

Manakeesh (*continued*)
   dough, 221
   labneh mint, 225
   lamb and tomato, 230
   muhammara, 227
   secrets to making, 218
   za'atar, 222
Manhattan, mulberry, 215
Matcha orange blossom latte, 176
Michigan cherries, 180
Michigan tart cherry bundt cake, 177
Michigan tart cherry limeade, 158
Millionaire ma'amoul mad, 117
Mint
   dried, 270; variation, 270
   lemonade, 115
Mocha brownies with olive oil and tahini swirl, 131
Mocha cardamom snack cake, 165
Mousse cake, pomegranate, with lime icing, 191
Mozzarella cheese
   cheese fatayer, 200
   cheese fatayer xl, 202
   cheese knafeh, 45
   cheese manakeesh, 226
   za'atar cheese dome, 235
Muhammara manakeesh, 227
Mulberry Manhattan, 215

N

Nests, baklawa, 24
Nests, knafeh, 53
Nigella seeds
   in cheese fatayer xl, 202
   in honey bun glaze, 67
Nut(s), xviii. *See also specific nuts*
   -filled knafeh, 49; knafeh nests with, 53; variation, 49
   -free baklawa, 31
   toasted, 266

O

Oils, xvii–xviii
Orange
   blossom cake, 146
   blossom caramel pecan rolls, 79
   blossom gin fizz, 245; variation, 245
   blossom madeleines with apricot glaze, 155
   blossom in walnut atayef, 154
   matcha orange blossom latte, 176
   orange date tea ring, 83; variation, 84
   walnut orange blossom mak'roun fingers, 91
Ovens (saj), 258

P

Pancakes. *See* Atayef
Panko bread crumbs, in knafeh crust, 40
Pecan(s)
   orange blossom caramel pecan rolls, 79
Pepitas, in nut-free baklawa, 31
Phyllo, xviii
   dough: baklawa cheesecake; baklawa cheesecake, 186; baklawa crinkle, 26; baklawa nests, 24; baklawa rolls, 20; burma baklawa, 22; cream baklawa, 29; nut-free baklawa, 31; triple chocolate baklawa, 33; baklawa diamonds, 15
   homemade, 2–3; baklawa diamonds with, 6; baklawa spirals with, 10
   store-bought, 3
Pies. *See* Fatayer
Pine nuts, in turmeric tea cake, 175
Pistachio(s)
   blanched, 267
   chocolate pistachio knafeh bars, 54
   cream atayef, 153
   crust, 191
   cupcakes with strawberry rose water buttercream, 162; variations, 164
   roasted, in nut-filled knafeh, 49
   rose water filling, 105
   white chocolate pistachio cookies, 134
Pita, 240
   chips, 243; variation, 244
Pomegranate
   molasses, xviii; in lamb and tomato manakeesh, 230; in muhammara manakeesh, 227; in sambousek, 213
   mousse cake with lime icing, 191; variation, 193

Q

Qurban holy bread, 73

R

Raspberry
   basil iced tea, 141
   rose water macarons, 96; variation, 99
Rolls
   baklawa rolls, 20
   honey buns, 67
   orange blossom caramel pecan rolls, 79
   za'atar garlic knots, 248
Rose water
   raspberry rose water macarons, 96
   rose water sauce and labneh, lemon yogurt cake with, 171
   strawberry rose water buttercream, pistachio cupcakes with, 162

S

Saj bread, 252
   secrets to making, 250
Saj ovens, 258
Sambousek, 213
   variation, 214
Sauce
   orange blossom caramel, 159
   strawberry rose water, 171
Savory yeast breads, 217
   arayes, 247
   cheese manakeesh, 226
   labneh mint manakeesh, 225
   lamb and tomato manakeesh, 230
   manakeesh, secrets to making, 218
   manakeesh dough, 221
   muhammara manakeesh, 227

INDEX

pita, 240
pita chips, 243
saj bread, 252
saj ovens saga, 258
sesame purse bread, 238
talami bread, 233
za'atar cheese dome, 235
za'atar croissants, 259
za'atar croissants, discovering, 263
za'atar garlic knots, 248
za'atar manakeesh, 222
Seeds. *See* Anise seeds; Nigella seeds; Pepitas; Sesame seeds; Sunflower seeds
Semolina
   coconut semolina cake, 185
   Lebanese nights cream cake with berry compote, 181
Sesame cookies, barazek, 123
Sesame ka'ak rings, 129
Sesame purse bread, 238
   knafeh bil ka'ak with, 46
Sesame seeds, toasted, 269
Sfeha, 204
   variations, 205
Shortbread
   apricot gems, 102
   ghraybeh, 138
   glazed ka'ak shortbread, 142
   ma'amoul, 105
Shortcut knafeh crust, 40
   cheese knafeh with, 45
   cream knafeh with, 57
   nut-filled knafeh with, 49
Shredded wheat knafeh biscuits, 50
   variation, 51
Smooth knafeh crust, 43
   cheese knafeh with, 45
   cream knafeh with, 57
   nut-filled knafeh with, 49
Snack cake, mocha cardamom, 165
Spinach fatayer, 206
   variation, 207

Spirals, baklawa, with homemade phyllo, 10
Squash. *See* Kousa fatayer
Strawberry
   rose water buttercream, 162
   rose water sauce, 171
Strawberry shortcake. *See* Lemon yogurt cake with strawberry rose water sauce and labneh
Sunflower seeds, in nut-free baklawa, 31
Sweet yeast breads, 61
   cardamom date rings, 70
   dough, secrets to making, 62–63
   glazed ka'ak bread, 76
   honey buns, 67
   orange blossom caramel pecan rolls, 79
   orange date tea ring, 83
   qurban holy bread, 73
   zalabia donuts, 64
Syrup, in baklawa, 3. *See also* Flower water syrup

T

Tahini
   in millionaire ma'amoul mad, 117
   swirl, 131
   in turmeric tea cake, 175
Talami bread, 233
Tart cherry bundt cake, Michigan, 177
Tart cherry limeade, Michigan, 158
Tea
   green, with warm spices, 85
   iced, raspberry basil, 141
Tea cake, turmeric, 175
Tea ring, orange date, 83
Toasted coconut mak'rouns, 95
Toasted nuts, 266
Toasted sesame seeds, 269
Tomato(es)
   lamb and tomato manakeesh, 230

Triple chocolate baklawa, 33
Turmeric tea cake, 175

U

Upside-down cake, apricot, 169

W

Walnut(s)
   apricot walnut cookies, 137
   atayef, 154
   orange blossom mak'roun fingers, 91; variation, 92
   toasted, 266
Whipped cream, 159, 169
   layer, 181
White chocolate pistachio cookies, 134
   variation, 135

Y

Yeast, xvii
Yeast breads. *See* Savory yeast breads; Sweet yeast breads
Yeasted doughs, secrets to making, 62–63
Yogurt, xviii. *See also* Greek yogurt; Labneh
   cake, lemon, with strawberry rose water sauce and labneh, 171
   in coconut semolina cake, 185

Z

Za'atar
   cheese dome, 235
   croissants, 259; discovering, 263; variation, 260
   garlic knots, 248
   manakeesh, 222; variation, 222
Zalabia
   donuts, 64
   glazed, 101